Creative Approaches to Planning and Local Development

This book highlights creative approaches to planning and local development. The dynamic complexity, diversity and fluidity which characterize contemporary society represent challenges for planning and development endeavours. While research and policy work has extensively focused on large cities and on metropolitan regions, there has been relatively little work on 'smaller places'.

This book shows that if these new challenges affect all places and regions, small and medium-sized towns (SMSTs) are suffering many specific problems that call imperatively for the design and implementation of very imaginative, creative approaches to planning and local development. What could enhance creativity in local development and planning? Is it possible to talk about creative capacity building at the level of a town that might release imaginative and innovative activities? Under what local and non-local conditions is creativity being initiated and flourishing? What are the major obstacles and in what way can these be contained in order to safeguard pockets of creative action?

Interdisciplinary and with case studies from France, Norway and other European countries, this volume presents a wide range of approaches and territorial contexts of small cities and towns in which spatial dynamics and the consequences of the city-region for urban planning theory and practice in Europe are highlighted, with a special focus on the challenges for – and understanding of – planning and development of SMSTs. It provides a significant body of critical, comparative and contextual perspectives on the quest for urban sustainability and resilience in SMSTs, therefore emphasizing collaborative and potentially innovative approaches that can be detected, but also the shortcomings, pitfalls and 'traps' that can lie behind the approaches aimed at concerting ecological, economic, and socio-cultural concerns, and the discourses promoting them.

Abdelillah Hamdouch is Professor of Urban and Regional Planning and Head of the Spatial Planning & Environment Department, Polytechnic School of the University of Tours, France.

Torill Nyseth is Professor of Community Planning at the University of Tromsø, the Arctic University of Norway.

Christophe Demazière is Professor of Urban and Regional Planning at the Spatial Planning & Environment Department of the Polytechnic School, University of Tours, France.

Anniken Førde is Associate Professor of Community Planning at the University of Tromsø, the Arctic University of Norway.

José Serrano is Associate Professor of Urban and Regional Planning at the Spatial Planning & Environment Department of the Polytechnic School, University of Tours, France.

Nils Aarsæther is Professor of Community Planning at the University of Tromsø, the Arctic University of Norway.

Creative Approaches to Planning and Local Development
Insights from Small and Medium-Sized Towns in Europe

Edited by
Abdelillah Hamdouch, Torill Nyseth,
Christophe Demazière, Anniken Førde,
José Serrano and Nils Aarsæther

LONDON AND NEW YORK

First published 2017
by Routledge

2 Park Square, Milton Park, Abingdon, Oxfordshire OX14 4RN

711 Third Avenue, New York, NY 10017

Routledge is an imprint of the Taylor & Francis Group, an informa business

First issued in paperback 2018

Copyright © 2017 selection and editorial matter, Abdelillah Hamdouch, Torill Nyseth, Christophe Demazière, Anniken Førde, José Serrano, Nils Aarsæther; individual chapters, the contributors

The right of the editors to be identified as the author of the editorial material, and of the authors for their individual chapters, has been asserted in accordance with sections 77 and 78 of the Copyright, Designs and Patents Act 1988.

All rights reserved. No part of this book may be reprinted or reproduced or utilised in any form or by any electronic, mechanical, or other means, now known or hereafter invented, including photocopying and recording, or in any information storage or retrieval system, without permission in writing from the publishers.

Notice:
Product or corporate names may be trademarks or registered trademarks, and are used only for identification and explanation without intent to infringe.

British Library Cataloguing in Publication Data
A catalogue record for this book is available from the British Library

Library of Congress Cataloguing in Publication Data
The LOC data has been applied for.

ISBN: 978-1-4724-7700-2 (hbk)
ISBN: 978-1-138-58874-5 (pbk)

Typeset in Sabon
by Out of House Publishing

Contents

List of figures and tables viii
Notes on contributors xi
Preface xvi

Introduction 1
ABDELILLAH HAMDOUCH, TORILL NYSETH, CHRISTOPHE DEMAZIÈRE,
ANNIKEN FØRDE, JOSÉ SERRANO AND NILS AARSÆTHER

PART I
Approaches to planning and local development: analytical landmarks and methodological challenges 11

1 Perspectives on creative planning and local development in small and medium-sized towns 13
   TORILL NYSETH, ABDELILLAH HAMDOUCH,
   CHRISTOPHE DEMAZIÈRE, NILS AARSÆTHER, ANNIKEN FØRDE
   AND JOSÉ SERRANO

2 Small and medium-sized towns: a research topic at the margins of urban studies? 22
   CHRISTOPHE DEMAZIÈRE

3 'Ordinary politics of planning' for socio-economic development: insights from European small and medium-sized towns 36
   ABDELILLAH HAMDOUCH AND KSENIJA BANOVAC

4 Governing place reinvention: the quest for an integrative approach 61
   TORILL NYSETH AND ANDERS TØNNESEN

PART II
Can place transformation be planned? Challenges to creative planning in small and medium-sized towns 79

5 Cultural industries as a base for local development: the challenges of planning for the unknown 81
ANNIKEN FØRDE AND BRITT KRAMVIG

6 Innovative actions for local development in small and medium-sized towns: the case of the Centre-Val de Loire region in France 97
CHRISTOPHE DEMAZIÈRE, ABDELILLAH HAMDOUCH AND KSENIJA BANOVAC

7 Inter-municipal cooperation as a means of creative territorial planning 114
JOSÉ SERRANO AND ABDELILLAH HAMDOUCH

8 Potential and obstacles to creative planning in a crisis context: the case of the city of Patras in western Greece 134
PAVLOS MARINOS DELLADETSIMA AND JOHN LOUKAKIS

9 Territory vs. function: ambitions and tensions in the creation of a new urban neighbourhood 155
NILS AARSÆTHER AND HALVARD VIKE

PART III
Social innovation, participatory governance and collective learning as levers of creative planning 171

10 Envisioning dialogues of new urban landscapes in Nuuk 173
KJERSTIN UHRE AND KNUT EIRIK DAHL

11 Social innovation as the common ground between social cohesion and economic development of small and medium-sized towns in France and Quebec 190
ABDELILLAH HAMDOUCH AND LEÏLA GHAFFARI

12 Renewed sustainable planning in the Arctic: a reflective,
    critical and committed approach   208
    GISLE LØKKEN AND MAGDALENA HAGGÄRDE

13 Quality of life and attractiveness issues in small and
    medium-sized towns: innovative or commonplace policies?   234
    HÉLÈNE MAINET AND JEAN-CHARLES EDOUARD

14 Postscript: pathways towards a critical and comparative
    approach to creative planning   249
    NILS AARSÆTHER, JOSÉ SERRANO, ANNIKEN FØRDE,
    CHRISTOPHE DEMAZIÈRE, TORILL NYSETH AND
    ABDELILLAH HAMDOUCH

    Index   258

Figures and tables

Figures

3.1	Case study countries and SMSTs	45
4.1	The Ypsilon Bridge. One of the new images of Drammen	70
6.1	Case studies situated in the proximity of the large cities of Paris, Orléans and Tours	106
8.1	Location of the city of Patras	137
8.2	Population growth in the Peripheral Unit of Achaia and the city of Patras	138
8.3	Transportation activity of the ports of Patras and Igoumenitsa (passengers)	141
8.4	Transportation activity of the ports of Patras and Igoumenitsa (private cars and commercial vehicles)	141
8.5	Transportation freight activity of the main ports of western Greece (commodities)	142
8.6	The Rio–Antirio Bridge	143
8.7	Workers and population by sector of economic activity, city of Patras, 2011	147
10.1	Paper planes of whitepapers, reports and research as they circumscribe Nuuk	179
10.2	Blok P was Greenland's largest housing project, once inhabiting one per cent of the entire national population. A new horizon appears after the disappearance of this housing slab	180
10.3	'Learning as catalyst' is the notion that opened up for inclusive and creative programming	183
10.4	Active city floor in the Blok P area is a question of the right to the city. Low threshold learning is the programmatic key	184
10.5	Civic landscapes indoors and outdoors at the ground floor of Tuujuk	185
10.6	*Ilaqutariit illuat – The House of Families* – was planned to help young parents support their children and to be like a small society within the larger society	186

11.1 The role of local policies in feeding social cohesive dynamics 194
11.2 Analytical framework: the role of proximity and social innovation in the development of SMSTs 200
11.3 The place of social innovation in social cohesion and economic development 200
12.1 The stories of the people in the landscape. The landscape and what exists here – the other stories. From the student project *No-one belongs here more than you* by Marianne Lucie Skuncke 219
12.2 From the student project *Extracts of culture – we talk about the same, do we?* by Silje Ødegård 220
12.3 The delight space in the cultural landscape. The crude space in the industrial landscape. The dying space in the drained landscape. From the student work *Flexibility in contradictory landscape* by Guðrún Jóna Arinbjarnardóttir 221
12.4 Kiruna is dying – fight!!!!! Bye. I'll be here forever. Historic and contemporary messages on the walls of Kiruna 223
12.5 The eight seasons of the Sámi landscape – time, space and practice connected 225
12.6 The move – a city inventory: programmes, buildings, functions to relocate, reinvent, reinforce, replace 226
12.7 The entrained – iconic items of nostalgia: mapping the existing/archives for the future/present history 228
12.8 The new – new programmes in existing context/existing objects in new context/new programmes in the new city centre/happenings and acts of attention, adieus and establishings 229
12.9 The everyday life – integrated movement, landscape, items of nostalgia 231

Tables

2.1 Definition of SMSTs in France: differences according to sources 25
3.1 The main characteristics of the socio-economic profiles of SMSTs 41
3.2 The socio-economic profiles and performance of case studies (*TOWN* research project) 46
4.1 Summing up dimensions and timeframes 73
7.1 Demographic and job data of urban areas selected 121
7.2 Institutional context 121
7.3 Features of the studied business parks implemented by SMSTs 123
7.4 Wildlife protected areas overlapped by business parks 124

7.5 Summary of strategic trends of SCoT and connections
between economic development and environmental issues 125
7.6 Features of business parks implemented by the SMSTs chosen 128
8.1 Evaluation of the international importance of ports
(western Greece) 139
13.1 Examples of images and words used to describe amenities
in small towns 239
13.2 Perceptions of quality of life by inhabitants of small towns 240
13.3 Residential mobility in French small towns 241

Contributors

Nils Aarsæther is Professor in Community Planning at the University of Tromsø, the Arctic University of Norway. His research fields are local democracy, policies of local development, and municipal planning in the Northern areas. Within education, he heads the board of the BA and MA programmes in Community Planning & Culture Studies. Besides co-authoring scientific articles and books on planning and innovation, he pursues dissemination activities including public lectures, magazine and newspaper articles, and media interviews concerning local/regional development and public health policies. In 2015, he co-edited *Lokalpolitisk lederskap i Norden* (*Local Political Leadership in the Nordic Countries*).

Ksenija Banovac is a PhD student in urban and regional planning at the University of Tours, France. Her research focuses on planning the socio-economic development in and for small and medium-sized towns. Her scientific interest is related to regional science, economic geography and new institutional economics. More recently, she was involved in two projects that aimed to study development and planning in small and medium-sized towns across Europe and particularly in France. The *TOWN* project was commissioned by the European Observation Network, Territorial Development and Cohesion (ESPON) and the *ODES* project was commissioned by the French Centre-Val de Loire region.

Knut Eirik Dahl is architect and partner of Dahl & Uhre Architects in Tromsø, Professor Emeritus at the Institute of Urbanism and Landscape at the Oslo School of Architecture and Design, and President of Europan Norway. He was also founder and partner in Blue Line Architecture. He was a jury member in the competition on the future of Kiruna and has recently been invited as a reviewer of planning strategies in the city of Malmö.

Pavlos Marinos Delladetsima is Professor at the Department of Geography, Harokopio University, Greece and has taught postgraduate courses in Europe and Greece. His academic and research interests are spatial planning, urban development, land values and property development, urban vulnerability and disaster management.

xii *Contributors*

Christophe Demazière is Professor in Urban and Regional Planning at the Spatial Planning & Environment Department of the Polytechnic School, University of Tours, France. His fields of expertise are strategic spatial planning, city-region governance and small and medium-sized towns. He has coordinated over 20 research programmes on urban and regional development issues in France and Europe. At present, he is Vice-President of the University of Tours and is in charge of partnerships and research valorization. He also chairs the French association of planning schools and research.

Jean-Charles Edouard is Professor in Geography at the University of Clermont-Ferrand II, France. He has undertaken research for many years on issues relating to small and medium-sized towns, urban geography, urban planning and development in non-metropolitan areas in France and Europe. He coordinates a master's degree in urban planning and management dedicated to small and medium-sized towns. His recent research deals with the issues of attractiveness of intermediate towns and on criteria of evaluation (both quantitative and qualitative).

Anniken Førde is Associate Professor of Community Planning at the University of Tromsø, the Arctic University of Norway. Her research fields are transformation processes of places and landscapes, innovation policies and practices, and the responsible development of tourism and creative industries. She teaches philosophy of science and methodology for students in Community Planning & Culture Studies, and is interested in methodological issues related to the exploration of complex, relational realities.

Leïla Ghaffari is Teaching Assistant in Geography at the University of Quebec at Montreal (UQAM), Canada. She is also a PhD candidate of Urban Studies in a joint programme of UQAM and the University of François Rabelais of Tours, France. Her research concentrates on the influence of urban strategies on social structure in small and medium-sized towns and also in deprived neighbourhoods. Her scientific interests focus on urban issues concerning vulnerable groups. Her most recent work deals with the relationship between gentrification and displacement, and strategies that can protect the local population from losing their sense of place in this process.

Magdalena Haggärde is an architect and partner of 70°N arkitektur, Tromsø, Norway. With an educational background from Sweden and Paris, she has developed an experimental, participatory and research-based approach to architecture and planning, developed through practice and teaching in Norway and abroad, and presented in articles, conferences and publications internationally. In her work, methods, investigations and proposals centred on notions of openness and planning for an unknown future encompass issues of multiplicity and indeterminacy – lately with a particular focus on Arctic landscapes and societies.

Abdelillah Hamdouch is Professor of Urban and Regional Planning and Head of the Spatial Planning & Environment Department, Polytechnic School of the University of Tours, France, and Senior Researcher at the CNRS research unit CITERES (CIties, TERritories, Environment and Society). His ongoing research focus on the territorial dynamics of innovation and sustainable development in relation to spatial planning approaches. His recent co-edited volumes include: *Quand l'innovation fait la ville durable* (2015); *The International Handbook on Social Innovation* (2013); and *Mondialisation et résilience des territoires* (2012).

Britt Kramvig is Professor in the Department for Tourism and Northern Studies at the University of Tromsø, the Arctic University of Norway. She is inspired by science and technology studies (STS) and postcolonial theories, and is interested in ontologies and the multiple encounters in the North involving tourism, indigeneity, industries, whales, dreams and science as intervention. She is a CAS fellow on the Domestication project on the subject of the Anthropocene in the Arctic, as well as work on the HERA project *Arctic encounters* and the NFR project *Reason to return*.

John Loukakis is a lecturer at the Department of Geography, Harokopio University, Greece. He has been a main researcher in many national and European research programmes. His principal academic and research interests are urban safety policy, location theory, financial evaluation, recovery-rehabilitation and emergency planning.

Gisle Løkken is an architect, founding partner and manager of 70°N arkitektur, Tromsø, Norway. Through architecture practice, teaching and writing, he aims to develop an experimental and critical approach to architecture, urban development and planning, both locally and in a broader Scandinavian and Arctic context. He teaches regularly and is in demand as a lecturer, assessor and jury member in competitions and prize committees, both nationally and internationally. Lately his work has specially focused on common rights to cities and landscapes under the impact of strong global currents.

Hélène Mainet is Associate Professor in Geography at the University of Clermont-Ferrand II, France. Her research concentrates on small and medium-sized towns in Europe (especially in France and Poland) and in Africa (in relation to their role in urban–rural relationships). Her scientific interests and lecturing focus on urban geography, urban planning and development in non-metropolitan areas. Her most recent works deal with the issues of quality of life and sustainable development policies. She coordinates a multi-disciplinary French research programme on the attractiveness of intermediate towns.

xiv *Contributors*

Torill Nyseth is Professor of Community Planning at the University of Tromsø, the Arctic University of Norway. She has been involved in a number of research projects. Among her research leaderships are the following projects: *Multicultural Arctic Cities* (Norwegian Research Council 2011–13), *Place Reinvention in the Nordic Periphery: Governance Perspectives* (NORDREGIO 2006–7), *Public Policy and Network Governance – Challenges for Urban and Regional Development* (Norwegian Research Council 2006–9) and *EVAPLAN* (2014–18). Her main research interests are place making, network governance and urban planning. Besides many articles in academic journals and scientific books, her recent publications include the book *CitySami: Skandinaviske byer i et samisk perspektiv* (*Scandinavian Cities from a Saami Perspective*) (2015).

José Serrano is Associate Professor of Urban and Regional Planning at the University of Tours, France. His research focuses on land use conflicts in peri-urban areas. He analyses strategic planning documents, operational planning actions and actors' projects in order to understand the decisions about land use. He analyses the balance of power or the alliances. His latest work is on the implementation of multifunctional spaces.

Anders Tønnesen is a human geographer and senior researcher at the Institute of Transport Economics, Oslo, Norway. His research focuses on environmental policy-making and climate-friendly urban development, themes on which he has published articles in international scientific journals. In recent years, he has paid particular attention to urban planning in relation to land-use and transport-system development. In 2015 he had his public defence of a PhD involving analysis of environmental transport policy in a set of Norwegian case cities.

Kjerstin Uhre is architect and founding partner of Dahl & Uhre Architects in Tromsø, Norway and PhD fellow at the Institute of Urbanism and Landscape at the Oslo School of Architecture and Design. Her PhD research deals with cartographies of future landscapes in the European Arctic relating to the environment, resource exploitation, indigenous rights and land-use contestations. It analyses how mapping and counter-mapping take part in negotiations, and it draws on learnings from Dahl & Uhre Architects' comprehensive projects of public discourses at the city level, such as the strategy plan entitled *In the Middle of the World, in the Middle of Nuuk*.

Halvard Vike is Professor of Welfare Studies at the University College of South-East Norway and Senior Researcher at Telemark Research Institute. Until 2015, he was Professor of Anthropology at the University of Oslo. His research has focused on local politics, organizations, policy, cultural history and the state. His recent work has dealt mainly with comparative and historical perspectives on the Scandinavian welfare states and their contemporary transformations.

Preface

The contributions in this book stem primarily from the academic cooperation between researchers from the University of Tours and the University of Tromsø, under the umbrella of the AURORA – HUBERT CURIEN French–Norwegian exchange framework started in 2011 onwards.

Over the last few years, the researchers from the Department of Planning and Environment at the University of Tours have been involved in several research projects at the regional, national and European levels, investigating strategic spatial planning and the development models of small and medium-sized towns (SMSTs). Some partners of these projects have also agreed to contribute to this book. Other research cooperative agreements in the Planning Department at the University of Tours with European researchers and universities also offer inputs in various chapters on the theme, drawing on various national experiences (particularly in Europe).

In the same vein, the researchers from the Department of Sociology, Political Science & Community Planning, University of Tromsø are involved in various research projects and networks with Nordic partners. Within the framework of the NORDREGIO-financed 'Place Reinvention' project, processes of place transformation in industrial SMSTs are studied. Other projects have highlighted the innovative element in planning and development strategies ('Innovations in the Northern Periphery', 'Innovative rural communities').

Each of the two research groups responsible for editing the book (Tours and Tromsø) has its strengths and specialities. While the Tours milieu has explicitly addressed the ecological and regional economic aspects of the sustainability concept, the Tromsø researchers have focused more strongly on the social, cultural and governance aspects related to sustainability. Together, and relying on the merits resulting from the close cooperation taking place between the two research teams, we envisage a unique contribution to the planning discourse on creative measures and models to enhance sustainability.

We would like to sincerely thank our respective institutions and the programmes which supported the cooperative research which formed the basis of this book, as well as Mrs Muriel Hourlier, Research Engineer at the CNRS research unit CITERES (CIties, TERritories, Environment, Societies) at the University of Tours, who kindly agreed to prepare the manuscript for publication.

Introduction

Abdelillah Hamdouch, Torill Nyseth, Christophe Demazière, Anniken Førde, José Serrano and Nils Aarsæther

This book highlights creative approaches in planning and local development. The dynamic complexity, diversity and fluidity characterizing contemporary societies represent challenges for planning and development endeavours (Hillier, 2007; Healey, 2010). There is ample evidence that the socio-economic challenges induced by the globalization process, and the profound redefinition of urban hierarchies that places and regions are confronted with cannot be tackled and managed adequately either within the neo-liberal perspective (Harvey, 2006) or with the intellectual technical-legal apparatus and mindset of traditional land-use planning (Jessop, 2000; Albrechts, 2010).

Cities are nodes in the global economy, but have different functions that emanate from particular urban qualities, and their role in the urban hierarchy influences their ability to cope with these challenges (Taylor et al., 2011). Depending on their size, national and regional institutional context, main economic sectors and social structures inherited from the past, etc., cities and towns find themselves in more or less favourable situations. Their resilience and adaptation capacity, especially in terms of redefining/reinventing the very bases of their socio-economic development, plays a crucial role. Small and medium-sized towns (SMSTs), particularly those which historical economic development based on traditional industrial sectors, are specifically confronted by such challenges. Being less diversified than larger urban centres, many SMSTs experience problems due to de-industrialization, unemployment, an ageing population, etc., and they also face competition with neighbouring territories, other SMSTs and larger urban areas, as they struggle to find a position within the new territorial organization and urban hierarchies that emerge in most regions and countries (Dicken, 1999; Servillo et al., 2014).

One key idea constituting the backbone of this book is that places, and especially SMSTs, could only find their way in this challenging new context if they are able to think, plan and act in creative and innovative ways. This means that SMSTs in general, though depending on their specific situations and national/regional contexts, are doomed to be creative in the way they envisage, design and implement local development strategies.

But then a crucial question immediately arises: what could enhance creativity in local development and planning? Is it possible to identify creative capacity building at the level of the city that might release imaginative and innovative activities? Under what local and super-local conditions is creativity being initiated and flourishing? What are the major obstacles and in what way can these be contained in order to safeguard pockets of creative action?

These are some of the questions that will be addressed in this book. By presenting examples of open processes, experiments, and new forms of facing and defining problems, the authors explore and discuss different creative approaches. Creativity to us means being open to new ideas and approaches that are sensitive to today's socio-economic complexities. Creativity means social innovation, experimentation and collective learning in dealing with people's needs and aspirations, and imaginative ways of solving common or community problems. Creativity also refers to approaches, attitudes and practices to include and empower those who perhaps are not, but should be, involved in planning processes. In this way, it means the practice of bringing imagined futures into being (Healey, 2010).

This book is not intended to produce a generic theory or a 'ready-to-use recipe' for introducing or implementing local development strategies in SMSTs. Rather, it is an attempt to identify some key entries for analysing how SMSTs cope with contemporary socio-economic challenges and are able to engage in 'new ways of doing things', which are in some cases unique, while in other cases are new in their specific regional or national context.

This exploratory orientation of the book is justified by the fact that SMSTs remain understudied in the planning and urban development literature as compared to cities and metropolitan areas. But it is also motivated by the new awareness in many countries and regions of the important bridging role played by SMSTs as intermediate spaces between large urban centres and low-density, rural and semi-urban areas. Indeed, this orientation is in tune with contemporary theories of social innovation and their translation into urban and local (community) development (Moulaert et al., 2013), and with creative and experimental planning theory (Healey, 2004; Albrechts and Hillier, 2010; Nyseth, 2011). Therefore, the aim of the book is to exploit the potentials of contemporary theories of planning, taking them as inputs to the debate of innovative thinking, hopefully with implications for local development and planning practices.

The contributions in this book also offer a critical and reflexive perspective, especially through discussing what can be learned from the approaches and cases offered. Finally, the book focuses on new and more interdisciplinary approaches to the study of local development that can help us to understand and better grasp the complexity of planning and development practices, linking economic, environmental, cultural and social dynamics.

Therefore, the book is organized as a scientific anthology, with contributions from researchers from various disciplines and nationalities. Planning and development are areas of research that require interdisciplinary approaches. Much of the planning literature has focused on the growth and transformations of larger urban regions, not unexpectedly, as the growth of metropolitan areas has been one of the driving forces in contemporary, global development. In this book, we want to complement the urban studies tradition with a searchlight on the SMSTs found in great numbers all over Europe, but rarely studied in the planning literature (Bell and Jayne, 2009; Servillo et al., 2014).

Case studies from France and Norway, as well as studies from Canada, Greece, Greenland, Italy, Poland and Sweden, illustrate how spatial dynamics are informed by innovative and creative planning practices. Our argument, however, is not to maintain that creativity and social innovation have replaced bureaucratic, representative democracy-inspired or business lobby modes of governing places and towns. What we contend is that more knowledge about the circumstances in which innovation and creative arise and thrive should have implication for how we theorize the field of contemporary urban planning.

In sum, the book aims at providing a template for critical, comparative and contextual perspectives on the quest for sustainability and resilience in SMSTs. Collaborative and potentially innovative approaches are therefore emphasized, as are the shortcomings, pitfalls and 'traps' that can emerge in the wake of processes aimed at concerting ecological, economic and socio-cultural concerns, and the discourses promoting them.

The book has 13 chapters organized into three parts, followed by a final 'postscript' in Chapter 14, summing up and discussing pathways towards a critical and comparative approach to creative planning for local development.

Part I: Approaches to planning and local development: analytical landmarks and methodological challenges

In Chapter 1 the editors introduce the reader to different approaches to planning and development in a European context and provide a framework for a critical and comparative understanding. This introductory chapter also discusses variation and implications of geography, size and formal institutional frameworks, and introduces analytical landmarks and methodological challenges.

The nature of SMSTs is addressed by Demazière in Chapter 2. SMSTs have not been sufficiently addressed, and the categories of 'small town' and 'medium-sized town' are poorly understood. An analytical challenge is that there are actually few theories fitted to the study of SMSTs (Daniels 1989; Bell and Jayne 2009). In this context, we should be aware of a tendency to copy/paste analytical frameworks developed for the study of the largest cities (Amin and Graham, 1997). The chapter reflects further on the contribution of research dedicated to SMSTs to the progress of urban studies. Demazière illustrates this issue by tracing the evolution of French urban studies tradition dedicated to towns throughout the twentieth century, from the first monographs to more recent studies that insert such places into urban and economic networks of major proportions. In response to the fact that studies of SMSTs are at the margins of urban studies, Demazière claims that being at the margins could be turned into an advantage. He argues that studies of SMSTs cannot copy methodologies used to account for metropolitan dynamics. Innovation also takes place outside metropolitan environments. Studies from France indicate that channels for the structuring and coordination of innovation play a leading role in the development of towns.

In Chapter 3 Hamdouch and Banovac discuss local actors dynamics as levers of socio-economic development. The chapter explores spatial planning approaches in 31 SMSTs from ten European countries and, above all, the importance of 'ordinary politics of planning' (Newman, 2008) for the socio-economic development in SMSTs. Interactions among the actors involved are in focus, and examples of successful and creative approaches to local development in European towns are explored. The authors present the main features of SMSTs in terms of their functional roles within the urban system, their socio-economic profiles and the way they have been addressed in European Union (EU) policies. There then follows a discussion of the key characteristics and particularities of the national/regional institutional frameworks in which the case studies are embedded. The dynamics of the interaction between local actors involved in local development are discussed along with local actors' ways of addressing challenges, opportunities and incentives that affect a town's socio-economic trajectory.

A process of urban reinvention in the medium-sized Norwegian city of Drammen is the focus in Chapter 4. Nyseth and Tønnesen emphasize the numerous reasons behind the new image and reputation that Drammen has accomplished. From one viewpoint, this process manifests itself as a traditional regulative type of planning On the other hand, new forms of governance involving both market and civil society actors cannot be overlooked. Consensus building involving a number of stakeholders and collaborative efforts is also a part of the success story. Altogether, the Drammen 'model' seems to rest on flexible, innovative and integrative approaches to planning and urban development. The authors argue that an integrated planning approach can be creative. Integrative approaches to planning and development then are more than the approach promoted by the regulation school (Moulaert et al., 2013). Integration is no longer about creating one coordinated 'whole'; rather, it is about creating the partial, fluid and alternating integration of relations. Integrated approaches to urban development must keep economic, social and environmental considerations in conjunction to meet sustainability aims.

Introduction 5

Part II: Can place transformation be planned? Challenges to creative planning in small and medium-sized towns

Part II contains five chapters and presents innovative responses to competitive pressure and economic vulnerability. In this respect, resilience strategies of urban planning and promotion of local attractiveness are vital elements. Analyses of the *new economy* potentials are highlighted, especially within culture, tourism and conservation strategies.

In Chapter 5 Førde and Kramvig discuss cultural industries as a basis for local development. In Norway, as in many European countries, cultural industries are regarded as a promising toolkit for future economic growth, strengthening the attractiveness of regions as well as contributing to local development. During the past decade, numerous policy programmes have been established, aiming at stimulating innovation and facilitating creative processes within this field. The authors discuss the challenges facing the actors in this field. Creativity and innovation are social processes which unfold in complex and often fluid networks. Through a study of a policy programme for cultural industries in the medium-sized north Norwegian city of Tromsø, the authors discuss the challenges of planning for the 'unknown'. As traditional models are perceived as unfit to meet the complexities of cultural industries, the need for new methods and more flexible and sensitive approaches in planning and development policies emerge. The chapter addresses the ambivalence of facilitating creativity through public policy and programmes. By examining the effort of creating an experimental policy model, the authors show how technocratic understandings of innovation are challenged and more sensitive and reflexive approaches are presented. They argue for a relational perspective on innovation to make planning and policy programmes that are open to complexity and difference, 'allowing the presence of the non-present'. This implies changing the focus from the end-product to creative processes, applying a multifaceted concept of value and taking the risk of emphasizing the unknown.

Next, in Chapter 6 Demazière, Hamdouch and Banovac explore innovative actions for local development in SMSTs in the Centre-Val de Loire region in France, a region which has been badly hit by the current economic crisis. The chapter particularly focuses on how social cohesion and cultural and creative activities are planned in SMSTs and the way in which they contribute to the local development. Many local governments are engaged in such policies. Social cohesion policies are seen as the 'social glue', fostering socio-economic inclusion and diversity, and contributing as innovative drivers to local (re)development. Case studies show that municipalities, supported by national policies, have succeeded in implementing creative and innovative policies promoting social cohesion. The chapter also gives an overview of the key features of social cohesion and cultural and creative activities relevant to local development. In its conclusion, the 'innovativeness' in the French case studies and the lessons for other SMSTs that are looking for new and creative ways of doing planning and local development policies are discussed.

Serrano and Hamdouch present a case study of two SMSTs located in the peri-urban areas of Marseille and Rennes in France in Chapter 7. The focus is on economic projects, in particular through the planning both at the urban region and the two municipalities scale for the implementation of new business parks. The conceptualization of the creative approach and the kind of relationships presupposed by this approach are discussed. The authors show how municipalities coordinate their economic strategy at the urban regional level and implement it at the local level. Business parks are regarded as important tools for economic development, but they also consume green spaces. The case studies show that it is difficult to favour the protection of natural spaces and the biodiversity they host when the modernization or extension of business parks is given priority by municipalities and local economic actors.

In Chapter 8 Delladetsima and Loukakis discuss potentials and obstacles to creative planning in a crisis context. Based on a case study of the port city of Patras in Greece, the authors elaborate upon the role of planning and its creative potential in contributing to sustainable local development and innovation. In the context of the current crises, they ask whether creative planning can contribute to overcoming the negative trends. Through identifying factors determining the development potentials of the city, they show how spatial planning relies on a physical deterministic blueprint rationale detached from other economic, environmental and cultural policies. This results in developmental and innovation policies that could be characterized as being ad hoc in nature. The situation urges for more creative planning, combining physical, social, economic, cultural and environmental policies.

In Chapter 9, the final chapter of this section, Aarsæther and Vike discuss 'the Fornebu experiment' – the transformation from an airport site to a new urban neighbourhood, addressing creativity in terms of what may be the planners' ultimate dream: starting from scratch to create a new suburban area in the former national airport area near Oslo. The chapter focuses on the innovative ways of delivering educational, cultural and healthcare services to the new inhabitants, in which the fundamental principle was to assemble a multitude of functions in 'village centres'. However, this territorial integrationist strategy of village centres, as multifunctional areas located within people's immediate neighbourhood, was abandoned by the municipal administration. The chapter discusses why the integrated model for service provisions failed in a context that should in theory have offered the optimal preconditions for its successful implementation.

Part III: Social innovation, participatory governance and collective learning as levers of creative planning

Part III contains five chapters dealing with sustainability and environmental issues. An extended understanding of sustainability includes analyses of social cohesion and social innovation as key inputs for the development of SMSTs. Novel types of governance processes and participation as crucial dimensions of a more creative approach to urban planning are also addressed. These issues are severe challenges to planners in SMSTs as they demand a radical change in mentalities and the way in which planning should be performed through continuous and sharing processes of learning.

In Chapter 10 Uhre and Dahl address the appearance of the new urban landscape of Nuuk, the capital of Greenland. Based on experiences as architects in an award-winning planning project in Nuuk and from citizen participatory processes in Tromsø, the authors show how broad and inclusive *city dialogues* – combined with visual representations of ideas along the way (visualizing futures) – open up new opportunities to address a broad spectrum of questions in planning projects. Concrete examples of dialogue as a basis for planning are presented, e.g. a dialogue through which the relevance of taking into account historical, present and geopolitical contexts for designing spatial inventions emerges among the actors. This is explored from the architect's point of view regarding the acts of drawing and modelling as ways of understanding and mediating complex and often contradictory knowledges and desires in the becoming of spatial futures. The authors demonstrate the opportunities of producing visual and material arguments, using the slogan 'they shall see what we hear', in participatory processes. They also discuss the concepts of city dialogues, exploring dialogical capacity building in negotiation and discourse.

The relation between economic development and social cohesion is the focus of Chapter 11. Hamdouch and Ghaffari here suggest that social innovation is a common ground between economic development and social cohesion. Based on case studies of SMSTs in France and Canada, the authors argue that the analytical approach proposed still requires theoretical elaboration and empirical evidence to support it. Indeed, several important questions deserve further investigation. Particularly important is to better document the effect of growing size on the ability of a town to preserve a high potential of local networking among actors that could support and sustain social innovation dynamics. Likewise, the variability of national policies (especially in times of crisis and sharp global competition) in the funding of SMSTs' policies may represent a threat to the efforts of local actors. Finally, one may wonder if SMSTs are able to develop and/or sustain planning approaches and policies balancing economic development and social cohesion when key actors weaken their engagement or simply 'fly away' to places (including large cities) offering better financial or institutional opportunities. The functional role that SMSTs can play in evolving urban hierarchies is clearly an issue; equally crucial is their ability to plan for sustained cooperative commitments with other cities and towns they can complement/work with in the mid- to long term.

In Chapter 12 Løkken and Haggärde present a reflective, critical and committed approach on sustainable planning in the Arctic. Arctic landscapes and societies are more than ever affected by the impact of global incidents beyond local influence or control. Severe environmental challenges due to demographic change, escalating urbanization, economic crisis and the over-exploitation of nature have evoked awareness of the vulnerability of Arctic ecosystems. The authors argue that studying and practising in an Arctic landscape requires knowledge, curiosity and an open mindset. The landscape must be investigated and understood as an assemblage of spatial narrations, events and practices – as an experience that acknowledges both the objective and the subjective, including natural processes and history. An open, inviting and experimental planning approach can be relevant for the local inhabitants only if they feel that it is based on their experience of issues that they consider to be important and that it allows for extensive participation; at the same time, this approach requires from the actors that they recognize the impact of the global forces of transformation. Because the nature and the reality of life are by no means static, future planning primarily has to be formulated as a tool in a process that is always looking for new knowledge, making use of this knowledge and at the same time facilitating for experimentation with new solutions. Planning and architecture must strive towards a continuous reformulation and renewal, and thus will always emerge as a work in progress.

In Chapter 13 Mainet and Edouard explore the quality of life and attractiveness issues in SMSTs. They develop a critical perspective on the role of quality of life in attractiveness discourses and policies of SMSTs. In changing contexts linked to economic restructuring process, the effects of metropolization impact on the lower levels of the urban hierarchy. A growing residential mobility of the population linked to increased social demands for better amenities and quality of life are factors that challenge the implementation of development policies in SMSTs. Local actors are confronted with different and sometimes ambivalent options: to develop productive and/or residential economies; to retain and attract businesses and/or people; to compete or cooperate with other policy-makers; and to reproduce successful models and/or try to promote innovative actions. Affordability and liveability stand out as the primary drivers of the attractiveness of SMSTs, supported by specific qualities of community and place, including the non-economic dimensions of everyday life. Mainet and Edouard suggest that local and national governments need to pay closer attention to the local context rather than adopting a 'one-size-fits-all' approach (Bishop and Han, 2013). The question for SMSTs is that being really innovative is probably closely linked to quality of life, to a limited growth-rate and to a controlled attractiveness. SMSTs could then become models of quality cities and towns and could function as reference points for larger cities looking for solutions to improve their own quality of life. Some already do.

Finally, Chapter 14 sums up the book and draws the lines between the different contributions and discussions in the preceding chapters. In addition, the editors develop some new ideas toward a critical and comparative perspective of planning relevant to both academics and practitioners, but also in the context of a prospective research agenda.

References

Albrechts, L. (2010) Enhancing creativity and action orientation in planning. In J. Hillier and P. Healey (eds), *The Ashgate Research Companion to Planning Theory: Conceptual Challenges for Spatial Planning*. Farnham: Ashgate, pp. 215–32.

Amin, A. and Graham, S. (1997) The ordinary City. *Transactions of the Institute of British Geographers*, 22(4): 411–29.

Bell D. and Jayne, M. (2009) Small cities? Towards a research agenda. *International Journal of Urban and Regional Studies*, 22(3): 683–99.

Bishop, A. and Han, S.S. (2013) Growth of the creative economy in small regional cities: A case study of Bendigo. Paper presented at the State of Australian Cities Conference. Available at: http://www.soacconference.com.au/wp-content/uploads/2013/12/Bishop-Economy.pdf.

Daniels, T. (1989) Small town economic development: Growth or survival? *Journal of Planning Literature*, 4: 413–29.

Dicken, P. (1999) *Global Shift: Transforming the World Economy*. London: Paul Chapman Publishing.

Harvey, D. (2006) *Spaces of Global Capitalism: Towards a Theory of Uneven Geographical Development*. New York: Verso.

Healey, P. (2004) Creativity and urban governance. *Policy Studies*, 25(2): 87–102.

—— (2010) *Making Better Places. The Planning Project in the Twenty-First Century*. Basingstoke: Palgrave Macmillan.

Hillier, J. (2007) *Stretching beyond the Horizon. A Multiplanar Theory of Spatial Planning and Governance*. Aldershot: Ashgate.

Jessop, B. (2000) Globalization, entrepreneurial cities and the social economy. In P. Hamel, M. Lustiger-Thaler and M. Mayer (eds), *Urban Movements in a Global Environment*. London: Routledge, pp. 81–100.

Massey, D. (2007). *World City*. London: Polity.

Moulaert, F., MacCallum, D., Mehmood, A. and Hamdouch, A. (eds) (2013) *The International Handbook on Social Innovation. Collective Action, Social Learning and Transdisciplinary Research*. Cheltenham: Edward Elgar.

Newman, P. (2008) Strategic spatial planning: Collective action and moments of opportunity. *European Planning Studies*, 16(10): 1371–83.

Nyseth, T. (2011) The Tromsø experiment: opening up for the unknown. *Town Planning Review*, 82(5): 573–95.

Servillo, L., Atkinson, R., Smith, I., Russo, A., Sýkora, L., Demazière, C. and Hamdouch, A. (2014) *TOWN – Small and Medium-Sized Towns in their Functional Territorial Context*. Final Report, Luxembourg: ESPON.

Taylor, P.J., Ni, P., Derudder, B. Hoyler, M., Huang, J. and Witlox, F. (eds) (2011) *Global Urban Analyses: A Survey of Cities in Globalization*. London: Earthscan.

Part I
Approaches to planning and local development
Analytical landmarks and methodological challenges

1 Perspectives on creative planning and local development in small and medium-sized towns

Torill Nyseth, Abdelillah Hamdouch, Christophe Demazière, Nils Aarsæther, Anniken Førde and José Serrano

Since the 1980s, regional and local governments have adopted a proactive stance in order to face the challenge of economic decline, under conditions of scarce resources, rising citizen needs and often with inadequate or ineffective planning instruments (Moulaert, 2000). The traditional planning model, which tried to manage growth by defining zones and building densities, has been replaced (with considerable variation between countries) by strategic spatial planning, whose aim is to foster growth by focusing on larger projects (Douay, 2010). Whereas the traditional planning model was dominated by experts and elected politicians, private sector actors and civil society groups today influence planning decisions through a number of means. Added to this, the social composition of towns and cities has become less homogeneous, requiring sensitivity to cultural issues. Obviously, planners need new methods for staging inclusive processes as well as for selecting, designing and implementing projects which are to make real the orientations of the negotiated plan (Albrechts, 2004).

Goals in conflict: a challenge for planning

Planning institutions have also been exposed to the urgent needs for climate-adaptive solutions and environmental sustainability – to be worked out in societies in which the electoral behaviour of the voters does not always promote ecological solutions. Campbell (1996: 296) has argued that 'planners face tough decisions about where they stand on protecting the green city, promoting the economically growing city, and advocating social justice. Conflicts among these goals are not superficial ones'. Nahrath et al. (2009: 5) added that the implementation of sustainability principles at the local level implies significant transformations of spatial scales where issues are identified and where public policies are conceived, decided upon and implemented. Also, after several decades of local experiments towards sustainability, local actors have increasingly taken into account national (and supra-national) legislation and norms, focusing on climate change within the sustainability agenda. At the same time, local planners must also observe the restrictions on action placed by strong norms of protecting property rights, free competition and the principles of promoting the mobility of goods, services and people. This requires a capacity to adapt to top-down change as well as to tap into the many possibilities proposed by regional, national or European calls for projects.

Creative orientation in planning

All these challenges call for an innovative and creative orientation in planning and development work. As the terrain demanding planning practices is changing into a more complex situation, there is a pressing need for an open, dynamic and flexible approach to planning and local development that is adaptable to changing circumstances and to uncertainty. Or, as Jean Hillier puts it, 'we need to look into the sun, think at the edge, and cross boundaries' (Hillier, 2008: 281).

But is planning in itself an adequate tool to counter the multitude of challenges in urban development? One type of opposition to planning is represented by neo-liberals who argue that the innovative energy is driven by market processes, while planning never will be able to depart from a bureaucratic, standardized rule-following activity with no room for new ideas or flexibility (Pennington, 2000). This is not necessarily the case as planning theory and practice have moved away from technocratic practices and incremental approaches. Over the last two decades or so, spatial planning has become a field of experimentation where new tools are deployed, based on communicative practices and with the involvement of multiple actors, i.e. practices that have replaced the top-down imposition of goals and policies (Balducci, 2008). Still, planners need to grasp the momentum and to challenge mental models that limit their creativity and look at prospects for 'breaking-out-of-the-box' (Albrechts, 2005: 263).

Innovation and creativity, however, have been regarded as opposites to planning. Creativity and innovation are fuzzy and broad concepts that need to be defined in order to be useful as analytical concepts. Creativity has also become a buzzword triggered off by Richard Florida (2002) and his ideas about the creative class and linked to new economy entrepreneurialism, place-marketing and urban growth (Pratt, 2008).

Three meanings of creativity

Creativity in our view can be linked to at least three different meanings. The first one is the most straightforward, and links creativity to innovation and the search for 'new' policies, products, practices or participants. It places value on non-routine practices, on the ability of individuals to learn, on the actor's capacity to draw in new ideas from outside and to link them to the specifics of local situations, and it emphasizes the importance of experimentation and exploration (Balducci, 2011).

The second meaning moves beyond an individualist concept of creativity, also criticizing the mere economistic view on innovation (Jessop et al., 2013) and addressing the dimensions of urban and regional dynamics (Landry, 2000). A long-running critique of notions such as creativity and entrepreneurship, as well as innovation, has been that they have been conceived of as individualistic and not social phenomena (Pratt, 2008). But creativity is socially embedded; being creative in a vacuum is not productive. New planning frameworks and an increased awareness of the importance of culture, art and creative capacities in cities and towns are much in evidence (Landry, 2000; Kunzmann, 2004; Knox and Mayer, 2009; Tremblay and Pilati, 2013, Young and Stevenson, 2013).

A third meaning focuses on creativity as the *process* of making new 'products', whether these are material or immaterial. Ingold and Hallam (2007) argue that creativity must be understood by way of its processes rather than its products. They challenge what they see as a backward reading of creativity in terms of its results, and propose a forward reading by seeing creativity as improvisation. As improvisation is generative, relational, temporal and performative, this implies challenging the polarity between novelty and convention, and accepting a world always in the making (Ingold and Hallam, 2007: 3).

In this book, we lean on Michalko's definition of creativity as 'the ability to view problems, situations and challenges in new and different ways and to invent and develop original, imaginative futures in response to these problems, situations and challenges' (Michalko, 2001, cited in Albrechts, 2005). Planners need the assistance from reflexive social theory to break free from concepts, structures and ideas that are mainly there through the process of continuity (Albrechts, 2005: 253). Recognition of the need to encourage innovation in a context of dynamic complexity suggests a mode of planning and development projects allowing for experimentation and promotes an understanding of experiments as models that may fail as well as succeed. Experiments are speculative methods of knowing, working with doubt and uncertainty (Healey, 2008; Hillier, 2008; Nyseth, 2011). But what kind of creativity does planning require and, in turn, what kind of planning is needed to facilitate creative activities for local development? How can planning become more innovative and more creative in dealing with places? These pertinent questions were asked by Louis Albrechts in an article in *Planning Theory* entitled 'Creativity as a drive for change' (Albrechts, 2005) and his arguments for creativity are followed up in this book.

Creativity to us means to be open to new ideas and approaches that are sensitive to social and cultural complexities, where social innovation, experimentation and collective learning are key inputs for thinking about people's needs and aspirations, and imaginative ways for solving common or community problems. Creativity also refers to approaches, attitudes and practices that include means to empower those who are or should be involved in planning processes. It means the practice of bringing imagined futures into being (Healey, 2010).

Since planning and local development capacities are firmly linked to national institutional systems, we also need to reflect on the change for places induced by neo-liberal reforms such as the adoption of a free-market system throughout Europe or by democratic moves in the form of legal and fiscal decentralization in Western European countries (Sager, 2013). Does devolution foster creativity in local development strategies, or does it lead to a zero-sum territorial competition? The process of policy change 'is not just about the formal design of regulatory legislation and resource allocation: it also involves changing the discourses in all arenas which are significant for policy to have an effect' (Vigar et al., 2000: 50–1). For instance, the rhetorics of competitiveness or of sustainable development at the national or European level have to be translated into ideas and arguments that have salience for actors at the local level. This translation work is also part of the planning processes, and so is the need to procure an awareness of the tensions between neo-liberal regulations and measures to enhance ecological and social sustainability. If this translation work is not competently carried out, habits and traditions of action may resist change or channel processes in unforeseen directions. As a result, creativity is not only inspired by the will of local actors to explore new ways of imagining a future for a place; it is also a characteristic of place-based approaches advocated at the national and European levels (Ingold and Hallam, 2007; Barca, 2009; Jessop et al., 2013). In this respect, the literature on local and regional development has already made key contributions on creativity at work within territorial development strategies (Blakely, 1989; Stöhr, 1990), often stressing the social and cultural embeddedness of economic dynamics (Mingione, 1981; Fua and Zacchia, 1983). Such approaches can be updated by examining the current challenges identified by place-based actors across Europe. Several paradoxes can be seen. For instance, whereas planning for sustainability revolves around the preservation of a core reproduction potential, it is more often based on a principle of change management rather than the characteristic of a status quo (Bagheri and Hjorth, 2007). At the same time, the notion of sustainability gives way to different and sometimes divergent interpretations in the planning field (Berke and Conroy, 2000). We can also argue that since large cities are considered as the type of spatial organization most capable of containing and adapting to global economic changes, rural areas and towns especially need to be creative in their search for novel planning models (Knox and Mayer, 2009; Servillo et al., 2014), otherwise they are at risk of being increasingly marginalized.

Creative co-thinking

Indeed, too often, developmental strategies address economic sectors, social welfare and cultural issues, or the natural environment, without taking into account the demanding task of 'co-thinking' or sorting out how a coherent and sustainable 'whole' can be approached at the level of the town, district or neighbourhood. In this respect, strategic spatial planning makes up a template for visions which may inspire creative attempts to link together the various sectorial challenges faced by places, but can itself run the risk of becoming disconnected from the decision-making sphere (Albrechts, 2005).

The debate on creativity in planning has a strong territorial dimension. Within the scope of the new post-industrial and information/knowledge-based economy, large cities are seen as catalysts and nodal points for global processes to land locally (Capello, 2013). Whereas research and policy work has focused to a large degree on big cities and on metropolitan regions, there has been relatively little work on 'smaller places' such as smaller cities and towns (McCann, 2004; Bell and Jayne, 2009). However, in Europe, the large cities are not the primary economic drivers in the way they seem to be in North America or Asia (Dijkstra et al., 2013). Considering the 264 metropolitan city-regions of more than half a million people in the Organisation for Economic Co-operation and Development (OECD) countries, those situated in Europe represented only 36 per cent of the total population and 43 per cent of gross domestic product (GDP), as compared to respectively 53 per cent and 58 per cent in North America, and 69 per cent and 70 per cent in Asia (OECD, 2012). While only 30 per cent of the European Union (EU) population lives in cities of more than 100,000 people, 38 per cent live in small and medium-sized towns having between 5,000 and 100,000 residents (European Commission, 2011).

As the globalized economy puts pressure on local firms and on the local welfare system, many small and medium-sized towns (SMSTs) suffer employment losses in the wake of economic restructuring processes. In addition, the metropolitan environments appear increasingly attractive to young people seeking better educational and employment opportunities, cultural and leisure facilities, etc. This tendency must be considered when discussing future revitalization and growth in the smaller urban settings. Finally, as geographically close SMSTs are often competing for new residents and commuters, new businesses, tourists, etc., planners must also think of policies or actions that could promote more cooperative arrangements and strategies with neighbouring towns. All in all, demographic and economic factors may thus exert much influence on local development, and attempts at creating sustainability at the level of a SMST are today highly challenging (Servillo et al., 2014).

No standardized responses

As the terrain of community practices is thus changing, there are no standardized responses to meet the challenges. Integrated area development, which emphasizes the key role of socially innovative initiatives and strategies (Moulaert, 2000), is one example of a creative response to particular challenges faced by neighbourhoods within a participatory framework. What we know, however, is that expert knowledge no longer has a particular status and is often questioned, and that collective learning, democratic participation and representation are closely linked to planning and development work. In other words, several stakeholders and citizen groups will be involved in networking, negotiations and outright competition in planning and development processes (Moulaert et al., 2013). But there is a lack of literature on how the quest for innovative and sustainable planning is to be met (Mieg, 2010). Addressing these aspects explicitly, and in different contexts, this book will contribute to a better understanding of the 'ingredients' that may foster and feed creative approaches in planning and development.

From an analytical point of view, our approach to creative planning and development in SMSTs builds on four key ideas (or assumptions):

1. All towns and cities are facing huge challenges due to global pressures from inter-territorial competition, rapid technological change, and increasing societal concerns (environmental, social, cultural, etc.). These challenges and their very consequences (de-industrialization, poverty, social fragmentation, urban fragmentation, identity erosion, harms to the environment) create a bundle of radical uncertainties.
2. Consequently, planning in (and for) a fast-changing world cannot be done with planning tools that have been designed for a rather stable and linear process of industrial modernization. Paraphrasing organization theory, one may say that every city or town must now 'negotiate' with its environment and develop planning capabilities allowing for a dynamic resilience rather than a mere ex-post adaptation to change and new challenges and pressures (on this, see the introduction to Hamdouch et al., 2012). To be sure, many planning tools have evolved considerably over the last two decades (particularly as designed and implemented in large cities), introducing large-scale participation, selectiveness of objectives and evaluation. These changes may emerge as bottom-up approaches, but increasingly they result from changes in the national and EU legislations. Still, we believe that significant further progress towards 'planning differently' remain at stake, notably in smaller towns and cities.
3. Thus, 'creative planning' for local development is a must, a crucial need and no longer a matter of choice. This is particularly decisive for SMSTs that have usually, as compared to larger cities and metropolises, other resources and capabilities (including in planning), less diversified economic activities, and which may, as a consequence, be more vulnerable to shocks and external threats.
4. Accordingly creative planning has to rely on open-ended but at the same time productive networks and relations. A commitment to the city and its future is perhaps the only common denominator, but such a

Perspectives on creative planning and local development 19

commitment can be a powerful tool, because no one is by definition excluded from participating in, or contributing to, the planning process. The professional planners, together with elected politicians, will not always be the driving forces when creativity and innovative moves are in need. The local business community, professional networks, cultural and environmental activists, and the large number of voluntary organizations may individually or in concert produce initiatives, mobilize resources or open new network connections that may impinge on the strategies pursued. In the following chapters, the authors describe and analyse how innovative and creative processes may engage a very broad range of actors, institutions and projects, certainly operating within different legal frameworks and socio-economic contexts, but all highlighting the potentials of creative and innovative planning practices.

References

Albrechts, L. (2004) Strategic (spatial) planning re-examined. *Environment and Planning B*, 31(5): 743–58.

—— (2005) Creativity as a drive for change. *Planning Theory*, 4(3): 247–69.

Bagheri, A. and Hjorth, P. (2007) Planning for sustainable development: A paradigm shift towards a process-based approach. *Sustainable Development*, 15(1): 83–96.

Balducci. A. (2008) Constructing (spatial) strategies in complex environments. In J. van den Broeck, F. Moulaert and S. Oosterlynck (eds), *Exploring the Planning Field: Ethics, Creativity and Action*. Leuven: Acco, pp. 79–99.

—— (2011) Strategic planning as exploration. *Town Planning Review*, 82(5): 529–47.

Barca, F. (2009) *An Agenda for a Reformed Cohesion Policy, A Place-Based Approach to Meeting European Union Challenges and Expectations*. Independent Report prepared at the request of Danuta Hübner, Commissioner for Regional Policy, Brussels.

Bell, D. and Jayne, M. (2009) Small cities? Towards a research agenda. *International Journal of Urban and Regional Studies*, 22(3): 683–99.

Berke, P.R. and Conroy, M.M. (2000) Are we planning for sustainable development? *Journal of American Planning Association*, 66(1): 21–33.

Blakely, E.J. (1989) *Planning Local Economic Development*. Newbury Park, CA: Sage.

Campbell, S. (1996) Green cities, growing cities, just cities? Urban planning and the contradictions of sustainable development, *Journal of the American Planning Association*, 62(3): 296–312.

Capello, R. (2013) Recent theoretical paradigms in urban growth. *European Planning Studies*, 21(3): 316–33.

Dijkstra, L., Garcilazo, E. and McCann, P. (2013) The economic performance of cities and city-regions: Myths and realities. *European Planning Studies*, 21(3): 334–54.

Douay, N. (2010) Collaborative planning and the challenge of urbanization: Issues, actors and strategies in Marseilles and Montreal metropolitan areas. *Canadian Journal of Urban Research*, 11(1): 50–69.

European Commission (2011) *Cities of Tomorrow – Challenges, Visions, Ways Forward*. Brussels: European Commission.

Florida, R. (2002) *The Rise of the Creative Class*. New York: Basic Books.
Fua, G. and Zacchia, C. (eds) (1983) *Industrializzazione senza fratture*. Bologna: Il Mulino.
Hamdouch, A., Depret, M.-H. and Tangy, C. (eds) (2012) *Mondialisation et résilience des territoires. Trajectoires, dynamiques d'acteurs et experiences*. Québec: Presses de l'Université du Québec.
Healey, P. (2008) Making choices that matter. The practical art of situated strategic judgement in spatial strategy-making. In J. Van den Broeck, F. Moulaert and S. Oosterlynck (eds), *Empowering the Planning Fields. Liber Amicorum Louis Albrecht*. Leuven/Voorburg: Acco, pp. 23–41.
—— (2010) *Making Better Places: The Planning Project in the Twenty-First Century*. Basingstoke: Palgrave Macmillan.
Hillier, J. (2008) Plan(e)speaking: A multiplanar theory of spatial planning. *Planning Theory*, 7: 24–50.
Ingold, T. and Hallam, E. (2007) Creativity and cultural improvisation: An introduction. In. E. Hallam and T. Ingodl (eds), *Creativity and Cultural Improvisation*. Oxford: Berg, pp. 1–24.
Jessop, B., Moulaert, F., Hulgård, L. and Hamdouch, A. (2013) Social innovation research: A new stage in innovation analysis. In F. Moulaert, D. MacCallum, A. Mehmood and A. Hamdouch (eds), *The International Handbook on Social Innovation: Collective Action, Social Learning and Transdisciplinary Research*. Cheltenham: Edward Elgar, pp. 110–30.
Knox, P.L. and Mayer, H. (2009) *Small Town Sustainability*. Basel: Birkhäuser Verlag AG.
Kunzmann, K. (2004) Culture, creativity and spatial planning. *Town Planning Review*, 75(4): 383–404.
Landry, C. (2000) *The Creative City: A Toolkit for Urban Innovators*. London: Earthscan.
McCann E.J. (2004) 'Best places': Interurban competition, quality of life and popular media discourse. *Urban Studies*, 41(10): 1909–29.
Michalco, M. (2001) *Cracking Creativity*. Berkeley, CA: Ten Speed Press.
Mieg, H. (2010) Sustainability and innovation in urban development: Concept and case. *Sustainable Development*, Published online by Wiley InterScience (www.interscience.wiley.com). DOI: 10.1002/sd.471.
Mingione, E. (1981) *Fragmented Societies*. Oxford: Basil Blackwell.
Moulaert, F. (2000) *Globalization and Integrated Area Development in European Cities*. Oxford: Oxford University Press.
Moulaert, F., MacCallum, D., Mehmood, A. and Hamdouch, A. (eds) (2013) *The International Handbook on Social Innovation: Collective Action, Social Learning and Transdisciplinary Research*. Cheltenham: Edward Elgar.
Nahrath, S., Varone, F. Gerber, J.-D. (2009) Les espaces fonctionnels: nouveau référentiel de la gestion durable des ressources? *Vertigo*, 9(1): 1–14.
Nyseth, T. (2011) The Tromsø experiment: Opening up for the unknown. *Town Planning Review*, 82(5): 573–95.
OECD (2012) *Redefining 'Urban': A New Way to Measure Metropolitan Areas*. Paris: OECD.
Pennington, M. (2000): *Planning and the Political Market: Public Choice and the Politics of Government Failure*. London: Athlone Press.

Pratt, A. (2008) Creative cities: The cultural industries and the creative class. *Geografiske Annaler; Series B, Human Geography*, 90(2): 107–17.

Sager, T. (2013) *Reviving Critical Planning Theory: Dealing with Pressure, Neoliberalism and Responsibility in Communicative Planning Theory*. London: Routledge

Servillo, L., Atkinson, R., Smith, I., Russo, A., Sýkora, L., Demazière, C. and Hamdouch, A. (2014) *TOWN – Small and Medium-Sized Towns in their Functional Territorial Context*. Final Report, Luxembourg: ESPON.

Stöhr, W. (ed.) (1990) *Global Challenge, Local Response*. London: Mansell.

Tremblay, D.G. and Pilati, T. (2013) Social innovation through arts and creativity. In F. Moulaert, D. MacCallum, A. Mehmood and A. Hamdouch (eds), *The International Handbook on Social Innovation: Collective Action, Social Learning and Transdisciplinary Research*. Cheltenham: Edward Elgar, pp. 67–79.

Vigar, G., Healey, P., Hull, A. and Davoudi, S. (2000) *Planning, Governance and Spatial Strategy in Britain*. London: Macmillan.

Young, G. and D. Stevenson (eds) (2013) *The Ashgate Research Companion to Planning and Culture*. Farnham: Ashgate.

2 Small and medium-sized towns

A research topic at the margins of urban studies?

Christophe Demazière

Introduction

In various European countries, the field of urban studies has the distinction of being largely developed and structured based on concerns of public authorities, which led to the commission of studies and experimental research (Scherrer, 2010). This is certainly the case in France, where scholars (geographers, sociologists, economists, etc.) showed interest in small and medium-sized towns (SMSTs) during the 1970s, when such places were the focus of national policies (see Chapter 6).

For the last 10–15 years, spatial policies in developed countries have tended to focus on metropolitan areas that have been seen as the main centres of economic growth and innovation (OECD, 2006). Within the European Union (EU), SMSTs have often disappeared of the list of priorities of the national government (Servillo et al., 2014). This is a serious problem for such towns, because many sectoral policies (in the field of housing, transport, education, etc.) can affect their development, mostly negatively, in the sense of inadvertently undermining their local potential. In France, for instance, such schemes as the innovation cluster policy, the call for metropolitan cooperation or the ongoing labelling process known as 'French Tech' all ignored dynamic medium-sized towns and their economic actors. At the same time, the downsizing of the army or of administrations can lead to a significant reduction of employment opportunities in public sector-led secondary towns. Devising creative strategies is all the more necessary, but it is also difficult as the former sources of social stability and economic prosperity erode.

In the current globalization era, many scholars argue that large cities and metropolitan city-regions constitute major parts of a society based on knowledge, innovation and creativity (Sassen, 1991; Castells, 1996; Scott, 2001; Florida, 2002). Nevertheless, half of the European population lives in a city with fewer than 100,000 inhabitants, many of them in towns with between 5,000 and 100,000 people (Servillo et al., 2014). Furthermore, services of general interest are typically located in small towns and address local populations and people in the rural hinterland. Therefore, SMSTs may have a strategic importance in terms of territorial cohesion. Besides, does economic globalization bring only threats and no opportunities for non-metropolitan settlements? While some scholars believe that outside forces determine whether or not a small town will grow, others argue that local efforts can generate sustainable growth (Daniels, 1989). Some economic theories focus primarily on the external or exogenous determinants of growth, such as exchange rates, labour markets or agglomeration economies (Henderson, 1997). But more recently it has been argued that economic development depends heavily on the mobilization of social capital (Putnam, 2000). The smaller scale of medium-sized towns and the relatively lower level of complexity compared to metropolitan areas can make it easier for communities to have a comprehensive understanding of the local situation and to respond in a creative way (Tallec, 2014).

Most of the chapters in this book analyse how various sets of actors in a range of non-metropolitan settings respond to the ecological, social or ecological challenges of the day and how they mobilize local and external resources in a creative way. In a complementary manner, this chapter reflects on the contribution of research works dedicated to SMSTs to the progress of urban studies. Urban studies form a vast and always-expanding field of scientific activity, and research on secondary towns is part of it; hence, its development is influenced by more general debates about urbanization. One of the aspects of research on secondary towns, which has not been sufficiently addressed, is that the categories of 'small town' and 'medium-sized town' are uncertain. I shall try to illustrate this issue by tracing the evolution of French works dedicated to towns throughout the twentieth century, from monographic works to more recent research that insert such places into major urban and economic networks.

A second analytical challenge is that there are actually few theories suited to the study of SMSTs (Daniels, 1989; Bell and Jayne, 2009). In this context, we should beware of a tendency to copy/paste analytical frameworks developed for the study of the largest cities (Amin and Graham, 1997). The low visibility of SMSTs is due to the focus of the majority of urban research on very large cities.

Yet, I hypothesize that SMSTs remain singular objects and their studies enhance the pieces of research on large cities rather than copying them.

SMSTs: a heterogeneous category but common issues?

Giving more attention to the cities that are at the bottom of urban hierarchies should certainly not mean idealizing them. By the 1970s, the French geographer Michel (1977: 657) observed the creation of an 'ideology' by public policies in their emphasis on medium-sized towns:

> The discourse on medium-sized towns is not justified or even concerned by a statistical or functional definition. They associate it with

an emotional and flattering description based solely on consideration of appearances and subjective impressions, hence the medium-sized town became decorated by appeal, qualities and virtues. The key words are acceptable, charm, discretion, modesty, humanity, harmony, balance ... (1977: 657)

At the time, more than 70 French towns with the population of 20,000–100,000 benefited from a contract for medium-sized towns provided by and signed with the state (Tellier, 2014). As towns experienced strong growth, which was particularly due to the arrival of those from rural areas and industrial decentralization, the objectives of such contracts were to improve the quality of life, the provision of services, and the social and economic development of medium-sized towns.

Three decades later, Mainet (2011) studied how the local authorities of small French towns present their town through their website. In order to do this, she analysed the websites of 110 small towns located in different geographical contexts. Some places are isolated, while others are integrated into a larger conurbation. She argues that the images and discourses that are used swing between traditional rural attributes and urban mimicry, which reveals the existence of an ambiguous identity for small towns. On the one hand, the websites highlight the friendliness and village-like-proximity, while on the other hand, they promote the quality of provided services and a development of public spaces that is equal to those present in the largest cities. According to her, the images produced by the local authorities are part of a territorial competition to attract and/or retain population and economic actors. By promoting access to the countryside and nature, as well as the functional centrality for many services, local policy-makers formulate a discourse that tries to marry the expectations of future residents and tourists, in the hope of benefiting from the manna that is the contribution of external revenues.

In link with the advantageous presentations of secondary cities by their leaders, a crucial question is whether these towns, called 'medium', 'small' or 'intermediate', form a relevant category for social sciences. By describing a medium-sized town as an 'unidentified real object', the famous geographer Roger Brunet (1997: 188) noted that such places are undeniably a stratum of the urban system, although it is hard to define them by specific criteria. In fact, when undertaking a cross-national comparison, one is confronted with a variety of criteria for identifying SMSTs (Santamaria, 2000). Most authors use the size of the population as a reference point, but there are almost as many thresholds as researchers and organizations in charge of collecting and processing data on towns. For example, a lower limit for identifying a 'small town' is 250 inhabitants in Denmark, 4,500 inhabitants in Northern Ireland, 5,000 in Austria and 30,000 in Japan (Servillo et al., 2014). In France, a 'small town' is often considered to have between 3,000 and 20,000 inhabitants. Nevertheless, the threshold that is often used

Table 2.1 Definition of SMSTs in France: differences according to sources

	According to associations of elected officials	According to researchers	According to the state (the French Ministry for spatial planning)
Small towns	Municipalities from 2,500 to 25,000 inhabitants (Association of Small Towns of France)	Urban centres from 5,000 to 20,000 inhabitants (Laborie, 1978; Edouard, 2012)	-
Medium-sized towns	Municipalities-centres from 20,000 to 100,000 inhabitants and the area of their inter-municipal cooperation (Federation of Towns of France)	Urban centres from 20,000 to 100,000 inhabitants (Lajugie, 1974)	Travel-to-work areas from 30,000 to 200,000 inhabitants (Medium-Sized Towns Programme, 2005–9)

among researchers is 5,000 inhabitants (see, for example Kayser, 1972). In Poland, the threshold of 10,000 inhabitants is used in most cases to distinguish between a small town and a village. However, in some studies, the threshold is reduced to 5,000, or raised to 20,000 or 50,000 inhabitants (Servillo et al., 2014).

Regarding medium-sized towns in France, the most frequently chosen threshold defines a stratum of towns with 20,000–100,000 inhabitants (Table 2.1). However, within these limits, one can distinguish different meanings of the town. At first, the national policy of medium-sized towns conducted in 1973–82 targeted municipalities with 20,000–100,000 inhabitants. Later, the National Institute of Statistics and Economic Studies (INSEE) favoured the morphological definition of the urban space and proposed the term 'urban centres', while keeping the same interval. In the 2000s, in order to understand the actual role of medium-sized towns in the context of living and employment areas, the French Ministry in charge of spatial planning preferred to observe travel-to-work areas with 30,000 to 200,000 inhabitants (De Roo, 2007). In this context, Béhar (2007) argued that the former view of medium-sized municipalities dominating a hinterland had ceased to exist, and he pleaded for coalitions gathering urban and rural municipalities while selecting specific 'niches' for future development.

Actually, the various spatial notions that seize the current reality of SMSTs (urban centres, travel-to-work areas) can be combined in a multi-dimensional approach in urban studies. In recent research for the European Spatial Planning Observatory Network, Servillo et al. (2014) combined three complementary perspectives for defining SMSTs:

1. A morphological approach in which a town represents a continuous built-up area that concentrates a certain number of inhabitants.
2. An administrative definition according to which a town is a territorial unit of local government.
3. A functional vision in which a town concentrates jobs, services and functions for its hinterland.

By implementing the first criterion (a continuous built-up area with a density above 300 inhabitants per sq. km and a population of between 5,000 and 50,000 inhabitants), Servillo et al. (2014) identified 8,314 SMSTs across Europe with a total population of 109 million inhabitants in 2011 (21.6 per cent of the European population). In France, the INSEE noted that 869 urban centres have between 5,000 and 50,000 inhabitants, which represented 17.3 per cent of the population in 2010. In sum, even if the object is blurred, it is there.

'Small and medium-sized towns' appears to be a relative term, arising from upper and lower extremes of regional, national or continental hierarchy. The median of the urban framework is defined by statistical thresholds, by spatial parameters and by different polarization levels. In France, Blois, Bourges and Châteauroux (respectively with 120,000, 125,000 and 90,000 inhabitants in their travel-to-work areas) are considered at the national level to be medium-sized towns (De Roo, 2007). Nevertheless, the Regional Council of the Centre-Val de Loire considers them to be large cities. At the same time, the Council reserved the term 'medium-sized town' for 15 municipalities with fewer than 10,000 inhabitants that along with big agglomerations concentrate jobs and services, and play a role of urban centre vis-à-vis rural areas (see Chapter 6). It is always more appropriate to add other criteria and variables to that of population size depending on the question that is to be investigated: job commuting, functions and urban infrastructure, provision of services, accessibility, etc. (Santamaria, 2000). One realizes that the role of SMSTs varies considerably. Forty years ago, Lajugie already wrote:

> A small town ... should be considered as medium-sized town if it is located in a sparsely populated and less urbanized region. Nevertheless, a city twice or three times bigger in size and embedded in the urban fabric of a densely populated region may not play a role of a big city and does not always respond to this vocation. (Lajugie, 1974: 18)

For many researchers, it is often by immersing themselves in the territory, by observing the everyday practices and by meeting policy-makers that the most relevant approach to these towns can be developed. The aims are to analyse differences within the same regional space and to outline the development potentials. In France, such methodology is rooted in the research tradition of SMSTs within different branches of social sciences: geography (Veyret-Verner, 1969; Commerçon and

George, 1999), regional and urban economics (Lajugie, 1974), political science (Mabileau and Sorbets, 1989), sociology (Morin, 1965), etc. Through a systematic search on the Persée Portal, which provides over 120 journals and more than 150,000 scientific articles on the human and social sciences, Gaudin (2013) identified 190 articles published between 1920 and 2005 that explicitly focus on 'medium-sized towns'. The author drew attention to the presence of the monographic approach applied to industrial centres such as Briançon, Annonay or Lorient during the period between the two World Wars. Later, in the 1970s, the scientific work focused on the description of the integration of medium-sized towns in new economic and social conditions (Michel, 1977; Allain, 1984). In other words, medium-sized towns were observed within various subjects: urban growth, commercial and industrial changes, identity and image, local politics, etc. Regarding small towns, the monographic tradition was also vivid, which Edouard (2012: 28) qualified as 'essential and unavoidable research'. Nevertheless, since the 1970s, the research on small towns has turned towards the observation of mutations affecting Western societies as a whole. 'It is ... less about small towns and more about a clearly identified territory that enables easier exploration of evolutions and general knowledge at the spatial level, allowing a more comprehensive approach to observed phenomena' (Edouard, 2012: 26).

Overall, the research on SMSTs has led to a certain trivialization of the subject. Many studies on secondary cities have shown that they have been affected for a long time by wider economic and social changes, such as modernization or industrialization (Cooke, 1989; Demazière, 2015). In the context of expansion during the period of the post-war boom, companies that applied the Scientific Work Management were prone to locate their production facilities in medium-sized towns, thus adding a manufacturing component to the economic profile of towns that in some cases has been strongly based on administration and services to the population (Massey, 1984; De Roo, 2007). By offering a premium to land use, the national authorities sought to introduce modern industries such as automotive and electronic sectors into a number of areas considered to be under-industrialized. For companies, a medium-sized town became 'a means to exploit the labour force' that was unskilled and inexperienced in industrial work (Michel, 1977: 670). But three decades later, Hildreth argues that:

> A challenge for many [medium-sized] towns at the beginning of the 21st century is that the historic competitive advantage that enabled these industries to prosper no longer exists. Nearby raw materials may have been exploited, the industry may have been obsolete or other centres in the world may be able to produce the same goods at considerably cheaper prices due to lower labour costs. As a consequence, these cities may display characteristics that make their economies particularly vulnerable. (Hildreth, 2006: 26)

Since the 1980s, and with the further impact of the global economic slowdown of the last few years, many SMSTs have experienced a rapid process of de-industrialization and local economic crisis (ÖIR, 2006; Kwiatek-Soltys, 2011; Servillo et al., 2014). For example, in France, the industrial town of Dreux saw the closure of several major facilities, and the manufacturing sector today provides only 20 per cent of local jobs; the proportion was 60 per cent in the late 1980s (Demazière, 2015). However, there are cases of towns where new industrial specializations were built on existing experience and practices in the town. This is the case for many towns that developed marshallian industrial districts over decades, but also of more recently industrialised towns (Stöhr, 1990; Carrier et al., 2012). Such places offer a particular industrial knowledge and skills that local firms or firms relocating to the town can draw upon. For instance, we can quote the case of Châtellerault in France, where the industrial sector remains strong due to the transfer of traditional know-how to new sectors, including the aerospace and automotive sectors. In 2009, 42 per cent of the jobs in the Châtellerault employment zone were in the industrial sector and it took 15th place in the ranking of the most industrialized zones in France (Bouba-Olga et al., 2012).

These observations lead one to question the specificity of contemporary research on SMSTs in relation to the research on city-regions and 'global cities'.

SMSTs: a research subject at the margins?

One of the characteristics of urban studies is that since its beginnings, it has been dominated by the analytical frameworks of the research on large cities in developed countries (Robinson, 2002). In Europe, London and Paris have been the subjects of analyses so many times that it is impossible to list them all. In North America, the sociology school of thoughts was created in Chicago in the early twentieth century and the geography school of thoughts in Los Angeles in the 1980s. The continuous attention that has been given to very large cities is due to something other than their size. According to the historian Connolly (2008: 3), the 'key questions are urged by the emergence of major urban centres around the world: the flow of people, goods and ideas; the ways in which cultures and identities are formed and reformed; the distribution of the economic and political power. For all these reasons and many more, the analysis of the metropolitan context dominates the academic literature on cities of yesterday and of today'.

However, there are very few outstanding work on medium-sized towns such as *Middletown: A Study in American Culture* by R. Lynd and H. Lynd (1929) that focuses on the town of Muncie (30,000 inhabitants), 100 km from Indianapolis. In this book, which later became a classic of sociology, the authors applied for the first time the methods of cultural anthropology to study a town in the Western world.

Some theoretical and analytical frameworks have contributed to the metropolitan bias of urban research. Hence, Robinson (2002) observes that the shift from *gemeinschaft* to *gesellschaft*, described by Tonnies in 1887, has influenced many later works that considered cities to be *par excellence* the centres of emerging modernity, while other urban spaces experienced much less anonymity, pluralism and social mobility. Moreover, Bell and Jayne (2009) consider that the work of Christaller (1933) on central places laid the foundation for analyses of urban hierarchies that culminated over the last twenty years with appearance of many work on 'global cities' (Sassen, 1991) and 'world cities' (Beaverstock et al., 1999). This kind of approach usually starts with the analysis of relations between companies in order to draw links between remote places (flows of knowledge, values and people). Such research illustrates the concentration of economic, social and cultural power in a handful of cities. In doing so, it 'encourages the idea that smaller cities and towns are put to the last line of development designed on the top of the urban hierarchy and the experiences of their inhabitants deserve little attention' (Connolly, 2008: 4).

By studying very large cities, the scientific objective of many researchers is the understanding of patterns of urbanization applicable to all cities now or in the future. However, there is a risk that secondary cities are treated as not being of scientific interest due to the lack of trends already existing in some metropolises. According to Bell and Jayne (2009: 684), due to the work on 'world cities' over the last 20 years, 'small towns have been considered irrelevant. They have been seen as spaces that say nothing about urbanity, but rather evoke a failure of urbanization'. For example, a quick reading of the work on the global hierarchy of cities based on the presence of corporate financial and legal headquarters (Sassen, 1991; Beaverstock et al., 1999) confirms the increasing 'fragility', 'delay' and 'handicap' of other cities and towns facing globalization. The research on very large cities has raised some interesting considerations and illuminating comparisons. Nevertheless, they have not contributed to the interpretation of mutations in SMSTs. The urban world is not only comprised of a handful of globalized metropolises.

A theoretical background of recent research on very large cities includes the optimal city size theory (Alonso, 1971) that points to the increasing advantages of local economic activities as the size of the city increases, which is due to positive externalities deriving from public investment, diversified resources and better access of products to the market. Similarly, Krugman (1991) estimated that the spatial concentration is the cause of increasing returns. West (2012) argues that any city whose size has doubled has also experienced an increase in productivity of 15 per cent. Nevertheless, in Europe, the relationship between city size and economic performance has limited relevance. Indeed, if one observes the 264 metropolitan areas in the OECD countries that have more than 500,000 inhabitants, those located in Europe represent only 36 per cent of the total population and 43 per cent of the total gross domestic product (GDP). In North America, metropolitan areas represent 53 per cent of the total population and 58 per cent of the total GDP, and in Asia, 69 per cent of the total population and 70 per cent of the total GDP (OECD, 2012). In the most developed EU countries (EU-15), agglomerations with a population of over 250,000 inhabitants have increased their share of GDP by only 0.6 per cent in the 2000s (Dijkstra et al., 2013). In sum, all this suggests that urbanization based on large cities is not the key element of economic growth in Europe.

Moreover, if SMSTs are not part of the work on globalization, perhaps one should question the measuring instruments. The research on urban hierarchies has illustrated it. For instance, the Global Analysis of World Cities Group (GaWC) defined a global hierarchy of cities based on the concentration of economic activity (Beaverstock et al., 1999). It put an emphasis on advanced activities such as financial, legal and accounting services. By measuring the presence of company headquarters in these sectors, it came with a proposition of the urban hierarchy that assigned to world cities the status of alpha, beta and gamma city. It counted about 50 cities across the world, while all others are invisible.

This research has raised a number of critical remarks (Robinson, 2002; Bell and Jayne, 2009). First, the relationship between these cities and their position in the hierarchy was examined using a very small (albeit critical) number of activities. Therefore, a very small number of actors situated in a few cities or even parts of cities (business centres) were included in the research. As a consequence, the research does not say a lot on other cities, which do not benefit from the presence of such forms of activities and such kinds of actors. Second, the majority of the research on global cities has a Cartesian approach: 'A limited range of cities are being assigned to categories and ranked according to, *a priori*, analytical hierarchies' (Robinson, 2002: 535). The analytical categories are rigid and do not reflect intermediate situations. Third, the developed analyses ignore the scientific output already made regarding these areas. In fact, all these areas have been the subject of multiple studies that demonstrated the real knowledge of the area as their researchers were often involved in strategic discussions at the local and regional levels.

To conclude, I will outline the thinking of Clancey (2004: 2337–8): 'To analyse globalization as a connections network, such as the one of "world cities", is perhaps a scientific subject, but it is not of general importance.' In the same way, the research on SMSTs does not claim to explain the dynamics of New York, London and Tokyo. The focus on connections between 'global cities' leaves a very open space for research on SMSTs. Nevertheless, analysts of secondary cities face many challenges. How can they reflect the great diversity of situations in towns without just producing monographs? In a context where capital flows expand and infiltrate more and more geographical areas, how can they avoid the image of towns being dominated by globalization? In France and other European countries, the internationalization of companies and rising competitive pressure have affected the productive systems of some secondary cities. Nevertheless, one can highlight peculiarities and local pulses (Demazière, 2015). Some medium-sized French towns are distinguished by their dynamism of their productive economy or even by being innovative hubs. In fact, in his study of Albi, Alès, Fougères and Quimper, Tallec (2014) demonstrated how the development of innovation occurs outside the metropolitan areas through structuring and the coordination of innovative firms that play a leading role in the development of medium-sized towns.

More radically, Robinson (2002) highlighted the concept of 'ordinary cities', claiming that all cities, regardless of their size or location, show dynamic and innovative aspects at the same time as they face constraints and challenges. In fact, while studying cities of the Global South, Robinson argued: 'Instead of considering that only a few cities are the urban matrix … in the world of ordinary cities, the ways of transforming urban areas are various since they are created by the population of all cities' (Robinson, 2014: 35). Cities are places of crossings of flows of people, goods, information, waste, symbols, etc. (Graham, 2001). However, the experimental plans for capturing those flows in the biggest cities – through iconic urban projects, accessibility improvements and major events organizations – do not apply to most SMSTs. Secondary cities remind us that urbanized areas have a materiality that is strongly embedded in their local history and culture (Guay and Hamel, 2004). Studying secondary cities would therefore show that everyday life continues to coexist alongside the effects of the international flows of goods, capital, people and symbols. It would mean examining local practices, identities and autonomies.

Conclusion

Although the current political agenda in many countries is primarily focused on the role of large cities in promoting future development, should SMSTs be set aside? In the pre-industrial age, such towns performed essential trade and craft functions as well as being religious and administrative centres (Hohenberg and Lees, 1985). More recently, they expanded as a result of industrial development and they were also shaped by national or local development policies. Nowadays, SMSTs usually fulfil major functions, through the provision of housing and of public services. Even though their economic structure is in transition and the perspectives are blurred, such towns still perform a significant labour market function, while the provision of leisure and tourism is reinforced by city marketing (ÖIR, 2006; Servillo et al., 2014)

While SMSTs are part of the daily experience of many European citizens, they are still at the margins of urban research. Within the research tradition of secondary cities, the monographic approach that was originally developed seems outdated. It is even inadequate due to the fact that SMSTs face the challenges of mobility and of the opening of national economies.

France is a case where smaller towns accumulated population and benefited from industrial decentralization for three-quarters of the twentieth century. Today they offer a volume and a variety of jobs and services that cannot be compared to the dynamism of large urban areas. Also, they tend to experience an exodus of young population leaving for education and employment, as well as an exodus of dual-income couples and highly educated individuals.

As a research subject, secondary cities need to be re-examined. Depending on the academic disciplines, there are several avenues for future research since, as Queffélec has noted:

> Several images [of SMSTs] coexist: the one of the traveller who sees the monumental treasures and an atmosphere of the town-centre, the one of the resident who is sensitive to the environment but who is also looking in these places for services he needs for his daily life, and the one of the planner who tends to organize the urban space within its context. (2014: 67)

In any case, I argue that the dynamics of SMSTs should be analysed at different spatial scales: the town centre, the urban core, the functional urban region, etc. These various layers of analysis are complementary and help to show the reciprocal influence of places regarding housing, education, culture or the labour market (Servillo et al., 2014). The multiscalar approach is also important in policy terms. In many SMSTs, elected officials of the central municipality wish to strengthen the centrality functions of the town centre (through the planning of public spaces, commercial areas, cultural spaces, etc.), having in mind the broader attractiveness of the town. These interventions are made in a context of limited markets and of competition coming from other areas, sometimes even from within the same living area.

Seeing SMSTs as 'ordinary cities' may contribute to a critical (although partial) observation of the current urban research. The limitations of analyses of 'global' and 'world' cities are obvious when they lead to generalizations out of very specific cases and to making urban policy recommendations for all other areas, regardless of their size and their history. What should be a debate on specificity and diversity is often reduced to highlighting factors or key processes of urban change (Amin and Graham, 1997). In this sense, a research strategy to study creative approaches to the development of SMSTs should favour a 'territorial approach' (Lazzeroni et al., 2013). In such an approach, the town should be studied with a view to revealing its tangible and intangible ressources. For instance, the values and significance given to the cultural or industrial heritage of a place should be considered before they can become the pivot on which development policies can be defined (Lorentzen and Van Heur, 2011). Such an analytical perspective is present in several of the following chapters.

References

Allain, R. (1984) Croissance et urbanisme dans une 'ville moyenne': le cas de Fougères. *Norois*, 123(1): 393–406.
Alonso, W. (1971) The economics of urban size. *Papers and Proceedings of the Regional Science Association*, 10(1): 67–83.
Amin, A. and Graham, S. (1997) The ordinary city. *Transactions of the Institute of British Geographers*, 22(4): 411–29.
Beaverstock, J., Taylor, P. and Smith, R. (1999) A roster of world cities. *Cities*, 6(4): 445–58.
Béhar, D. (2007) La fin des villes moyennes? *Les Échos*, 14 December, p. 15.
Bell, D. and Jayne, M. (2009) Small cities? Towards a research agenda. *International Journal of Urban and Regional Studies*, 22(3): 683–99.
Bouba-Olga, O., Ferru, M. and Guimond, B. (2012) Organisation des activités et dynamiques territoriales: éléments d'analyse et application aux bassins de Cognac et de Châtellerault. *Revue d'Economie Régionale et Urbaine*, 2: 173–91.
Brunet, R. (1997) *Territoires de France et d'Europe*. Paris: Belin.
Carrier, M., Thériault, M. and Véronneau, E. (2012) Structure socio-spatiale des réseaux d'innovation en secteur manufacturier traditionnel d'une ville moyenne. *Revue d'Economie Régionale et Urbaine*, 2: 215–44.
Castells, M. (1996) *The Rise of the Network Society*. Cambridge: Blackwell.
Christaller, W. (1933) *Die zentrale Orte in Süddeutschland*. Iéna: Fischer.
Clancey, G. (2004) Local memory and worldly narrative: The remote city in America and Japan. *Urban Studies*, 41(12): 2335–55.
Coing, H. (1966) *Rénovation urbaine et changement social*. Paris: Editions ouvrières.
Commerçon, N. and George, P. (1999) *Villes en transition*. Paris: Economica.
Connolly, J. (2008) Decentering urban history. Peripheral cities in the modern world. *Journal of Urban History*, 35(1): 3–14.
Cooke, P. (ed.) (1989) *Localities: The Changing Fate of Urban Britain*. London: Unwin Hyman.
Daniels, T.L. (1989) Small town economic development: growth or survival? *Journal of Planning Literature*, 4: 413–29.
De Roo, P. (2007) *Les villes moyennes françaises: enjeux et perspectives*. Paris: La Documentation française.
Demazière, C. (2015) Systèmes productifs et villes moyennes. In G. Baudelle and J. Fache (eds), *Les mutations des systèmes productifs en France*. Rennes: Presses Universitaires de Rennes, pp. 261–70.
Demazière, C., Banovac, K. and Hamdouch, A. (2014) The changing profiles of small and medium-sized towns in the European context: Between residential economy, competitiveness and innovation. In A. Kwiatek-Soltys, H. Mainet, K. Wiedermann and J.-C. Edouard (eds), *Small and Medium Towns' Attractiveness at the Beginning of the 21st Century*. Clermont-Ferrand: Presses Universitaires Blaise Pascal and CERAMAC, pp. 29–40.
Dijkstra, L., Garcilazo, E. and Mccann, P. (2013) The economic performance of cities and city-regions: Myths and Realities. *European Planning Studies*, 21(3): 334–54.
Edouard, J.-C. (2012) La place de la petite ville dans la recherche géographique en France: de la simple monographie au territoire témoin. *Annales de géographie*, 683: 25–42.

Florida, R. (2002) The economic geography of talent. *Annals of the Association of American Geographers*, 92(4): 223–57.
Gaudin, S. (2013) Villes moyennes et rénovation urbaine. Discours et actions d'une transaction spatiale. Exemples pris en Bretagne. Unpublished PhD dissertation. Rennes: Université Rennes 2.
Graham, S. (2001) FlowCity, networked mobilities and the contemporary metropolis. *DISP*, 144: 4–11.
Guay, L. and Hamel, P. (2004) Les villes contemporaines à la croisée des choix collectifs et individuels. *Recherches sociographiques*, 3(4): 427–39.
Henderson, V. (1997) Medium size cities. *Regional Science and Urban Economics*, 27(4): 583–612.
Hildreth, P. A. (2006) Roles and economic potential of English medium-sized cities: A discussion paper. Available at: www.salford.ac.uk/__data/assets/pdf_file/0019/114733/061010_Medium_sized_cities_complete_final.pdf.
Hohenberg, P.M. and Lees, L.H. (1985) *The Making of Urban Europe, 1000–1950*. Cambridge, MA: Harvard University Press.
Kayser, B. (1972) Les petites villes françaises. *Revue de géographie alpine*, 60(2): 269–84.
Krugman, P. (1991) Increasing returns and economic geography. *Journal of Political Economy*, 99(3): 483–99.
Kwiatek-Soltys, A. (2011) Small towns in Poland: Barriers and factors of growth. *Procedia Social and Behavioral Sciences*, 19: 363–70.
Laborie, J.-P. (1978) Les petites villes dans le processus d'urbanisation. Unpublished PhD dissertation. Toulouse: Université de Toulouse.
Lajugie, J. (1974) *Les villes moyennes*. Paris: Cujas.
Lazzeroni, M., Bellini, N., Cortesi, G. and Loffredo, A. (2013) The territorial approach to cultural economy: New opportunities for the development of small towns. *European Planning Studies*, 21(4): 452–72.
Lorentzen, A. and Van Heur, B. (eds) (2011) *Cultural Political Economy of Small Cities*. London: Routledge.
Lynd, R. and Lynd, H. (1929) *Middletown: A Study in American Culture*. New York: Harcourt Brace and Company.
Mabileau, A. and Sorbets, C. (eds) (1989) *Gouverner les villes moyennes*. Talence: CERVL.
Mainet, H. (2011) Les petites villes françaises en quête d'identité. Ambiguïté du positionnement ou image tactiquement combinée? *Mots. Les langages du politique*. Available at: https://hal.archives-ouvertes.fr/halshs-00686442/document.
Massey, D. (1984) *Spatial Divisions of Labour*. London: Macmillan.
Michel, M. (1977) Ville moyenne, ville-moyen. *Annales de géographie*, 478: 641–5.
Morin, E. (1965) *La Métamorphose de Plozevet*. Paris: LGF.
OECD (2006) *Competitive Cities in the Global Economy*. Paris: OECD.
—— (2012) *Redefining 'Urban': A New Way to Measure Metropolitan Areas*. Paris: OECD.
ÖIR (Österreichisches Institut für Raumplanung) (2006) *ESPON 1.4.1 – The Role of Small and Medium-Sized Towns – Final Report*. Luxembourg: ESPON.
Putnam, R. (2000) *Bowling Alone: The Collapse and Revival of America's Civic Community*. New York: Simon & Schuster.
Quéffelec, C.-N. (2014) Portrait d'une ville moyenne: Quimper. *Pour mémoire*, 13: 40–73.

Robinson, J. (2002) Global and world cities: a view from off the map. *International Journal of Urban and Regional Research*, 26(4): 531–54.

—— (2014) Villes ordinaires: vers des études urbaines postcoloniales. In C. Gintrac and M. Giroud (eds), *Villes contestées. Pour une géographie critique de l'urbain*. Paris, Les prairies ordinaires, pp. 16–32.

Santamaria, F. (2000) La notion de 'ville moyenne' en France, en Espagne et au Royaume-Uni. *Annales de géographie*, 61: 227–39.

Sassen, S. (1991) *The Global City*. Princeton: Princeton University Press.

Scherrer, F. (2010) Le contrepoint des études urbaines et de l'urbanisme: ou comment se détacher de l'évidence de leur utilité sociale. *Tracés. Revue de Sciences humaines*. Available at: https://www.cairn.info/revue-participations-2011-1-page-36.htm.

Scott, A.J. (ed.) (2001) *Global City-Regions: Trends, Theory, Policy*. Oxford: Oxford University Press.

Servillo, L., Atkinson, R., Smith, I., Russo, A., Sýkora, L., Demazière, C. and Hamdouch, A. (2014) *TOWN – Small and Medium-Sized Towns in their Functional Territorial Context*. Final Report, Luxembourg: ESPON.

Stöhr, W. (ed.) (1990) *Global Challenge, Local Response*. London: Mansell.

Tallec, J. (2014) La construction socio-spatiale de l'innovation en ville moyenne face aux objectifs de compétitivité et d'attractivité des politiques d'aménagement. Unpublished PhD dissertation. Toulouse: Université Jean-Jaurès.

Tellier, T. (2014) L'essor des politiques contractuelles des villes moyennes dans les années 1970–80. *Pour mémoire*, 13: 17–21.

Veyret-Verner, G. (1969) Plaidoyer pour les moyennes et petites villes. *Revue de géographie alpine*, 1: 5–24.

West, G. (2012) The laws of the city. *The Economist*, 23 June, available at: www.economist.com/node/21557313.

3 'Ordinary politics of planning' for socio-economic development
Insights from European small and medium-sized towns

Abdelillah Hamdouch and Ksenija Banovac

Introduction

Traditional spatial planning in Europe has adopted a passive approach that generally aimed at controlling the use of land through zoning system and regulations (Albrechts, 2006b). However, since the 1960s and 1970s, the socio-economic changes, increasing concerns about rapid development, the problems of fragmentation as well as the growing strengths of the environmental and social movements have emphasized the need for a strategic approach to planning. As a consequence, by the end of the 1990s, the formulation of spatial strategies for cities, city-regions and regions became quite fashionable in Europe (Healey et al., 1997; Faludi, 2001; Albrechts et al., 2003; Martinelli, 2005; Healey, 2006a; Healey, 2006b). As remarked by Albrechts (2006b) and Scott (2001), the new spatial planning strategies embraced an agenda that was wider than the traditional regulatory approach to land-use management. In other words, they attempted to create an integrated policy that would more effectively link strategic and local planning:

> Strategic spatial planning creates solid, workable long-term perspectives and it creates strategies at different levels, taking into account the power structures – political, economic, gender and cultural – uncertainties and competing values ... It is about building new ideas and processes that can carry these structures, content, etc. forward, thus generating ways of understanding, ways of building agreements, and ways of organizing and mobilizing for the purpose of exerting influence in different arenas. Finally, strategic spatial planning, both in the short term and the long term, is focused on framing decisions, actions, projects, results and implementation, and it incorporates monitoring, feedback, adjustment and revision in its efforts to accomplish these aims. (Albrechts, 2006b: 1491)

Nevertheless, the critics underline that the normative conception of strategic spatial planning makes demands that actors may not be able to fulfil because they are not sufficiently reflexive or they are calculating opportunities in order to take action that will serve planners' interests (Newman, 2008). In other words, instead of seeking 'transformative' planning, actors may have more modest or even different ambitions (Healey, 2006a). Therefore, some authors propose giving more attention to the ordinary politics of planning and challenges, opportunities and incentives necessary for collaboration instead of focusing on the ideal norms of strategic spatial planning that are not applied in reality (Lowndes, 2005; Parker, 2007; Newman, 2008).

Indeed, strategic spatial planning in Europe (and for Europe) was associated with the development and promotion of the European Spatial Development Perspective (ESDP) in 1999 and the European Union (EU)'s encouragement of regional and local economic development policy (Newman, 2008) during the 2000s. Since its creation, the ESDP has focused on polycentric urban development, balanced spatial development, urban-rural partnerships and transborder/transnational planning which are concepts that have been increasingly translated into almost every EU member state's national and regional policies and strategies (Scott, 2001). Likewise, framing (decisions, actions and projects), implementing, monitoring, feedback, adjustment and revision represent the modus operandi of the strategic spatial planning process that was also adopted by the EU policy-making process.

The publication of the ESDP in 1999 has encouraged many authors to consider the effects of European spatial planning from the perspective of metropolises, city-regions and larger regional areas (Atkinson, 2001; Krätke, 2001; Albrechts, 2004, 2006a, 2006b; Healey, 2006a, 2006b, 2007). These areas have been considered as the main drivers of European development that provide opportunities for economic activities on a global scale and that enable the participation of actors in global interactions (Sassen, 1991; Castells, 1996; Graham, 2001; Scott, 2001; Huriot and Bourdeau-Lepage, 2009). At the same time, paradoxically, much less attention has been given to spatial planning in and for small and medium-sized towns (SMSTs) (5,000–100,000 inhabitants) which have been, on the one hand, conceived as 'immature, less developed or declining territories, in need of policy action from outside and from within in order to cope with present day economic dynamics ... On the other hand, SMSTs have been frequently celebrated as the last resorts of true urban ambience and idealised as the most appropriate linkage between the urban and the rural, a potentially sustainable form of urban structure' (OIR, 2006: 27). Arguably we need to move beyond this 'simple' duality to investigate the more varied and complex nature of SMSTs in their context.

Building on these arguments, this chapter aims to explore spatial planning approaches in 31 SMSTs from ten European countries and, above all, the 'ordinary politics of planning' (Newman, 2008) for socio-economic development in SMSTs. In other words, we examine the circumstances under which local actors plan for socio-economic development and the nature of interactions among involved actors, and, finally, we provide some illustrative examples of successful and creative approaches to local development in European towns. Hence, the first section presents the main features of SMSTs in terms of their functional roles within the urban system, socio-economic profiles and the way they have been addressed in EU policies. The second section examines the key characteristics and particularities of the national/regional institutional frameworks in which our case studies are embedded. Finally, the third section observes the dynamics between local actors involved in local development as well as their 'creative' ways of addressing challenges, opportunities and incentives that affect a town's socio-economic trajectory.

SMSTs and their key features

During the last century, Europe changed from being a largely rural to a predominantly urban continent. Around 70 per cent of the EU population live in urban agglomerations of more than 5,000 inhabitants (European Commission, 2011a). Compared to other countries such as the USA or China, Europe has a more polycentric urban structure that is characterized by numerous and dense SMSTs. In fact, in the territory of the EU, Iceland, Liechtenstein, Norway and Switzerland, there are more than 8,400 SMSTs, compared to 850 large cities (more than 50,000 inhabitants) and 69,000 villages and very small towns (fewer than 5,000 inhabitants) (Servillo et al., 2014).

The functional roles and position in the spatial hierarchy

European SMSTs not only gather a large part of the population together (European Commission, 2011), but they also perform important functional roles for their region and the rural populations surrounding them. Moreover, regardless of their size and national context, SMSTs are urban centres for services, local and regional knowledge production, innovation and infrastructure (Brunet, 1997). To give some examples, in the English context, Hildreth (2006) distinguishes industrial towns, touristic destinations, university towns, gateway towns, peripheral towns within a large city-region and regional services centres. Similarly, Bolay and Rabinovitch (2004) define several possible functions of SMSTs: regional market, service centre, regional capital, economic location, tourist centre, communication hub, metropolitan periphery, national/international interface, association of group of towns, etc.

As illustrated by Central Place Theory (Christaller, 1933), the type of goods and services provided by each town depends on its position in the functional spatial hierarchy as well as on proximity to other urban centres. In that respect, some authors argue that the functions of SMSTs depend on their proximity to larger cities, which might limit their influence on the territory (Henderson, 1997; Bellet and Llop, 2004; Taulelle, 2010; Santamaria, 2012). Some SMSTs during the process of agglomeration may be taken over by metropolises and become suburban towns (De Roo, 2007). In that case, as argued by Léo et al. (2012), the consequences for the local development of SMSTs are twofold. On the one hand, the development of SMSTs may benefit from good access to the services and infrastructure of the metropolis by avoiding costs of land, high taxes, congestion, etc. On the other hand, the larger city may block the development of an SMST by the effect of spatial competition for the provision of commercial activities and services (Léo et al., 2012). Nevertheless, there are also SMSTs that maintain their social and economic capacities independent of larger cities through networks with other SMSTs or by staying isolated as the only service centre in rural areas (De Roo, 2007).

One of the European Observation Network for Territorial Development and Cohesion (ESPON)'s research projects (Servillo et al., 2014) observed the functional roles of SMSTs across Europe and identified three basic forms of the positions of towns in the spatial hierarchy: autonomous (or isolated) towns, towns agglomerated with large cities and towns networked with other SMSTs. The position in the spatial hierarchy was identified by observing a daily job commuting of the working population between cities and towns from ten European countries. The results of the research project showed that the majority of towns are not isolated, but rather are networked and agglomerated within local, regional, national, supra-national and global systems. Moreover, the SMSTs studied play either a role of urban centres for their hinterland or a role of nodes within the urban system. However, the research project found remarkable differences between European countries. For instance, some countries such as Belgium have a highly urbanized landscape of large cities and SMSTs are densely linked to them. Consequently, all urban places in Belgium, including SMSTs, benefit from the polycentric pattern of the country. Also, some countries, for example, Slovenia, have two forms of spatial hierarchy that coexist in symbiosis. Besides the capital Ljubljana that has the role of prime national centre for the entire country, there is also an equally important polycentric network of SMSTs. Finally, some countries such as the Czech Republic, Spain and Poland have developed all three forms of the position of towns in the spatial hierarchy (autonomous, networked and agglomerated) and thus demonstrate the diversity of the situation of SMSTs within their urban hierarchies.

The socio-economic profile and shifts in the local economy

As SMSTs play different functional roles within the spatial hierarchy, some of them have more economic advantages than others. For example, towns located in a dynamic city-region are more likely to benefit from the economic success of the large city. In that case, highly qualified workers would choose to live in SMSTs and work in large cities. On the contrary, if the town is located in a weak or predominantly rural region, it may face difficulties in attracting and retaining highly qualified workers unless it offers some economic advantages, such as the presence of a university, an attractive business environment or natural amenities (Hildreth, 2006). This clearly illustrates that the socio-economic characteristics of SMSTs are related to the proximity of larger cities and to their performance in terms of their capacity to create jobs, to provide services, to attract new population and to engage in inter-territorial and innovation networks (Carrier et al., 2012; Demazière, 2012; Demazière et al., 2012).

Furthermore, a smaller labour market often leads to specialization in economic activities (manufacturing, tourism, etc.) whose dynamics are linked to economic and social changes at the national or even international levels. In his comparison of economic specializations between large cities and medium-sized towns in England, Hildreth argues that SMSTs benefit more from the economies of location in which firms agglomerate within the same sector so as to produce a variety of the same product (benefits of specialization), thus increasing their productivity (Hildreth, 2006; Huriot and Bourdeau-Lepage, 2009). Towns that have a strong knowledge-based economy are more likely to benefit from agglomeration benefits than those with an industrial economy. Moreover, towns with a strong knowledge base and innovation culture are more likely to gain from localization economies. By contrast, towns with economies that rely on one or very few specializations are more likely to be disadvantaged (Hildreth, 2006).

In order to classify specializations of local economies of SMSTs, we refer to the concept of socio-economic profiles that French scholars have used for some time now. The French National Statistics Office (INSEE) has been classifying specialization of economic activities into productive, residential and public spheres in order to analyse localized data concerning jobs and wages. In this chapter we refer to the classification of socio-economic profiles defined by Hamdouch and Banovac (2014) on productive, residential and knowledge-creative economies (Table 3.1).

Furthermore, scientific literature agrees that some cities and towns have been shifting towards new development models (Kourtit et al., 2012). For example, concepts of *smart cities*, *green cities*, *sustainable cities*, *healthy cities or cultural capitals* have been booming over the last decade. The common innovative characteristics of these new visions of cities are investment in human and social capital and modern infrastructure (ICT) in order to enable sustainable economic development and high quality of life, along with wise management of natural resources through participatory action and engagement. Our opinion is that such a vision is not exclusive to large cities. SMSTs can also share that orientation of their future (see Hamdouch and Banovac, 2014; Servillo et al., 2014).

The ESPON research project (Servillo et al., 2014) also examined the profiles of local economies in 31 SMSTs in ten European countries. The research discovered an ongoing sectoral shift from an industrial local economy to one that is more residential and knowledge-creative. A very significant observation was that half of the selected case studies were engaged in

Table 3.1 The main characteristics of the socio-economic profiles of SMSTs

	Residential	Productive	Knowledge-creative
Target groups	Residents, commuters and tourists	Business actors	Creative class and innovative firms
Factors of attractiveness	Good living environment, heritage, quality of provision of services, culture, health and schools, real estate conditions	Competitive business environment, labour skills	Creative environment, quality of provision of services
Characteristics	Diversity of equipment and amenities	Sectoral specialization, concentration of business activities	Innovation systems and knowledge-based activities, concentration of business activities
Policy focus	Culture and tourism, public services, private services to population, transport facilities	Quality of business areas, low taxes, subsidies	Clusters and networks

Source: Hamdouch and Banovac (2014)

creative and knowledge-based activities. Furthermore, the majority of the selected towns were dynamic in the sense that they have experienced an increase in both population and employment over the last decade. Other towns were in the process of restructuring, which means that they searched intensively for solutions to attract people and/or jobs. Finally, the research project found evidence that there may be a connection between performance and position in the spatial hierarchy. In fact, better performance (growth in population and in employment) was found in towns that were agglomerated and networked.

SMSTs and European Spatial Planning

The term 'European Spatial Planning' covers at least two concepts. The first concept is the already-mentioned ESDP, which introduced the idea of planning *for* Europe (i.e. strategies and policies for the development of the European territory). The second concept is the variety and diversity of national spatial planning systems within Europe, i.e. planning *in* Europe (Böhme, 2002).

SMSTs have been indirectly addressed within two EU policy domains: regional development and rural development. However, there is considerable overlap between these two domains with regard to how SMSTs are viewed. The regional development policy associated with the ESDP suggested the promotion of integrated spatial development strategies for city clusters within the framework of transnational and cross-border cooperation, including corresponding small cities and towns (ESDP, 1999: 21). In fact, the recommendation was to strengthen the role of SMSTs as development hubs, supporting partnerships and networks at the national and transnational levels, improving transport links and supporting their role as providers of services of general interest (ESDP, 1999). Yet, some authors argue that the ESDP failed to understand the wide range of places included in the SMST category and the functions they play in their territory. Also, they argue that SMSTs were 'primarily understood in terms of their location within particular metropolitan or city-regional contexts where it could be plausibly argued that polycentric urban structures existed' (Servillo et al., 2014: 191).

Only recently, with the publication of the *Territorial Agenda 2020*, was the role of SMSTs in Europe's spatial and territorial development recognized:

> In rural areas small and medium-sized towns play a crucial role; therefore it is important to improve the accessibility of urban centres from related rural territories to ensure the necessary availability of jobs opportunities and services of general interest. (European Commission, 2011b: 8)

The *Territorial Agenda 2020* was the document that followed the adoption of the ESDP in 1999 and the Leipzig Charter in 2007. It provided strategic orientations for territorial development and stressed the need for more efficient and synergetic policies that would promote balanced, polycentric territorial development and the use of integrated development approaches in cities and rural regions. The role of SMSTs was recognized as a pivotal for regional economies, since the objective for the EU is to have the 'most balanced urban system in the world':

> The generic features of SMSTs, particularly their human scale, liveability, the conviviality of their neighbourhoods, and their geographical embeddedness and historical character, in many ways constitute an ideal of sustainable urbanism. SMSTs are therefore essential for avoiding rural depopulation and urban drift, and are indispensable for the balanced regional development, cohesion and sustainability of the European territory. (European Commission, 2011a: 4)

Having discussed planning *for* Europe, in the second section we will turn to planning *in* Europe, in particular the issues that concern SMSTs.

The national institution framework

Institutional systems across Europe are very heterogeneous. The analysis of the political and fiscal decentralization in ten countries carried out as part of ESPON's research project 'TOWN' (Servillo et al., 2014) distinguished four types of institutional systems in Europe: federalized states, unitary 'regionalized' states, unitary 'Northern' states and unitary states. Federalized states (Belgium, Germany, Switzerland, etc.) have central government and regional authorities, both with their own legislative and administrative competences that are exercised independently and recognized by the Constitution. Unitary 'regionalized' states (Italy, Spain, etc.) have an intermediate level of government with a wide set of competences. Unitary 'Northern' states (Norway, Sweden, Denmark, etc.) have local governments with a wide range of responsibilities in relation to territorial development. Unitary states (France, the UK, Poland, Slovenia, the Czech Republic, Hungary, etc.) have a predominant central government and the degree of decentralization varies. It can be relatively high in some countries and very limited in others.

Furthermore, Newman and Thornley (1996) outlined the five planning groups in Europe according to legal and administrative styles: Nordic, British, Napoleonic, Germanic and East European. The Nordic group comprises Norway, Sweden, Finland and Denmark; it is characterized by unitary governments with strong local authorities. Due to advanced decentralization, spatial planning at the national and regional levels is reduced to a minimum while almost all responsibility is given to the municipalities. Members of the British group (Ireland and the UK) put a strong emphasis on the obligation of the central government to provide national coordination and consistency, while the majority of planning functions are implemented at a local level. Thus, a strong emphasis is placed on making a system plan-led and not plan-based (i.e. zoning is not as common as in other European countries). Members of the Napoleonic group (France, Portugal, Spain, Italy, Greece and the Benelux countries) base their centralized planning system on the use of abstract legal principles and theoretical debates in order to foresee in advance questions of possible dispute and to prepare a complete system of rules. Thus, planning is characterized by a market-led approach and the central government plays an important role in defining rules. The countries of the Germanic group (Germany, Austria and Switzerland) have federal government systems, and both federal and regional levels have autonomy and legislative power. Thus, planning is based on horizontal negotiations between federal and regional authorities. Finally, the East European group includes countries with a common communist heritage (Russia, Poland, Ukraine, the Czech Republic, Slovenia, and the Balkan and Baltic countries). The main characteristics of the planning systems is these countries are the creation of national codes that define planning hierarchies, rules and procedures. The code requires all cities to adopt general plans with 'functional territorial zoning'. Nevertheless, unlike in Soviet times, planning is linked to rules for private development: legally binding zoning plans.

As has been emphasized by scholars, institutional structures play a fundamental role in the performance of economic systems (Freeman and Perez, 1988; Hamdouch and Moulaert, 2006; Chen and Galbraith, 2012). Thus, patterns of behaviour, legal frameworks, power structures, local agents and their modes of interaction, policies and regulations, etc. are all structures combined in place-specific institutional dynamics (Ménard, 1995; Hodgson, 1998) that have an influence on local development (Hamdouch and Moulaert, 2006).

Equally, the scientific literature on relationships between policies and performance highlights the importance of decentralization processes and the power given to local authorities, local development policies and their correspondence to regional and national policies. The ESPON research (ESPON SGPTD, 2012) devoted to second-tier cities (non-capitals) and territorial development in Europe outlines two conclusions that we find adequate for our discussion on institutional factors affecting the local development of SMSTs. First, the performance of cities is significantly affected by national government policies – whether implicit or explicit, direct or indirect. Second, cities perform better where national, regional and local policy-making systems are horizontally and vertically aligned. Hamdouch and Moulaert (2006) argue that institutions shape the orientation and the content of public policies and regulations, which, in turn, influence strategies and coordination modes within development processes. On the other hand, economic actors and public authorities, through their decisions, actions and interactions, can modify the existing institutional framework or can even build a new one. Thus, the development process becomes a continuous flow of opportunities to influence the system and to initiate new forms of coordination (Hamdouch and Moulaert, 2006).

Other institutional factors that are important for the local development of SMSTs are the deconcentration of investment and the decentralization of decision-making and resources. Despite the uneven level of decentralization (Sorens, 2009), most European countries have engaged in the decentralization of their political and administrative structures, and have given more power to regional and local authorities (i.e. in relation to employment, industrial restructuring, higher education, research and development) (Hamdouch and Moulaert, 2006). Thus, benefits for SMSTs from the system where public and private investment and resources are spread across the (national) territory would in the long run be greater than in a more centralized system where investment is concentrated and shared between the capital and a few large cities.

Finally, the development of SMSTs depends upon the institutional mobilization of resources and partners to achieve agreed long-term objectives through systematic, coherent strategies and policies. Authors such as Pecqueur (1989), Stöhr (1990), Healey (1997), Magnaghi (2003), Knox and Mayer (2009), Demazière et al. (2012) and Hamdouch et al. (2012) stress the importance of strategic planning and integrated approach as important tools that may enable local actors to identify the advantages of their town and to address the real needs of their communities.

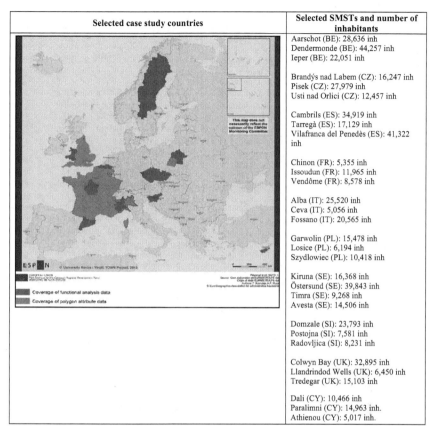

Figure 3.1 Case study countries and SMSTs
Source: Servillo et al. (2014)

Development practices in European SMSTs

By taking into account the national and regional institutional framework, in this section we observe the planning practices and dynamics between local actors in 31 case studies from ten European countries (the UK, France, Spain, Italy, Sweden, the Czech Republic, Cyprus, Slovenia, Poland and Belgium) (Figure 3.1). For this purpose we use case study reports from selected countries provided by local researchers for the ESPON research project 'TOWN' (Hamdouch and Banovac, 2014). These reports contain detailed information on the institutional systems, planning practices and socio-economic analysis of SMSTs.

In order to compare planning approaches to socio-economic development in SMSTs, we grouped case studies according to their socio-economic profile and performance during the period 1999–2011. Hence, we identified

Table 3.2 The socio-economic profiles and performance of case studies (*TOWN* research project)

	DYNAMIC (gaining population AND jobs)	RESTRUCTURING (losing population OR jobs)	DECLINING (losing population AND jobs)
Productive	Dali (CY)	Tredegar (UK), Vendôme (FR), Pisek (CZ), Szydłowiec (PL), Losice (PL)	Avesta (SW), Usti nad Orlici (CZ)
Residential	Brandýs nad Labem – Stará Boleslav (CZ), Östersund (SW), Colwyn Bay (UK)	Llandrindod Wells (UK)	
Mixed (productive-residential)	Tarregà (SP)	Chinon (FR), Kiruna (SW)	Timra (SW)
Mixed (productive-creative)	Athienou (CY), Alba (IT), Radovljica (SL)	Issoudun (FR), Domzale (SL), Postojna (SL)	
Mixed (residential-creative)	Aarschot (BE), Dendermonde (BE), Paralimni (CY), Vilafranca del Penedès (SP), Cambrils (SP)	Ieper (BE), Ceva (IT)	
Mixed (productive-residential-creative)		Fossano (IT), Garwolin (PL)	

Source: Hamdouch and Banovac (2014)

six possible socio-economic profiles: productive, residential and four mixed types (productive-residential, productive-creative, residential-creative and productive-residential-creative). In this section we examine how the socio-economic profile is a result of creative planning, institutional frameworks and the intertwined dynamics of local actors involved in socio-economic development. More precisely, we group SMSTs according to their socio-economic profile and describe some 'successful' cases; we also compare the approaches to development of involved actors and look for factors of success that are related to creative ways of policy-making and development planning (Table 3.2).

SMSTs with a dominant productive profile

SMSTs with a dominant productive profile come from the Unitary states (France, Sweden, Cyprus, the Czech Republic, Poland and the UK), which means that they have a predominant central government and a varying degree of decentralization (the highest is in Sweden). These towns did not have any shift in their local economy and the productive sector (traditional industry) has continuously existed as part of the economic fabric for several decades. Nevertheless, there are differences when it comes to their performance. The majority of them are undergoing a restructuring process, which means that they either lose population or jobs.

Dali (Cyprus) is the only example of a successful (dynamic) productive town that has been gaining population *and* jobs during the last decade. The town is agglomerated to the capital city Nicosia, which is a key advantage that puts it ahead of other municipalities on the island. The town's economy, which was formerly based on agriculture, has shifted to industry (manufacturing, repairing, wholesale, logistics, etc.), construction and services related to industry. Nevertheless, a significant proportion of the economy is still based on agriculture, mainly cattle rising and milk production – Dali is the biggest milk provider in Cyprus.

The success of Dali seems to be due to a common vision and complementary partnerships between actors at three levels (national, metropolitan and local). At the national level, the central government in cooperation with the local administration prepared a *Local Plan* for Dali and its surrounding settlements, with the objective of implementing policies to address that particular functional rural area. This process of 'territorial restructuring' is led by the state government across Cyprus and it is mainly based on strengthening existing partnerships between adjacent rural communities in order to facilitate their long-term alteration into new larger municipalities.

The metropolitan level seems to be the most important level of partnership for Dali. The *Local Plan for the Southern Area of Nicosia* involves Dali in the urban-rural metropolitan network with a common outlook and goals to exploit a strategic location and partnership within the Nicosia metropolitan area. Dali has obtained several benefits from cooperation with the capital city: participation in one of the rare committees established by municipalities located in the metropolitan area stimulates exchange and cooperation among local actors (for example, jointly reducing costs for common services such as rubbish collection). Equally important for Dali is the creation of a common development agency, ANEL, which focuses on applications for EU funding and a common programme for the active inclusion of foreign citizens.

The objective is to provide the information of different administrative levels included in the creation of policies in Dali. The first level is the national level, where the national government in cooperation with the local administration prepared a *Local Plan* for Dali. The second level is the metropolitan level, where the capital included Dali in its planning strategy. The third level is the municipal level, where local authorities adopted their own *Master Plan*. At the municipal level, Dali's *Master Plan* acts as a policy-guiding framework for local and national stakeholders concerning the municipality's growth. Besides propositions concerning transportation and the natural and built environment, this *Master Plan* recommends some interesting policies, such as the creation of a small incubator for innovative technology in the historical urban core, giving incentives for favouring multiple uses of existing public facilities, promoting collective identity in the community through schools' curricula and workshops, etc.

SMSTs with a dominant residential profile

The majority of SMSTs with a predominant residential profile is dynamic (gaining population *and* jobs) and agglomerated to neighbouring large cities. They all have their own development strategies that combine incentives for sectors such as services to population and tourism. Among them, Östersund (Sweden) and Colwyn Bay (UK) are towns that have benefited from a growth in terms of both population and jobs. Their success seems to be more related to local strategies based on cooperation and partnership between public, private and civil local actors than to national and regional directives.

Such towns display three common features: first, both towns are characterized by a high quality of life, residential attractiveness and touristic potential. *Östersund* plays the role of urban centre for eight surrounding municipalities by providing them with infrastructure and services: personal services and retail, a university, a hospital, an airport and high schools. Due to the absence of large industries, the town has maintained a healthy environment and high quality of living with lots of touristic activities. *Colwyn Bay* is characterized by the presence of strong residential and tourism sectors. In both towns, local authorities developed long-term strategies and plans that rely strongly on horizontal cooperation with local partners.

Second, both towns acknowledged a place-based approach in the creation of a policy of their own. Östersund and its larger area are driven by a common vision of sustainability in economic, ecological, social and political terms, which indeed influences all political discussions and decisions. The main policy instrument of the strategic planning is the *Growth Programme* accompanied by an action plan and an orientation plan. To give some examples, a strong local network is built between the Mid Sweden University and local businesses that work together on the development of a winter sports centre. The Mid Sweden Science Park and Association Quatro Helix also represent a platform for dialogue between the business community, the municipal council, the university and sport professionals. In Colwyn Bay, Conwy County Borough Council, which represents the local authority, led the process through the adoption of a range of plans for the whole of its territory. It developed a *Master Plan* that put focus on the regeneration of the town, the improvement of the town's retail facilities and the development of new forms of tourism. As such, a number of projects were launched, such as new sea defences, a seafront environmental development, a leisure park and improvements to the townscape.

Finally, besides the importance of horizontal cooperation, vertical (regional) cooperation and 'European' cooperation are not ignored. Östersund has maintained a close partnership (especially for funding its projects) with the Regional Council and the County Board. Indeed, it applied intensively for EU financing of its development projects such as the 'Peak Innovation' project, the 'Wind Power Centre', the integrated touristic project 'Sundvall, Östersund, Trondheim' (SÖT), etc. In the case of Colwyn Bay, Conwy County Borough Council found ways to work outside the box and come up with innovative approaches to accessing, combining and using different funds. Some examples are partnerships with the Welsh government (such as the Welsh Rugby and Bay Life Initiative) that were useful in terms of finding resources and implementing some planned projects. Nevertheless, despite well-developed and efficient public partnerships, the private sector seems to remain weak and not sufficiently involved in local development projects.

SMSTs with a mixed productive-residential profile

Case studies with strong residential and productive sectors can be found in France, Spain and Sweden. In most cases, they used to have a predominately productive economy, which over the last decade has been diversified by an increasing proportion of jobs in residential services. Among SMSTs with residential and productive profiles, the only dynamic case in terms of attracting population and jobs is Tarregà in Spain. Tarregà's advantage has been a continuous process of cooperation between the local authority and the Regional Catalonian authority.

Tarregà is situated in the western part of Catalonia, a region characterized by agriculture, agro-industry and trade services. The town is part of a network system with two other urban centres (Cervera and Guissona), to which it is connected by a highway. The town's key strength is its diversified economy, where agriculture is the dominant factor for the town and its hinterland. Tarregà also concentrates a significant proportion of public and private services, a large number of which are oriented towards agricultural activities and companies.

In terms of spatial planning, Tarregà and its hinterland are covered by the *Territorial Plan of Ponent*, which is the planning instrument used in Catalonia to define supra-municipal territorial strategies and to delimitate the main land uses and general disposal of future infrastructures. According to the *Territorial Plan*, Tarregà is seen as the key settlement for territorial balance with a potential of growth above the regional average; as such, the *Plan* provides guidelines that further strengthen the town's centrality. The most relevant development projects have been coordinated by local and regional authorities, such as the experimental model of governance for horizontal cooperation. In fact, this experiment was co-financed by EU funds and is jointly coordinated by a Consortium of two local county councils and 37 municipalities (among which Tarregà). Between 2007 and 2013, the Consortium worked on the implementation of several measures related to the improvement of the transformation and marketing processes of agricultural products, support for the creation of micro-enterprises, especially in relation to the diversification of the local economy, the promotion of touristic activities, and the conservation and improvement of the rural cultural heritage. Good cooperation among local and regional entities contributed to strengthening the commitment and participation of local economic agents in the implementation of the local development strategy. In fact, the Local Action Group, composed of mostly private actors, became the key forum to open the decision-making process.

SMSTs with a mixed productive-creative profile

In most of the case studies, SMSTs with a mixed productive and creative profile experienced a growth in population and jobs during the period 1999–2010. Their local economies have had the same mixed profile for decades now. At the same time, the share of employment in the creative and knowledge sectors has been continuously increasing. Among towns with this profile, we found the most dynamic and interesting examples in Cyprus, Italy and Slovenia. Alba (Italy) and Athienou (Cyprus) based their success on rooted local dynamics and entrepreneurial *local milieu* where private and civil actors construct the vision and the development of the town. Radovljica (Slovenia) is a successful case within this category; however, its dynamics are different from those in Alba and Athienou. Radovljica is part of a conurbation that lacks cooperation and a common vision in spite of numerous efforts and strategies coming from both the national and regional levels.

In some ways *Alba* and *Athienou* are not significantly different from one another. They are both autonomous towns with an important specialization in agriculture. Moreover, the agriculture has been developed and utilized to support local endogenous development. For example, Athienou focused on strengthening local entrepreneurship and minimal dependence on external (national or regional) capital. Its local development is based on local sources and investment from local entrepreneurs gathered in a cooperative. The cooperative contributes largely to the development of business activities and the local identity of the population. It supports local entrepreneurship through the common trade of local agricultural products, loans and the provision of storage facilities. At the same time, Alba has a strong agro-food and wine sector that is driven by a dense network of local small and medium-sized enterprises (SMEs) and some large-scale manufacturing plants. The most important actors in the economic and social growth of Alba have been local enterprises. There are mainly young entrepreneurs with high qualifications in the agro-food sector, which is a result of the national policy to open new facilities with specializations fitting the regional economic specificities.

In terms of spatial planning, both towns have local authorities leading the development projects more or less independently of the regional or national authorities. Athienou created its own *Development Plan* and a *Local Plan* that focus on boosting the organic agricultural productivity, local start-ups and local development clusters such as the Local Development Park, the Institute of Integrated Rural Development, the Environmental Information Centre and the Centre for Entrepreneurship and Innovation. These clusters gather local actors involved in the valorization of local traditions, products, culture and innovation on internal and external markets. Alba has the *Local Development Plan* and an *Integrated Territorial Plan* coordinated with regional authorities. Furthermore, since 2000, Alba has been directly involved in ten European programmes which provide funding to enhance agro-food and tourism in the area. The aims of these projects were to promote sustainable, quality tourism, cultural, artistic and architectural heritage, as well as to improve the offer of social and healthcare services to the population by implementing the *Local Health Plan*.

Radovljica (Slovenia) is a service and tourist centre located in an Alpine region. It is networked with two neighbouring towns, Jesenice and Bled, with which it forms a conurbation. The town has developed its own strategy and has been performing quite well by investing in infrastructure projects. Most of the jobs are in the manufacturing industry, such as furniture, recycling, the production of electricity and optical equipment, the production of vehicles, ski equipment, trade and construction.

Unlike in Alba and Athienou, the development of Radovljica was addressed by several sectoral policies created by the national government. In fact, according to the *National Spatial Development Strategy*, the town is seen as one of 15 centres of national importance. At the sub-national level, there are several strategies and spatial plans that guide the development of

Radovljica and its urban area. *The Development Programme of Radovljica 2020, the Municipal Spatial Strategy and the Municipal Planning Order*, and *the Regional Development Programme of Gorenjska NUTS 3 Region 2014–2020* define more or less the same development goals, such as infrastructure, entrepreneurship, tourism and quality of life. Nevertheless, one of the main issues is a traditional rivalry between Radovljica and its neighbouring towns Jesenice and Bled. There is a lack of cooperation, which leads to a failure to develop a wider cooperative and 'polycentric vision' for the region.

SMSTs with a mixed residential-creative profile

A large majority of SMSTs with a mixed residential and creative profile have been gaining population and jobs over the last decade. We find that during the period 1999–2010, most of those towns had a shift in their economic profile in the sense that there has been a growth in residential and creative activities. The examples given in this chapter are Dendermonde and Aarchot in Belgium and Cambrils in Spain. These cases base their success on a well-established culture of regional and inter-municipal cooperation that benefits from collective political representation and a focus on developing approaches to common issues. This may not mean that there is no competition between towns, but overall the collective action to develop a common vision prevails.

Dendermonde and *Aarschot* are located in the very centre of the 'Flemish Diamond' (Brussels–Ghent–Antwerp) and are both agglomerated to larger cities (Dendermonde to Brussels and Aarschot to Leuven). They are both easily accessible by public transport and there are no remote rural areas in the vicinity. Both towns play the role of service centres for the hinterland, particularly due to their large number of shops and schools. The main objective of local authorities in both Dendermonde and Aarschot is to attract young families and a qualified population. Therefore, significant effort has been expended on urban renewal and the provision of services to the population, such as a new library, a cultural centre, the refurbishment of the central square, etc.

In terms of strategic planning, Dendermonde is not part of any national or regional spatial planning scheme since it does not meet the national criteria of becoming a 'centrum city'. Nevertheless, a group of local politicians and businessmen united in a committee that later on grew into an inter-municipal Dender–Durme–Scheldt (DDS) partnership. The role of the DDS partnership is to plan for the economic development and prosperity of the area. As a result, the *Strategic Regional Plan Dendermonde*, created by the DDS committee, proposed a concrete vision and projects for the development of the area.

In the case of Aarschot, the local authorities were successful in attracting grants from the Flemish government and the EU Regional Development

Fund. An important initiator of cross-community initiatives and the mobilization of funding has been the inter-municipal partnership with Leuven called Interleuven. This partnership complements the work of municipalities by providing expertise in terms of housing, environment, economic activity and spatial planning. Besides Interleuven, local authorities participate in another inter-municipal partnership, the IGO partnership, which focuses on the social sector, culture, rural development and the management of green areas.

Cambrils is located in the centre of the Costa Daurada, one of the main tourist destinations in Catalonia and the largest resort area in terms of accommodation capacity. It is part of the networked metropolitan system that also includes two large cities: Tarragona and Reus. Tourism has been the main factor of transformation of the local economy. Cambrils is also a founding member and promoter of the Spanish Association of Destination for Culinary Tourism Promotion, which is a partnership created to develop and promote food-based tourism products from raw materials to the restaurants. The partnership involves different local stakeholders: town authorities, tourist companies, the fishermen's association, the agricultural cooperative and the tourism school.

Regarding spatial planning, Cambrils has not received outstanding direct attention in the planning and policy initiatives that have been developed at the provincial and metropolitan levels. Nevertheless, the town's authority set three important policy and planning instruments that oriented the growth of Cambrils in recent years: the *Town's Urban Planning Document* (POUM), the *Mobility Plan* and the *Urban Regeneration Plan*. All three documents set a goal for development based on quality tourism, giving priority to family, gastronomic and sports tourism. Furthermore, local authorities and the private sector made partnerships with other destinations in the Costa Daurada. These alliances allow greater efficiency in touristic promotions through shared costs between contiguous municipalities and offer complementary products in the region.

Lessons from the case studies

Overall the case studies confirmed the *importance of the regional context for the development of SMSTs*. On the one hand, towns located in growing metropolitan regions such as Dendermonde and Aarschot (Belgium), Vilafranca del Penedès (Spain), Brandýs nad Labem – Stara Boleslav (the Czech Republic) and Dali (Cyprus) have benefited from suburbanization effects and metropolitan policies and planning approaches. Their economies are conditioned by the commuting of goods and population between them and a metropolitan area, by specialization in the residential and cultural sectors and by offering attractive land stocks to firms and people coming from large urban-metropolitan areas. As a result, these towns have a growing population and economy with relatively low levels of unemployment compared to the national average, a good quality of life and few social problems. However, they 'face the potential problem of becoming dormitory towns for a large metropolis and all this entails in terms of possible negative effects on the local economy and society' (Servillo et al., 2014: 197).

On the other hand, towns located in rural and peripheral regions have different challenges that are often related to the loss of population, an ageing population, the lack of services and an 'old' economic base. Nevertheless, our successful case studies demonstrate that it is possible to be located in a remote rural area and have community development and endogenous growth based on local assets, inter-municipal cooperation and regional support. Among our case studies located in peripheral regions, there are three scenarios. The first is development based on a particular local 'milieu', a strong local identity and an entrepreneurial spirit of the population. Athienou (Cyprus) and Alba (Italy) are examples of a local economy benefiting from embedded social relations and a sense of community. Both towns are autonomous and located in rural regions. Agriculture and agro-tourism have been developed and utilized to support local endogenous development. In these towns dynamic private and civil actors are already mobilized and are leading the local development.

The second scenario is development characterized by the leading role of the local authority, which acts as the driving force in creating strategies and partnerships with other private and civil stakeholders. Östersund (Sweden), Paralimni (Cyprus) and Cambrils (Spain) have their own long-term development visions that have been implemented through synergy with a wide range of stakeholders. These towns try to understand and use the strengths and weaknesses of their remote positions, and are engaged in the mobilization of local actors by using all possible policy instruments available to them.

The third scenario is a development guided by a regional or county public authority, such as in the cases of Colwyin Bay (UK), Tarregà (Spain) and Radovljica (Slovenia). In other words, in some successful cases, the Welsh, Catalonian or Slovenian governments have been more directly committed to the local development of SMSTs. The precondition of their engagement was the recognition of the importance of a balanced territorial development and the role that SMSTs play in their respective areas. Once their choice has been made, the regional and county governments (with the help of EU funds) started investing in the region and contributed to a sustainable regeneration of SMSTs.

If we leave aside the differences between SMSTs located in metropolitan regions and peripheral areas, and therefore decide to focus on what is common to all successful case studies, we find that inter-municipal cooperation with the objective of sharing competences and a vision of development is the key factor in achieving success. The form and intensity of inter-municipal cooperation vary among the case studies. In some countries, it is part of broader territorial reforms and its implementation has been more or less compulsory (Belgium, Slovenia and France). However, in other countries the cooperation between municipalities was an obvious need and it was initiated by the local actors themselves (Italy, Spain and Cyprus). As we have highlighted in the description of development practices, the coordination of inter-municipal cooperation is complex and may result in territorial competition. In other words, while SMSTs may be particularly interested in cooperating because of their limited resources and action capacities, there are cases where towns cooperate to the extent that they gain funding from the county/regional level while trying to preserve their specific economic advantage over others.

Conclusion

Since the creation of the *European Spatial Development Perspective* in 1999, the EU Member States have been increasingly implementing the concepts of polycentric development, balanced spatial development, urban–rural partnerships, transborder cooperation, etc. in their national and regional policies and strategies. The modus operandi of such policy-making suddenly became known as 'strategic spatial planning', which was conducted through six steps: (i) framing decisions, plans, actions and projects; (ii) implementing; (iii) monitoring; (iv) feedback; (v) adjustment; and (vi) revision. This cycle of steps was in most countries applied in metropolises, city-regions and large regional areas, since they were considered to be the main drivers of development. In that context, SMSTs, despite their large number on the European continent, seem to have been left out.

In this chapter we have called for a profound analysis of SMSTs by providing two key arguments. First, SMSTs have an important role to play in regional and national development. They are part of networks and agglomerations within local, regional, national, supra-national and global systems. SMSTs in some cases may contribute to and complement the development of metropolitan or regional areas as industrial towns, touristic destinations, university towns, gateway towns, peripheral towns within a large city-region and regional service centres. They also may be important regional markets, service centres, regional capitals, attractive economic locations, tourist centres, communication hubs, metropolitan peripheries, national/international interfaces, associations of group of towns, etc. Second, planning for development in SMSTs has as many dynamics as there are contexts. In fact, despite attempts by some scholars to distinguish the 'European approach' to spatial development and types of European institutional systems, planning families and types of economies in order to link institutional structures and the performance of economic systems, it seems that the context (geography and local institutions) matters most and varies from town to town, city to city and region to region.

Having this in mind, we analysed and compared spatial planning approaches in 31 SMSTs from ten European countries. Above all, we focused on what Newman (2008) called the 'ordinary politics of planning' and its implications on the socio-economic development of towns. More precisely, we examined to what extent the functional roles of towns in their territory and socio-economic trajectories are the result of the nature of interactions between local actors. More precisely, we demonstrated the relevance of contextual factors such as geography and the institutional framework in creating a structural role for SMSTs. Geographical factors affecting the development of SMSTs are closely related to the effects of spatial proximity and the concentration of economic activities. As they fulfil diverse functions in the urban hierarchy, the development of SMSTs depends on the usage of comparative advantages and the nature of relations with other surrounding urban and rural settlements. Likewise, a flexible institutional setting including patterns of behaviours, a legal framework, a power structure, local agents and their modes of interaction, policies and regulations may create an encouraging environment for SMSTs.

Building on the results of the ESPON research project 'TOWN' and case study reports from ten European countries, we examined the way in which socio-economic profiles are the result of planning, institutional frameworks and the intertwined dynamics of local actors involved in local development. In that context we presented the development practices of dynamic and successful European SMSTs.

Our research confirmed the importance of the regional context for the development of SMSTs. On the one hand, towns that are located in a metropolitan region may build on the advantages of proximity to larger and diversified markets. On the other hand, towns in rural and peripheral regions seem to have different development dynamics and it is necessary to observe them from a broader perspective: some of them have developed their own strategy based on an endogenous development, some of them have not any 'written' strategy, but there is a 'visible' development dynamic driven by private and civil sectors, and, finally, some of them are the object of regional and county policies and planning.

It seems that the majority of SMSTs with a predominantly productive (industrial) profile face long-term decline. In fact, we found only one case (Dali in Cyprus) where a productive town had a dynamic local economy. Its success was due to its proximity to the capital city and to continuous technological and socio-economic improvements. Furthermore, towns with a mixed productive-creative profile (such as Alba in Italy and Athienou in Cyprus) seem to have a development trajectory that benefits from a particular local 'milieu', a strong local identity and an entrepreneurial spirit of the population. These towns are interesting examples of endogenous growth with mobilized private and civil actors. When it comes to the profile based on services to residents and tourism, we found that in those towns, the vision and strategies have been carefully planned and implemented at the municipal and regional/county levels. Moreover, the majority of them have experienced a shift in their local economy from a productive to a residential profile. Thus, we may presume that such a shift has been foreseen and guided by public authorities (at the municipal, regional or county level) in synergy with other local stakeholders.

When it comes to the sectors identified as local potentials for the economy, it is not surprising to see that the majority of selected cases highlight services to the population and traditional industry as being their major assets. There may be several explanations for this choice. First, many SMSTs experienced rapid growth (in terms of population and jobs) during the period of industrialization of the post-war boom. Therefore, a town's industrial heritage represents a strong feature in its landscape as well as in the mindset of local decision-makers. Second, attracting and keeping the population is naturally in the interests of local authorities. Hence, many local development plans include the provision and improvement of services to residents, such as construction services, retail services, social services, proximity services or administration services.

Interestingly, agriculture in SMSTs seems to be directly related to tourism and SMEs. We found several case studies in Spain, Italy and Cyprus that successfully linked the sectors of agro-food and wine production to a touristic offer of the town. Such a sectoral connection was rarely a result of strategic planning; on the contrary, it was a bottom-up process in which private and civil society actors engaged in activity that was later on supported by local or regional authorities.

Yet, we may outline that inter-municipal cooperation was a common factor in the success of dynamic SMSTs. The approach to sharing competences and a vision of development has been articulated differently across Europe. In some countries, inter-municipal cooperation is part of territorial reforms and its implementation has been more or less obligatory (for example, in Belgium, Slovenia and France). However, in other countries, cooperation between municipalities was recognized as crucial and it was initiated by local actors themselves (for example, in Italy, Spain and Cyprus).

Indeed, the interconnectedness of contextual factors and their co-evolution over the course of time reflect the complex relationships of mutual influences. Hence, it would be difficult to replicate the factors that underlie the success of some SMSTs, such as social relations, use of territorial capital and modes of mobilization of those assets elsewhere, because they are deeply embedded in the local social structure and reflect a very particular history.

References

Albrechts, L. (2004) Strategic (spatial) planning re-examined. *Environment and Planning B*, 31(5): 743–58.

—— (2006a) Shifts in strategic spatial planning? Some evidence from Europe and Australia. *Environment and Planning A*, 38(6): 1149–70.

—— (2006b) Bridge the gap: From spatial planning to strategic projects. *European Planning Studies*, 14(10): 1488–500.

Albrechts, L., Healey, P. and Kunzmann, R. (2003) Strategic spatial planning and regional governance in Europe. *Journal of the American Planning Association*, 69: 113–29.

Atkinson, R. (2001) The emerging 'urban agenda' and the European spatial development perspective: Towards a EU urban policy?. *European Planning Studies*, 9: 385–406.

Bellet, C. and Llop, J.-M. (2004) Miradas a otros espacios urbanos, en Scripta Nova. *Revista electrónica de geografía i ciencias sociales*, VIII(165), available at www.ub.edu/geocrit/sn/sn-165.htm.

Böhme, K. (2002) *Nordic Echoes of European Spatial Planning: Discursive Integration in Practice*. Nordregio Report, Stockholm.

Bolay, J.-C. and Rabinovich, A. (2004) Intermediate cities in Latin America: risk and opportunities of coherent urban development. *Cities*, 21(5): 407–21.

Brunet, R. (1997) *Territoires de France et d'Europe. Raisons de géographe*. Paris: Belin.

Carrier, M., Thériault, M. and Véronneau, E. (2012) Structure socio-spatiale des réseaux d'innovation en secteur manufacturier traditionnel d'une ville moyenne. *Revue d'Economie Régionale et Urbaine*, 2: 215–44.

Castells, M. (1996) *The Rise of Network Society – The Information Age: Economy, Society and Culture*. Oxford: Blackwell.

Chen, J. and Galbraith, K. (2012) A common framework for evolutionary and institutional economics. *Journal of Economic Issues*, XLVI(2): 419–28.

Christaller, W. (1933) Die Zentralen Orte in Suddeutschland. In C.W. Baskin (ed.), *Central Places in Southern Germany*. Englewood Cliffs: Prentice Hall.

Demazière, C. (ed.) (2012) *Observation des dynamiques économiques et stratégies des villes petites et moyennes de la région Centre*. Interim research report for Région Centre, Université François-Rabelais, UMR CITERES, Tours.

Demazière, C., Banovac, K. and Hamdouch, A. (2014) The changing profiles of small and medium-sized towns in the European context: Between residential economy, competitiveness and innovation. In A. Kwiatek-Soltys, H. Mainet, K. Wiedermann, K. and J.-C. Edouard (eds), *Small and Medium Towns' Attractiveness at the Beginning of the 21st Century*. Clermont-Ferrand: Presses Universitaires Blaise Pascal and CERAMAC, pp. 29–40.

Demazière, C. and Wilson, P. A. (eds) (1996) *Local Economic Development in Europe and the Americas*. London: Mansell.

Demazière, C., Serrano, J. and Vye, D. (2012) Villes petites et moyennes. *Norois*, 223: 5–13.

De Roo, P. (2007) *Les villes moyennes françaises: enjeux et perspectives*. Paris: DIACT.

ESDP (1999) *European Spatial Development Perspective: Towards Balanced and Sustainable Development of the Territory of the European Union, Committee on Spatial Development*. Luxembourg: European Commission.

ESPON SGPTD (2012) *Second Tier Cities in Territorial Development in Europe: Performance, Policies and Prospects*. Final Report. Luxembourg: ESPON.

European Commission (2011a) *Cities of Tomorrow – Challenges, Visions, Ways Forward*. Brussels: European Commission.

—— (2011b) *Territorial Agenda of the European Union 2020: Towards an Inclusive, Smart and Sustainable Europe of Diverse Regions*. Brussels: European Commission.

Faludi, A. (2001) The application of the European spatial development perspective: Evidence from the north-west metropolitan area. *European Planning Studies*, 9: 663–75.

Freeman, C. and Perez, C. (1988) Structural crises of adjustment, business cycles, and investment behavior. In G. Dosi, C. Freeman, R. Nelson, G. Silverberg and J. Soete L. (eds), *Technical Change and Economic Theory*. London: Pinter Press, pp. 38–66.

Graham, S. (2001) FlowCity, networked mobilities and the contemporary metropolis. *DISP*, 144: 4–11.

Hamdouch, A. and Banovac, K. (2014) Socio-economic profiles and performance dynamics of European SMSTs: Methodological approach and lessons from 31 case studies. In L. Servillo (ed.), *TOWN – Small and Medium-Sized Towns in their Functional Territorial Context*. Final Report, Luxembourg: ESPON, pp. 162–86.

Hamdouch, A. and Moulaert, F. (2006) Knowledge infrastructures, innovation dynamics and knowledge creation/diffusion/accumulation processes: A comparative institutional perspective. *Innovation: The European Journal of Social Science Research*, 19(1): 25–50.

Hamdouch, A., Depret, M.-H. and Tanguy, C. (eds) (2012) *Mondialisation et résilience des territoires. Trajectoires, dynamiques d'acteurs et experiences*. Québec: Presses de l'Université du Québec.

Healey, P. (1997) *Collaborative Planning, Shaping Places in Fragmented Societies*. Vancouver: University of British Columbia Press.

—— (2006a) Transforming governance: Challenges of institutional adaptation and a new politics of space. *European Planning Studies*, 14(3): 299–320.

—— (2006b) Relational complexity and the imaginative power of strategic spatial planning. *European Planning Studies*, 14(4): 525–46.

—— (2007) *Urban Complexity and Spatial Strategies*. London: Routledge.

Healey, P., Khakee, A., Motte, A. and Needham, B. (eds) (1997) *Making Strategic Spatial Plans: Innovation in Europe*. London: UCL Press.

Henderson, V. (1997) Medium size cities. *Regional Science and Urban Economics*, 27: 583–612.

Hildreth, P.A. (2006) Roles and economic potential of English medium-sized cities: A discussion paper. Available at: www.salford.ac.uk/__data/assets/pdf_file/0019/114733/061010_Medium_sized_cities_complete_final.pdf.

Hodgson, G.M. (1998) The approach of institutional economics. *Journal of Economic Literature*, XXXVI: 166–92.

Hotelling, H. (1929) Stability in competition. *Economic Journal*, 39: 41–57.

Huriot, J.-M. and Bourdeau-Lepage, L. (2009) *Economie des villes contemporaines*. Paris: Economica.

Ismeri Applica (2010) Distribution of competences in relation to regional development policies in the Member States. Study for DG REGIO.

Knox, P. and Mayer, H. (2009) *Small Town Sustainability: Economic, Social and Environmental Innovation*. Basel: Birkhauser.

Kourtit, K., Nijkamp, P. and Arribas, D. (2012) Smart cities in perspective – a comparative European study by means of self-organizing maps. *Innovation – The European Journal of Social Science Research*, 25(2): 229–46.

Krätke, S. (2001) Strengthening the polycentric urban system in Europe: Conclusions from the ESDP. *European Planning Studies*, 9: 105–16.

Léo, P.-Y., Philippe, J. and Monnoyer, M.-C. (2012) Stratégie de développement tertiaire des villes françaises. *Revue d'Economie Régionale et Urbaine*, 2: 150–72.

Lowndes, V. (2005) Something old, something new, something borrowed ... how institutions change (and stay the same) in local governance. *Policy Studies*, 26(3/4): 291–309.

Magnaghi, A. (2003) *Le projet local*. Liège: Editions Mardaga.

Martinelli, F. (ed.) (2005) *La planificazione strategic in Italia e in Europa: Methdologie ed esiti a confront*. Milan: Franco Angeli.

Ménard, C. (1995) Markets as institutions versus organizations? Disentangling some fundamental concepts. *Journal of Economic Behavior and Organization*, 28: 161–82.

Nelson, A.C. (1993) Theories of regional development. In R.D. Bingham and R. Mier (eds), *Theories of Local Economic Development*. Newbury Park, CA: Sage, pp. 27–57.

Newman, P. (2008) Strategic spatial planning: Collective action and moments of opportunity. *European Planning Studies*, 16(10): 1371–83.

Newman, P. and Thornley, A. (1996) *Urban Planning in Europe: International Competition, National Systems and Planning Projects*. London: Routledge.

ÖIR (Österreichisches Institut für Raumplanung) (2006) *ESPON 1.4.1 – The Role of Small and Medium-Sized Towns – Final Report*. Luxembourg: ESPON.

Parker, R. (2007) Networked governance or just networks? Local governance of the knowledge economy in Limerick (Ireland) and Karlskrona (Sweden). *Political Studies*, 55(1): 113–32.

Pecqueur, B. (1989) *Le développement local*. Paris: Syros.

Santamaria, F. (2012) Les villes moyennes françaises et leur rôle en matière d'aménagement du territoire: vers de nouvelles perspectives? *Norois*, 223: 13–30.

Sassen, S. (1991) *The Global City*. Princeton: Princeton University Press.

Scot, M. (2006) Strategic spatial planning and contested ruralities: Insights from the Republic of Ireland. *European Planning Studies*, 14(6): 811–29.

Scott, A.J. (ed.) (2001) *The Rise of Global City-Regions*. London: Routledge.

Servillo, L., Atkinson, R., Smith, I., Russo, A., Sýkora, L., Demazière, C. and Hamdouch, A. (2014) *TOWN – Small and Medium-Sized Towns in their Functional Territorial Context*. Final Report, Luxembourg: ESPON.

Sorens, J. (2009) The Partisan Logic of Decentralization in Europe. *Regional and Federal Studies*, 19(2): 225–72.

Stöhr, W. (ed) (1990) *Global Challenge, Local Response*. London: Mansell.

Taulelle, F. (2010) La France des villes petites et moyennes. In L. Cailly and M. Vanier (eds), *La France: une géographie urbaine*. Paris: Armand Colin, pp. 138–54.

4 Governing place reinvention
The quest for an integrative approach
Torill Nyseth and Anders Tønnesen

Introduction

Contemporary urban governance is populated by a more diverse and varied set of institutions, networks and processes. First of all, it relates to a new role of government, moving from being a strong, dominant provider of all kinds of services towards the involvement of a number of different actors and agencies in the process of governing. What we see in several Norwegian cities is that local government leaders, in cooperation or partnership with non-public actors, have engaged in sometimes very strategic place-branding and place-promotion policies. Intentions behind such strategic efforts are often expressed as efforts 'to attract investments and people', which are conceived of as needed when overall economic restructuring processes continuously challenge local industries and institutions. This form of urban transformation stands in contrast to traditional forms of transformation and development through state-led planning and regulation. The aim of this chapter is to look more closely at the governance processes related to urban planning and development.

The discussion will focus on governance structures in the reinvention of Drammen, a medium-sized Norwegian town that has had great success. We will look more closely at the reasons for this success. On the one hand, what seem to be traditional regulative forms of planning appear to have been important. On the other hand, new forms of governance involving both market and civic society in urban development cannot be overlooked as explanations. Consensus building on strategies between a number of stakeholders and collaborative efforts in urban planning are also part of the success story. Altogether, the Drammen 'model' seem to rest on flexible, innovative and integrative approaches to planning and urban development.

Alternatives to entrepreneurialism in urban governance?

'The entrepreneurial city' is laid out as the currently dominant response to problems of urban transformation. The evolving entrepreneurial governance structure can be understood because of the increased competition between cities within the global discourse (Hall, 2001; McGuirk et al., 1998). Entrepreneurialism is reflected in new forms of governance institutions, for instance, public–private partnerships and other lasting alliances between public agencies and private actors. Since the 1970s, the rise of this type of entrepreneurialism is illustrated in local authorities' increasing involvement in economic development, supporting small firms and forging closer links between public and private sectors, and promoting certain areas to attract new businesses. The rise of urban entrepreneurialism as the dominant policy strategy transcends the traditional local government roles of delivering services towards risk-taking, inventiveness, self-reliance, profit motivation and promotion.

The city governments themselves act in a self-interested manner to promote economic growth and they use public sector resources to achieve this. However, when local governments become partners and facilitators in public–private consortia, growth coalitions, etc., they risk losing their overall coordination role for and on behalf of local community interests. In Bob Jessop's words:

> I suggest that we can begin to make sense of the twin facts that: (a) the city is being re-imagined – or re-imaged – as an economic, political, and cultural entity which must seek to undertake entrepreneurial activities to enhance its competitiveness; and (b) this re-imag(in)ing is closely linked to the re-design of governance mechanisms involving the city – especially through new forms of public-private partnerships and networks. (Jessop, 1997: 40)

However, 'entrepreneurial imagineneering' approaches to construct more competitive place brands (Kearns and Philo, 1993) are not the only urban development strategy.

Patsy Healey, for instance, argues that transformative strategies such as image-building need to build on real changes that are going on in the community, on analysis of the interests that are involved, and on the deeper movements in cultural assumptions and values, the ground upon which identities are shaped. Without such a grounded strategy, the risk is that people disconnect from the process and feel alienated from what is going on (Healey, 2002).

In addition, attempts to construct new place images are not necessarily limited to advertising campaigns alone, but are often linked to other strategies, for instance, the fabrication of a new urban landscape, flagship projects, mega-events and other cultural attractions (Healey, 2010; Hubbard and Hall, 1997). It is possible to identify a transition from a more disembedded promotion practice towards a toolbox of planning instruments based on a broader understanding of places (Kavaratzis and Ashworth, 2005). Celebrating diversity is, for example, present in urban branding profiles, particularly in multicultural contexts (Johansson and Cornebise 2010). A brand could also be a designation of heritage, and as such anchored in local history, and identity, and 'authenticity' (Skogheim and Vestby, 2010). Place promotion of this type is anchored more heavily in local identity. Promotion activities, however, need to find ways to increase awareness of diverse conceptions of place and to work out what is broadly shared and where deep conflicts lie (Healey, 2010). Place promotion is more than 'fine words' and should be more closely linked to place making and place development. Stephen Ward invites us to a much broader understanding: 'Yet marketing, narrowly defined, is not enough. Behind the fine words and images there has to be at least some physical reality of buildings, public spaces and activities that give some genuine promise of a re-invented city' (Ward, 1998: 193).

In this chapter we suggest that we may analytically distinguish between place promotion understood as boosterism and place reinvention as a broader perspective. While the first strategy represents the entrepreneurial and place-as-commodity-oriented form, place reinvention relates to a more complex and broader understanding of place transformation (Nyseth and Viken, 2009), and therefore, as will be argued later on, is potentially more inclusive and integrative than in the first case. Place reinvention goes beyond place branding and may involve both economic and symbolic transformations constituting a changed sense of place. It is a less strategic, but more analytical approach that tries to understand how different processes are linked together in place transformations. In place branding, all these strategies could be performed, either in combination or with an emphasis on only one of them. If, however, such projects encourage local participation and are embedded in collective strategies, they might stimulate increased engagement locally, create enthusiasm and improve the place attractiveness for locals and outsiders. In other words, such projects may contribute to turn around or slow down a negative spiral of economic and social development.

Place reinvention thus invites a radically different approach, moving from seeing places merely as products or destinations to be promoted towards a practice which views places (metaphorically) as living, breathing, cultural entities. From this perspective we move away from marketing as a decoupled project that is not linked to anything else and towards a more integrated approach that links place marketing to place development, urban renewal, community development and urban planning. The symbiotic relationship between people and place is a point of departure; places are shaped and made by people's actions and by their perceptions. At the core of the identity of place are local people as well as businesses, facilities and local landscapes. Without the involvement of their knowledge, concern and imagination, place marketing will be unable to move away from fictitious stereotyping and towards a more diverse set of messages about places. Place reinvention switches and broadens the perspective on place development and place promotion towards underlying processes of identity transformation and a sense of place that is always at stake (Nyseth, 2013).

Place reinvention addresses the numerous ways in which places are being produced and reproduced. Such strategies direct attention towards the relationship between symbolic and imaginative change and planned regeneration. Place reinvention relates to the transformations resulting from the interplay between actors such as industries, authorities and the public, between projects of construction, promotion and consumption, and processes related to information, identity and imagery. It involves a complex dialectic between material space and discursive representation, and the complexity involved in place transformation which the branding literature seems to ignore or simplify. It relates to both economic and symbolic transformations constituting a changed sense of place; for instance, changes in a place's industrial base are accompanied by changes in how a place is represented. The term 'reinvention' indicates that something has to be re-created, renewed or redefined, indicating that something else is left behind or forgotten. Place reinvention is a concept that focuses on both inventions and interventions as vehicles for change (Robinson, 2006: 251). Inventions are the continuous changes going on all the time, while interventions are linked to those more direct, planned and intentional processes attempting to achieve change.

Places change for a number of reasons and often out a necessity; industries and businesses adapt to changing circumstances in order to survive, and authorities urge change to keep up employment and settlement patterns. Over the years, the character of most places changes – sometimes radically, sometimes more modestly. Some processes change the *raison d'être* of a place or its genius loci, as, for instance, with changes to a town or region's industrial basis or nature. Other processes are more closely related to changed landscapes and townscapes, although often these two processes merge with changes due to shifts in their industrial bases. Changes in the modes of production followed by an ongoing restructuring of the local economy may lead to changes in place identities and place images. Place reinvention links place making to both material and symbolic processes of change, and to the discourses and narratives that are associated with place images. The material production and the symbolic production of place are intimately linked and are not two different processes. Materiality as landscapes and industrial base, and their representations, are tied together in the construction of narratives that create activities and reinvent places. Changes in the mode of production followed by an ongoing restructuring of the local economy may lead to changes in place identities and images – the symbolic representation of a place.

Reinvention of places is both random and a matter of intention; it is both planned and something that just happens as a more or less unintended consequence of other ongoing processes. Thus, new place images are not only the results of strategic development processes aimed at profiling and promoting place, but are also products of people's everyday life. Thus, reinvention takes place in the encounters between different types of actors; it is relational, dealing with the complex and multi-layered identities of place.

But place reinvention is also guided by traditions, norms and values. And at the same time, different actors tell different stories about the same place.

Integrative planning through place reinvention approaches

As argued above, the place reinvention perspective is seen as potentially more inclusive and integrative compared to the entrepreneurial-oriented place promotion. This makes relevant research typically related to *collaborative planning*. Here, the inclusion of stakeholders is not only treated as normative necessity, but also seen as providing better governance processes (Edelenbos et al., 2010). According to Healey, such collaboration enhances the 'capacity to work across sectoral divisions and single-issue politics' (2007: 282). This approach can be seen as a response to fragmented power in urban development issues. Typically, new development will require coordination not only across tiers of government (local, regional and national), but also between public agencies. There is thus a range of actors, each holding parts of the puzzle of how to achieve positive development in a given city. Fragmented lines of responsibility are also found between the public and private sectors. For instance, while the decision-making power over land use is delegated to municipal authorities, planning initiatives are increasingly developed by private actors (Falleth and Saglie, 2012; Saglie and Harvold, 2010). This is part of a tendency where private interests increasingly play a key role in urban planning.

Cooperation between policy actors may involve different degrees of commitment. Stead and Meijers (2009) describes this by distinguishing between *policy cooperation*, *policy coordination* and *policy integration*. Policy integration involves the highest level of dedication and complexity of the three. Here, decision-making is managed in a way that transcends the boundaries of established policy fields, resulting in joint new policy. At the city level, which is the topic of this chapter, this transcendence of borders would involve integration between public and private actors in the governance of place transformation.

In the following section we will apply these theoretical tracks to the case study of Drammen. Do we find entrepreneurial or collaborative and integrative forms of governance in the policies of urban transformation and reinvention in this city? And what are the factors that produce the specific planning and governing style that we observe there?

Research design

Data is based on a study of governance networks in Drammen, a medium-sized Norwegian city. The study was conducted in 2007 and was supplemented in 2012. The research design is based on two primary data-collection methods; first, a mapping of all collaborative arrangements in Drammen; and, second, semi-structured interviews with network members, business representatives, political leaders and administrative staff in the municipal administration.

The mapping was conducted through interviews with the city government leadership and studying the council minutes over four years. In addition, various types of documents, including cooperation agreements, municipal plans, information brochures and newspaper articles, were subjected to textual analysis. The mapping revealed a large number of collaborations and a multitude of types, ranging from limited companies involving the city government as a part-owner, via formalized collaborative projects with civil society or business sector as partners, to informal networks (Vabo et al., 2011; Tønnesen, 2015).

Drammen: the story of successful urban reinvention

The case study was conducted in Drammen (population in 2014: 66,214). Compared to other large Norwegian cities, Drammen has experienced relatively high population growth over the last decade (Statistics Norway, 2013).[1] Located 45 km east of Oslo, Drammen is a part of the large metropolitan region with Oslo and has struggled to be seen as something other than a part of the suburban area surrounding the capital. The town was originally established based on rug floating in the nearby river, then later on shipping, and cellulose and paper production characterized the industry here until the 1970s and 1980s.

In the early 1990s Drammen stood out as a city with a very negative image. It was a physically ugly, working-class city dominated by heavy industry. Moreover, the river was badly contaminated by sewage and paper industry waste. One of the planners in this period says:

> The Drammen River was more or less open sewage, the city physically decayed, the social life dominated by a tiered bourgeoisie stemming from an earlier period of greatness. (Bull, 2014)

The city was also dominated by a highway with heavy traffic passing through the city centre, splitting the public access to the river, and it was characterized by central areas being devoted to industrial storage facilities which also affected the city's aesthetic qualities. These industries also added to the volume of traffic in an already strained transport infrastructure. One of the consequences of this was a weak city centre, with much trade taking place at the malls on the outskirts of the city. Another planner described the crises that in this period had become widespread like this:

> I recognized a city with some basic and nature given qualities, however followed by some human produced environmental challenges and a proclaimed and outspoken sadness. This sadness lead to more of the same, it grew stronger instead of using this as an opening towards other possibilities that also can come out of an understanding of crises. From previous work on community development, I brought with me the

concept of optimal understanding of crises. That is when the crises have grown to a level where everybody understands that something has to be done. (Bull, 2014: 69)

Even if the population was not declining, it was not increasing for a long period and there was a lack of businesses willingness to invest there. With its working-class image and labour party majority over a long time period, powerful trade unions and a limited role for private capital, the governance regime was traditional and hierarchical, with a high emphasis on the delivery of basic public services. The negative image was also related to conflicts in some of the neighbourhoods with high numbers of immigrants. About 20 per cent of the population were immigrants from non-Western countries, which in the Norwegian context was the highest after Oslo. At the beginning of the 1990s, Drammen still experienced a population decrease and a weakened municipal economy. As a result, it served as a national reference town for everything ugly and depressing (Carlson, 2001). The sociologist Yngve Carlson, studying Drammen over many years, claimed that a form of 'place-masochism' nurtured the inhabitants' self-image of Drammen during these years.

Visiting Drammen today gives quite a different impression. It is now a vibrant city with a radically different profile compared to 20 years ago. And the change from a negative to a positive image is documented in a number of surveys. How can this success be explained?

'New Drammen' – the becoming of a renewed city

In the last few decades, much has changed. A number of severe transformations relating to major shifts in the economic basic structures has been going on. A number of new projects to regenerate and reinvent Drammen have emerged, many of them organized as networks like business park organizations and development agencies. The political climate has also changed. At present, there is a conservative majority in the municipal council. What has happened can be summarized in seven points:

1. Massive physical regeneration of the city centre, 'taking back the river' and the river banks.
2. Tunnels and other infrastructure investments leading traffic outside the city centre.
3. Densification.
4. New activities and institutions.
5. A successful strategy for the promotion and selling of the new urban image.
6. Strengthening of the local identity both at the level of the city and in the neighbourhoods.
7. Population growth: since 1990, the number of inhabitants has increased by more than 10,000.

Basic urban planning!

The physical regeneration that Drammen has undergone is remarkable. The city today has resumed contact with the river, the river itself has been cleaned and a public park has been developed along the riverside. The cleaning of the river was important in increasing the attractiveness of the urban centre. So too was the making of tunnels, leading traffic underground and away from the inner city. Though these tunnels did not reduce car use, they provided an opportunity to develop a strong city centre.

Basically these transformations have been well planned and anchored in a municipal comprehensive urban planning process for the city centre, including the complicated infrastructure issues relating to the highway passing through it. However, some of these projects, like cleaning the river, were ordered by the environmental authorities, and the new transport system could not have been established without the involvement and co-financing provided by state authorities. However, these larger projects did provide momentum to the process of change in the municipality; an opportunity to break with the past and build a new course through comprehensive planning. The city centre square has been significantly upgraded and the riverside and a brownfield area have given the inhabitants new opportunities for recreation and leisure. Together they cement the position of the city centre in the development strategy of Drammen.

The municipal planning process has been the basic instrument for the physical restructuring of the city, especially the planning of the riverbanks and the highway solutions. The plan has become a reference point for everything that has happened afterwards. The combination of professionalism, political representation and being able to cooperate with relevant partners who in their turn influence their respective organisations represent important success factors. Therefore, the first important explanation to this development is the proactive role played by the municipal government. The municipal council and in particular the political and administrative leadership have played a leading and controlling role in designing and implementing a regeneration policy through planning regulation and mobilizing funding from other public sources for investments in infrastructure, cleaning up the river, etc. The projects have been financed in part by public money – from the state, regional funds, and mobilizing municipal resources and toll money. The cleaning of the river and the tunnels relieving the city centre from traffic overload provided new opportunities for densification and investments. The municipality has been awarded a number of prizes related to this urban development and planning. The ways in which policy-makers grabbed this window of opportunity highlight Drammen as an example of positive urban development in the Norwegian context (Tønnesen, 2015).

City-centre densification

By private means, a number of apartment buildings along the riverside have been built, which together with the public investments have contributed to the development of a new urban space and a more compact city.

The city centre plays an important role in these new development strategies. Reflecting on the change, an informant in the county administration stated:

> [I was] excited about whether Drammen would manage to bring out the potential that was revealed with the tunnels being completed. I remember thinking that there never was a construction crane to be seen in Drammen [before the tunnels]. There was so little happening there. I think they have performed very well.[2]

The emphasis on city centre development is reflected in statistics showing increased population density for urban settlements (Haagensen, 2012). Strikingly, the densification strategy is used both to reduce car use and maintain city-centre vitality (Municipality of Drammen, 2007). The following comment from a public official illustrates the integration of the two:

> We want to increase city-centre density and use the major bulk of resources to develop the centre and thereby contribute to its vitality. More people living and working in the city centre gives a basis for doing something with the transport patterns and investments in the transport sector.

City-centre dynamics and the management of retail trade

The issue of city-centre vitality and trade transcends inner-city dynamics. It also involves questions of what types of trade are being allowed outside the city centre and in neighbouring municipalities. When trade statistics indicate a decline in urban-centre trade in Drammen (like all larger cities in Norway), this is a result of combined competition from car-based shopping centres situated inside and outside the municipal borders. Amongst the tools that Drammen has applied to counter this tendency are planning strategies for regulating trade within the municipality. Comparing Norway's largest cities in terms of such regulation, Tennøy et al. (2010) found such strategies to be strong in Drammen. This has resulted in the rejection of the new establishment of shopping centres on the outskirts of the city. In another instance, concerning the expansion of an existing shopping centre outside the city, it turned out to be larger than intended by the municipality. Here, the municipality demanded changes to be made if the shopping centre was

Figure 4.1 The Ypsilon Bridge. One of the new images of Drammen

to avoid coercive fines (Municipality of Drammen, 2007). This illustrates the municipality's intention to protect the city centre from competition with car-based shopping centres.

In Drammen, densification strategies are matched with strategies targeting increased city-centre attractiveness. Here the upgrading and maintenance of public space is seen as an 'important basis for the will of private actors to establish, especially in the city centre' (Municipality of Drammen, 2007: 13). As illustrated by this informant, there are high hopes in the municipal administration that the strategy will be beneficial:

> [The urban development] strategy has caught the attention of the surroundings. I think it's just a matter of time before we get the big fish on the hook in terms of investment.

Branding Drammen: the municipal hierarchy in tune with public–private partnerships

Since the beginning of the 1990s, a number of networks, partnerships and corporations operating in the field of place reinvention have been established.

The most important network was organized as a limited company called 'Our City Drammen'. The major shareholder was the municipality (33 per cent), with the major part of the shares being held by local private firms. This company's main goals were twofold: to develop the city centre area, and to coordinate and implement activities to strengthen the city as a commercial and cultural centre in the region. The network was then subdivided into several other companies, among them the 'Branding Drammen' project, which aimed to get rid of the old negative image of the city and create a new image. 'Our City Drammen' received fees from the businesses holding shares and full-time positions paid for by the city government. The process of city branding was put in the hands of inter-organizational networks outside the municipal administration.

The 'Our City Drammen' partnership as an umbrella network operated as a coordinator of a number of other organizations, networks and partnerships that were created in order to work on more specific projects and policy areas. The network also carried out the important function of communicating and mediating in potential conflicts between different actors, both between businesses and between public and private actors. One of the projects organized under 'Our City Drammen' was a project based on selling and promoting the city's new brand, 'The River City Drammen'. This was a long-term project, lasting from 2005 until 2011,[3] when there was a celebration of the city's 200-year jubilee. The argument for the long duration of this project was that it takes time to change a negative image. What was also stressed in this project was the emphasis on selling a 'true image'. The promotion of the city has a message. There is a consciousness of not trying to sell a false or empty image, but what the city actually can offer in terms of urban qualities, services, cultural activities, housing, etc. As one respondent stated:

> If you are carrying out place-marketing and people come in large bulks to Drammen asking, 'What was this all about?', then it will unravel completely. Here, I feel we have succeeded, when those who come saying that, 'Yes there was actually something to talk about!' Conducting place-marketing without a product does not work, everybody who has been into sales knows that.

The strong links between local business actors and the municipality are also obvious in the Drammen City Image Project. Established in 2005 as a governance network with the municipality and businesses in the city centre as participants, its overall goal is to develop a positive city image through festivals, events and campaigns. As such, it fits into typical place-marketing strategies, where events are used to create an appealing urban atmosphere. Moreover, it has an important function as an arena for the communication, coordination and mediation of views between public and private actors. As a public official stated:

> We have a very close relationship with landlords and trade actors in the city centre. It is necessary, because the centre has been continuously threatened due to failed land use over 20 years. [We want to] ensure that we have a functional centre, with dynamic trade as an important pillar.

All informants from Drammen pointed to the successful cooperation between the local authorities and private actors over many years as a reason for the success. Looking at how things have been organized, there are a lot of networks, partnerships and other forms of cooperation involving public and private actors, including the local newspaper.

Civic society – involved, engaged, mobilized

Following the regeneration projects, commercial activities have returned to the city centre, together with cultural activities, festivals and sport events, and have contributed to its success. These processes has been anchored in civil society, involving a broad number of inhabitants, business actors and NGOs. A whole range of associations, cultural and professional artists have contributed to filling these new urban spaces with a whole range of cultural, commercial and other forms of activities on an all-year-round basis. This cultural and commercial expansion is also a radical change. By 1990, the city centre had suffered the loss of a number of commercial activities, with new shopping centres being created outside the urban area.

The planning processes around the millennium, where a new municipal plan were carved out, were also characterized by broad public involvement. Central here was local authorities presenting a set of scenarios, asking the population of what they considered to be the most desired direction for the city to take. The choice, anchored among both politicians and the public, fell on *Naturbania* – a strategy emphasizing both urban and nature qualities. However, today the city centre still struggles with competition from shopping centres located on the outskirts of the city.

However, the question remains: what would the situation today have been if strategic and integrative planning had not taken place? This is of course a speculative question that we cannot answer fully. Nevertheless, it is not very provocative to claim that the situation then had been much worse.

Summing up

Table 4.1 below gives the most important dimensions summing up the development in Drammen.

The interdependency between the municipal administration, the businesses in the city centre and a various set of actors involved in creating new activities in the centre, from sport organizations to festival organizers and

Table 4.1 Summing up dimensions and timeframes

Dimensions/ Timeframe	Common understanding of crises and interdependence	Coordinated planning initiatives	Mobilizing the greater public in image-building activities	Organizational and institutional dynamics
1980s	Bad image, black shopping-windows, shopping centres established outside of city centre, decrease in industry	Public renovation initiatives: cleaning up the river, physical improvements	Negative externalities relating to pollution of water (sewage) and air (traffic) came on to the agenda	Public funding mechanisms available
1990s	Collective awareness of the need to turn the tables	City centre development, main road moved outside city centre, renovation of public spaces	Mobilization of creative and productive resources within civil society	Governance networks coordinating and mobilizing initiatives such as 'Our City Drammen'
2000s	Alliances with local media among others on creating a positive city image. Political agreements on urban development strategies	The Green River Park, the Ypsilon Bridge, Bragernes Square	Identity building through long-term branding and place reinvention activities, the new brand: The River City Drammen	A number of annual events and cultural activities in the city centre take place
2010s	Strong political attention given to avoiding decisions which may increase city centre traffic or draw customers out of the city centre	Densification, regeneration and regulation of trade localities	National prize-winner: the best environmental city of the year, broad involvement and celebration of the city jubilee	Hybrid forms of government and governance

civil organizations, was officially declared as the grounding of the success of the planning and implementation process. Interestingly, the city centre regeneration process in Drammen has been used as a strategy to address a wide range of societal goals, including improving local living conditions, reducing the volume of traffic, and attracting high-income residents, highly qualified workplaces and capital investments. 'Our City Drammen' was also a successful exercise in collaboration based on a shared understanding of the problems facing the city centre.

Drammen is a city with industrial traditions that during the 1990s experienced setbacks due to a decrease in traditional industrial activities. However, the response was an active one. Drammen has undertaken a number of activities to reinvent the urban images and thus to counter the downward trends at work at the end of the twentieth century. This was a part of a master strategy to brand the city through the formation of alliances and partnerships between municipal authorities and business and civil society actors. The outcomes of these new governance approaches in urban development are quite remarkable. As a medium-sized Norwegian city, close to the capital city Oslo, Drammen is of course in a position to mobilize competences and institutions in its immediate environment. On the other hand, it also faced massive challenges: competition from the capital, a very negative image which in any case would be very difficult to erase, an urban centre filled with traffic, a polluted river with no access from the urban centre, and a population containing a high number of immigrants, either from other parts of the country or from abroad.

Perhaps the explanation for Drammen's success also lies here; if Drammen were to face these challenges in an appropriate way, it had to address a number of issues that didn't seem to be related to each other, but turned out to be very much so; city branding would have been a complete failure without the physical improvements and the building of a new identity. It is thus a self-reinforcing process where change becomes a driving force to generate more change. In this way Drammen has become a reference town in Norway for change. It is an example of the possibility of combining hierarchical local government authority with new forms of collaborative governance.

Another striking characteristic of the Drammen model is the broad approach taken in relation to place reinvention strategies, working on projects and activities directly aiming at strengthening the local identity rather than only promoting a slogan, and demonstrating the ability to coordinate a large number of stakeholders and organizations so that they work in the same direction. The branding project in Drammen was therefore never only about branding – it was integrated into a broader strategy of urban development. The process undertaken in Drammen seems to have led to collaborative institution-building. The form of outsourcing that took place in Drammen never led to fragmentation, as could have been the case. Even if public–private agencies were handling a large number of policies, fragmentation was not an issue. The networks and agencies were coordinated, partly through active public leadership in the networks and partnership-based companies.

The case described indicates that the role of the municipalities in governing place-branding processes is in flux. The growth of networks, particularly in the local development field, seems to be nurtured first of all by the ideas of New Public Management, entrepreneurialism and neo-liberalism (Sager, 2013). The outsourcing of development tasks and promotion strategies to agencies like business parks and developing companies with private as well as public shareholders nurture these trends, but this does not have to be accompanied by fragmentation (Cars et al., 2002). Place branding can be performed in a number of ways, from the most simplistic advertising campaigns and 'boosterism' to more comprehensive strategies (Moor, 2007; Nyseth, 2013). It is possible to identify a transition from a more disembedded promotion practice towards a toolbox of planning instruments based on a broader understanding of places (Kavaratzis and Ashworth, 2005), as the Drammen case illustrates. Place promotion is therefore more than 'fine words' and should be more closely linked to place making and place development. In order to respond to these challenges, a transformation of existing governance cultures in the municipalities is required, so that new actors, discourses and perspectives are integrated into city-promoting activities.

We therefore argue that integrative planning can be creative. Integrative approaches to planning and development go beyond the standard integrative planning model promoted by the regulation school claiming that a coherent, integrative urban development strategy suited the logic of an industrial mode of accumulation, providing sites, buildings and transport to make production more efficient (Healey, 2010). Today, transformative dynamics seeks to swing established governance processes locked into old integrated and managerial models of governance towards more entrepreneurial approaches in order to develop the assets of urban areas. This is a more relational approach to planning. Integration is no longer about creating one coordinated 'whole'; rather, it is about creating partial, fluid and alternating integration of relations. Integrated approaches to urban development must keep economic, social and environmental considerations in tandem in order to meet sustainability aims.

Notes

1 In all instances when referring to larger cities in Norway, comparison is done with the 12 municipalities with the highest populations.
2 Informant quotes and policy document extracts have been translated from Norwegian.
3 www.drammen.no/TopMenu/OmOss/Omdommeprosjektet.aspx.

References

Bull – Nettverk for Byutviklingens lange linjer (2014) *Hvordan Drammen reiste seg. Hva seks byplansjefer forteller om byutviklingen 1980–2011*, Oslo.
Carlson, Y. (2001) *Et sted mellom Venezia og Harry-by?: En utredning om stedsidentitet, stedsimage og stedskvalitet i Drammen og Drammensregionen*. Report No. 2001:3. Oslo: Norwegian Institute for Urban and Regional Research.
Carlson, Y. and Onsanger, K. (2005) *Trekk ved historien i bykommunene i Østfold og Buskerud*. Oslo: Norwegian Institute for Urban and Regional Research, Working Paper 2005:130.
Cars, G., Healy, P., Madandipour, A. and De Magalhaes, C. (eds) (2002) *Urban Governance, Institutional Capacity and Social Milieux*. Aldershot: Ashgate.
Edelenbos, J., Steijn, B. and Klijn, E.-H. (2010) Does democratic anchorage matter?: An inquiry into the relation between democratic anchorage and outcome of Dutch environmental projects. *American Review of Public Administration*, 40(1): 46–63.
Falleth, E. and Saglie, I.-L. (2012) Planning a compact Oslo. In M. Luccarelli and P.G. Røe (eds), *Green Oslo: Visions, Planning and Discourse*. Farnham: Ashgate, pp. 267–83.
Haagensen, T. (2012) *Byer og miljø: Indikatorer for miljøutviklingen i 'Framtidensbyer'* (Report no. 27/2012). Oslo-Kongsvinger: Statistics Norway. Available at: www.ssb.no/a/publikasjoner/pdf/rapp_201227/rapp_201227.pdf.
Hall, T. (2001) *Urban Geography*. Florence, KY: Routledge.
Healey, P. (1997) *Collaborative Planning: Shaping Places in Fragmented Societies*. Hong Kong: Macmillan Press.
—— (2002) On creating the city as a collective resource. *Urban Studies*, 39: 1777–92.
—— (2003) Creativity and governance. Paper given at *Nordic Symposium: Local Planning and change*. Lillehammer, Norway, 14–16 August.
—— (2007) *Urban Complexity and Spatial Strategies. Towards a Relational Planning for Our Times*. London: Routledge.
—— (2010) *Urban Complexity and Spatial Strategies. Towards a Relational Planning for Our Times*. London: Routledge.
Hubbard, P. and Hall, T. (1997) The entrepreneurial city and the new urban politics. In T. Hall and P. Hubbard (eds), *The Entrepreneurial City. Geographies of Politics, Regime and Representation*. Chichester: John Wiley & Sons, pp. 1–23.
Jessop, B. (1997) The entrepreneurial city. Re-imaging localities, redesigning economic governance, or restructuring capital? In N. Jewson and S. Macgregor (eds), *Transforming Cities*. London: Routledge, pp. 28–41.
Kavaratzi, M. and Ashworth, G.J. (2005) City branding: An effective assertion of identity or a transitory marketing trick? *Tijdschrift voor Economische en Sociale Geografie*, 96(5): 505–14.
Kearns, G. and Philo, C. (1993) *Selling Places: The City as Cultural Capital, Past and Present*. Oxford: Pergamon Press.
Moor, L. (2007) *The Rise of Brands*. Oxford: Berg.
Municipality of Drammen (2007) *Kommuneplan for Drammen 2007–2018, Strategisk samfunnsdel*. Drammen: Municipality of Drammen.
Nyseth, T. (2013) The reinvention of place: Complexities and diversitties. In G. Young and D. Stevenson (eds), *Planning and Culture: The Ashgate Research Companion*. Farnham: Ashgate, pp. 325–39.

Nyseth, T. and Viken, A. (eds). (2009) *Place Reinvention: Northern Perspectives*. Farnham: Ashgate.

Robinson, J. (2006) *Ordinary Cities: Between Modernity and Development*. London: Routledge.

Sager, T. (2013) *Reviving Critical Planning Theory: Dealing with Pressure, Neoliberalism, and Responsibility in Communicative Planning*. London: Routledge.

Saglie, I.-L. and Harvold, K. (2010) Arealplanlegging. In K. Harvold, L. Innbjør, S. Kasa, V. Nenseth, I.-L. Saglie, A. Tønnesen and C. Vogelsang (eds), *Ansvar og virkemidler ved tilpasning til klimaendringer*. Report No. 1-2010. Oslo: CIENS, pp. 19–29.

Skogheim, R. and Vestby, G.M. (2010) *Kulturarv og stedsidentitet. Kulturarvens betydning for identitetsbygging, profilering og næringsutvikling*. Report No. 2010:14. Oslo: Norwegian Institute for Urban and Regional Research.

Statistics Norway (2013) Population statistics, 21 November. Available at: www.ssb.no.

Stead, D. and Meijers, E. (2009) Spatial planning and policy integration: Concepts, facilitators and inhibitors, *Planning Theory & Practice*, 10(3): 317–32.

Tennøy, A., Loftsgarden, T., Hansen, J.U. and Strand, A. (2010). *Erfaringer med handelsanalyser i Framtidens byer*. Report No. 1071/2010. Oslo: Institute of Transport Economics.

Tønnesen, A. (2015) Barriers and opportunities to car-use reduction. A study of land-use and transport policy in four Norwegian cities. PhD dissertation. Oslo: University of Oslo.

Vabo, S., Røiseland, A. and Nyseth, T. (2011) Evaluating performance in urban development networks: The Nordic context. *Urban Research and Practice*, 4(1): 72–84.

Ward, S. (1998) *Selling Places: The Marketing and Promotion of Towns and Cities, 1850–2000*. London: E & FN Spon.

Part II

Can place transformation be planned? Challenges to creative planning in small and medium-sized towns

5 Cultural industries as a base for local development
The challenges of planning for the unknown

Anniken Førde and Britt Kramvig

Introduction

In Norway – as in many countries – cultural and creative industries are seen as a promising toolkit for urban and regional development. Cultural industries are seen as a means to achieve future economic growth and strengthen the attractiveness of cities and regions. In recent years, cultural industries have become a high-profile public policy arena. Numerous policy programmes have been established, aiming at local regeneration through stimulating innovation and facilitating creative processes within this field. But this involves many challenges, as the cultural industries operate with a more multifaceted concept of value than the one often used in such policy programmes. Creativity and innovation are social processes unfolding in complex and often fluid networks. The field of cultural and creative industries thus challenge traditional planning endeavours and enhance more creativity in policy development. In this chapter we address the dilemmas that emerge in the encounters of creativity and public management. What kinds of practices and modelling are needed to facilitate creative activities within the cultural industries? And what happens when creative processes are to be embodied into regional policy programmes? Creativity within this field implies processes where the outcome is not known. Facilitating such creativity thus means plans and programmes allowing for the unknown to appear. Investigating the attempt to facilitate creativity through public policy and programmes in the city of Tromsø, Norway, we discuss the challenges of planning for the unknown.

The tension between creativity and planning is well known in the planning literature. So is the critique of neo-liberal models serving as a solution to manage complexity and create more creative practices. Regarding cultural industries, the main critique implies that creativity and the production of culture are often overruled by economic aims, interests and thinking. Adorno (1964) claimed that creativity loses when profit gains hegemony in culture. Consumers are reduced from subjects to objects; the people are turned into 'accesoires de la machine' (Adorno, 1964: 12). Adorno argued that turning culture into industry implies streamlining and preservation rather than creativity and innovation. Despite such critiques, policy programmes for facilitating creativity and growth within the cultural industries are gaining ground in urban and regional development (Oakley, 2009). These programmes realize the discussion in planning and development theory and practice of how to deal with the unexpected and the unknown. Recent planning theorists have urged for an urban planning process that acknowledges the complexities and multiplicities of postmodern cities, a planning stressing openness, temporality and respect for difference (Hillier, 2007; Nyseth, 2011; Pløger, 2004). Facilitating creativity in the cultural industry demands models that are sensitive to complexity. In order to build such models, knowledge of obstacles as well as enhancement to creativity is required. There is a lack of knowledge about the role of creative industries in urban and regional development (Oakley, 2004). We argue that in order to gain an understanding of how to target cultural industries-led local development, we need empirical studies of specific encounters of cultural industry entrepreneurs and policy programmes.

This chapter offers studies of such encounters. Through analyses of INTRO, the funding programme for cultural industries in Tromsø, as well as of some of the performing artists in the city and their concrete innovation practices and the networks at work, we explore the challenges of creating policies and plans facilitating creativity. The INTRO programme was created as a pilot to explore and create methods and models for innovation in the cultural industries. This involves taking into account the unknown, formulated by the INTRO programme as 'the x-factor'. Our concern is how the x-factor is performed in the encounter of the cultural industry actors and the public support system, and the implications of the perspectives on innovation and creativity materialized in such development policies and programmes. We argue for a more relational perspective on innovation in order to achieve planning and policy programmes more open to complexity and difference, and thus allowing the presence of the non-present.

Cultural industries as a tool for development

Developing and strengthening cultural industries are seen as crucial in the development of postmodern towns and regions. In the emerging cultural economic landscape, cultural products and experiences have become influential in urban and regional economic development (Pine and Gilmore, 1999; Hutton, 2009). As cities and regions compete over people as well as material and symbolic resources, and especially over 'the creative class' (Florida, 2002), cultural experiences become essential factors to their attractiveness. Cultural industries are also seen as important in the creation and maintenance of local and regional identities, and hence to people's experiences of place and sense of belonging. Culture further becomes a more important part of different economies (Lash and Urry, 1994), and the way in which art work is organized – as project-based companies – become more widespread in the economy as a whole (Oakley et al., 2008). In Norway, the government has introduced an action plan for cultural industries, focusing on the growth and professionalization of cultural industries, but also on the role of cultural industries in strengthening the attractiveness of local communities and cities for their inhabitants, visitors and other businesses (Ministry of Culture, Norway, 2013).

According to Adorno (1964), the concept of cultural industry was first applied in 1947 in the book *Dialektik der aufklärung* by Adorno and Horkenheimer. Further, the concept of creative industries was introduced as a discourse and policy concept in England in the late 1990s and was used as a tool in the 1998 Department for Culture, Media and Sport (DCMS) *Creative Industries Mapping Document*. The definition given by the document was: 'those industries which have their origin in individual creativity, skill and talent and which have a potential for wealth and job creation through the generation and exploration of intellectual property' (DCMS, 1998: 3). Cultural and creative industries entered the stage in many countries and policy documents. Different countries and regions use different concepts; creative industries, experience industries and cultural industries became the most frequently applied. Which businesses are included in the definition also differs. In Norway, the concept of cultural industries was chosen, focusing on the product and its characteristics (Haraldsen et al., 2004). 'Cultural industry' is used as a collective term for the following sectors: music, film, photography, television and radio, architecture, design, printed media, commercials, cultural heritage and artistic activities (Espelien and Gran, 2011). Cultural products are characterized as communicative, symbolic and aesthetic. Within the definition of cultural industries in Norway, multiple enterprises are included, and distinctions between private and public, and small and large scale are not drawn. Along with the increased emphases on cultural industries as a tool for urban and regional development came new national and regional programmes and institutional arrangements.

With the initiative from the former Norwegian government, *Kulturløftet 3* (Joint effort for Culture 3; Ministry of Culture, Norway, 2013), high ambitions were established for the cultural sector. While this sector has experienced dramatic curtailment in other countries, the culture budget in Norway has doubled since 2005. In 2013, the Prime Minister stated: 'Culture creates good experience and life quality. It creates participation, coping and enlightenment. This is the reason for the government to present a new *Kulturløft* with wide-ranging priorities.'[1] Cultural industry as a means for creating attractive communities is a central element of this policy programme, and activity at the municipal and regional levels is given priority. The process of developing this national programme has been open and inclusive, where the government has invited all different milieus within the cultural sector to participate in the process as well as setting up regional conferences across the country. The result is a programme with multiple and complex aims, encompassing 'culture to the people' (i.e. to children, youngsters, adults and elders, including the new, complex ethnic diversity) as well as strengthening the quality of art and culture and improving the conditions for artists. In addition to covering film, performing arts, literature, music, museums, design, architecture, gaming and the voluntary sector, the policy programme also includes libraries, media, cultural schools for children and efforts to integrate immigrants. Local and regional anchoring is seen as crucial for creating 'a cultural foundation wall' (Ministry of Culture, Norway, 2013).

In Tromsø, INTRO, a regional fund for cultural industries was established in 2010. The aim of this fund was twofold: in addition to strengthening the cultural industries and thus the attractiveness of the city and the surrounding region, it was created as a national pilot project for cultural industries. Tromsø is the regional centre in Troms, northern Norway. With 70,000 inhabitants, it is one of the largest cities in the Arctic region. The compact city centre is situated on a small island. Historically Tromsø was an important harbour for fishing, arctic hunting and trade. More recently, the city has experienced a rapid expansion, and with the establishment of the University and other academic institutions. It has established itself as a regional centre for knowledge-based activities. It has for a long time acted as an international city and, especially due to its dramatic climate and landscapes, it attracts increasing numbers of visitors from all parts of the world. Tourism is becoming an important sector, with international, highly educated visitors travelling in for shorter trips, asking for high-quality cultural experiences and adventures such as Arctic academic conferences, film and music festivals, skiing on mountain summits, Northern Lights tours, whale-watching, dog-sledding and various cultural activities. Cultural industries are growing in Tromsø, a process characterized by many small enterprises with relatively marginal revenues (Hauge et al., 2013). With the recent investments in oil, gas and mineral activities in the Arctic, it has become urgent to attract new actors to the city. Establishing a fund for cultural industries must be seen as a part of a wider strategy to strengthen the city's attractiveness to highly educated workers as well as visitors and investors.

The main objective of INTRO was defined as 'being an active promoter for increasing Tromsø's attractiveness through creating will, ability and opportunity for innovation and commercialization based on cultural activity'.[2] Further, it aimed at identifying defects of existing public policy and support systems and initiating interaction with public and private actors. The idea was that more flexible programmes were needed in order to meet the specific needs of cultural actors. An important premise for the project was to include research to evaluate the methods applied. It was explicitly formulated that the project should address the challenge of planning for the unknown, 'the X-factor', and should contribute to develop new methods and models. The city of Tromsø has experience of experimental planning. The Tromsø Experiment described by Nyseth (2011) represented a radical critique of mainstream planning and new forms of market-based project-oriented planning. Established planning structures were challenged as outsiders were invited in. Nyseth argues that projects like the Tromsø Experiment can have transformative power, with interventions coming from actors not trapped in taken-for-granted institutional practices, rules and regulations. INTRO also aimed at releasing such transformative powers.

In 2014, Tromsø's application to continue the INTRO fund was turned down by Troms county. The fund was closed and replaced by a new, permanent fund for the whole county, managed by Innovation Norway. From 2010 to 2013, INTRO allocated 40 million NOK to cultural industry actors and projects. The County Council of Culture insists that the ambitions of the INTRO fund are maintained in the new fund. As the ambitious pilot project in Tromsø is ended and transformed into permanent funds, enrolled into the established funding system of Innovation Norway, and as the project has undergone a process of evaluation, it is interesting to look at the experience of INTRO and the attempts to address the x-factor. Our investigation dates from the period before INTRO was brought to close, and thus relates to the explorative pilot project. What we are concerned with in this chapter is the attempt to create policy for cultural industries and its consequences in the encounters with creative practices. We will examine specific encounters of the regional policy programme in Tromsø, cultural industry actors and their creative projects.

Theoretical approach

We are interested in the concepts of innovation, culture and creativity, and how these are enacted in specific encounters between cultural industry actors and public policy programmes targeting cultural industries as a means to achieving urban and regional development. We aim to query the celebrated transportation of culture into the cultural industry and innovation policy. Investigating both the connections and disconnections that have been made, we emphasize the new dilemmas that emerge. Exploring such encounters requires concepts and understanding of planning, creativity and innovation that acknowledge complexity and contestation.

Within planning theory, there is a growing interest in theorizing transformation and exploring possibilities for creative change. Hillier's multiplanar theory (Hillier, 2007) is an important contribution. She argues for a theory of planning as becoming rather than fixing; a planning open for what might come – for the unknown. We share her concern in how planning and planning theory can deal with postmodern thinking and the acknowledgement that everything is partial. We can never grasp the entire flow. But even in a world of flux, there are moments of temporary fixity (Law, 1992). Hillier criticizes outcome-focused planning for imposing a futile certainty on a contingent world and argues for performance-based planning – a more flexible planning willing to compromise. This is highly relevant for planning and policy development for cultural industries, where the object is to facilitate innovative performances and the appearance of the non-present. Inspired by the French philosophers Deluze and Guattari, Hillier encourages an ontology that recognizes the dynamic complexities of time and space, and the importance of relations – as a politics of the possible. Like Hillier, we urge for a planning theory that aims at making sense of disorder, variability and difference, and dealing with an unpredictable future. The object of such a theory is not to unfold the universal, but to 'find conditions under which something new is produces' (Deluze, quoted in Hillier, 2007: 18).

The concept of creativity has become a buzzword in the contemporary Western world. It is seen as a universal problem-solving tool for people and enterprises as well as cities and regions. Before the concept of cultural and creative industries was applied in the 1990s, creativity was mainly connected to art. Dating back to Romanticism, the source of creativity and art has been related to the inner feelings of individuals. Art work cannot be disconnected from the person, unrestrictedly unfolding the imagination of the artist. As Meyer (2007) argues, this way of thinking has become crucial for our way of thinking about identity. In later years, the strong belief in individuality and creativity has been adopted by all sectors and has entered into business as well as public policies. In this process, creativity is renamed as innovation and is seen as the key to economic growth as well as social cohesion. In an English context, Oakley (2009) shows how the shift of terminology from 'cultural' to 'creative' and from 'creativity to 'innovation' reflects changing priorities. As the cultural sectors have been linked to innovation policy, traditional arts or cultural policy and funding have been downplayed. The term 'creativity' has to a large extent been decoupled from specifically cultural activities. Innovation then becomes where the big money is, and the cultural industry must adopt the economic models in order to benefit from it (Oakley, 2009). Adorno's old critique of the cultural industry is re-actualized; while art was traditionally defined by the presence of the non-present, the new imperative of cultural industries might lead to conformism and restriction to what already exists (Adorno, 1964).

These dilemmas and how they are continuously played out are rarely addressed in research on entrepreneurship and innovation. We are concerned with which concepts of creativity and innovation are articulated in the INTRO regional cultural industry programme and how they are enacted in entrepreneurial practices. Involving themselves in innovation programmes can be risky for artists and cultural entrepreneurs. Their ideas and creativity can, in the worst-case scenario, end up only being seen as input to innovation, where others take ownership and control of the output: the product, event or company. The 'problem-solving' idea of creativity emphasizes the instrumental utility, while diminishing notions of fantasy and play, which have a long history in discussions of artistic creativity (Oakley et al., 2008). We argue that it is crucial for planning and policy, as well as for research on cultural industry development, to address these dilemmas. We need to develop concepts of creativity and innovation that allow for the complexity of relations and connections involved in entrepreneurial practices and processes. And we need reflexive approaches in planning and policy development that recognize these complexities.

One way to grasp this complexity is to focus on innovation as creative processes. Ingold and Hallam (2007) argue that innovation should be studied as improvisation. They criticize the hegemonic way of understanding creativity, where innovation is seen as the opposite of convention. They wish to challenge what they see as a backward way of understanding creativity and argue that rather than reading creativity out of results, we should read it out of the processes that created them. They apply the terms 'improvisation' and 'innovation' where the first characterizes the creative process and the latter the product. By focusing on improvisation, it becomes possible to explore the productive processes of innovation.

Inspired by Ingold and Hallam's take on innovation as improvisation, we are concerned with the complex fluidity of entrepreneurial practices. We need to be concerned about the effects of policy programmes and new institutional arrangements within this field. Planning for the unknown as an approach to local development requires knowledge about the manifold connections and disconnections made within specific projects at specific places. It also requires an ongoing striving to improve our methodology, both in terms of planning and research. Through analyses of specific relational networks, practices and encounters, we aim to contribute to theory building exploring the concepts of becoming and creative experimentation.

Methods

The following analyses are based on multiple methods. First, we have investigated national, regional and local policy documents, applications, resolutions, websites and the evaluation report by Hauge et al. (2013). We have also conducted a session of reflection where we gathered four cultural industry actors to discuss 'the x-factor'. These actors are all members of RadArt, a network organization for performing arts in the Tromsø region. And they all have a long history of experience with public support programmes for cultural industries, including INTRO. They were selected in order to cover different cultural activities: theatre, lyrics, music and film making. In the session, they were invited to reflect on their experiences from the processes of establishing cultural industry activities, with an explicit focus on their encounters with public support systems in general and INTRO in particular. The dialogue dealt with how the policy programmes and funds intervene in their creative practices, and the accuracy of the programmes in facilitating creativity. The reflection session involved encounters between different experiences and knowledge, where difference and disagreements as well as common understandings were discussed. In addition, one of the authors – Britt Kramvig – was herself involved in INTRO as member of the board from 2009 to 2011. She thus knows the programme well and has followed the transformation of the ambition of the project into policy implementation.

Our research practices are far from innocent techniques; they produce not only different perspectives but also different realities (Mol, 2002; Law, 2004). Law (2004) criticizes the dominating research ideals aiming at order and unambiguity; rather than suppressing the fluidity and disorder of the worlds we are studying, we need to find ways of getting to terms with messy realities. Innovation and policy development within the cultural and creative industries is a complex and fluid field of study, and thus requires complex-sensitive methods. This is a field that eschews simple categories. It is in the complex composites, the ambivalences and movements that we can achieve knowledge and create change. As Alvesson (2011) argues, we must acknowledge the complexity and uncertainty of our research practices, and must strike a balance between endless reflexivity and radical scepticism. Through the multiple methods applied in this study, we have strived to increase our sensibility towards ambiguities and explore multiple meanings.

INTRO: a pilot project

INTRO was introduced in 2010 as a three-year pilot project for cultural industries in the Tromsø region, which was designed as a proactive programme to strengthen and develop creative businesses in the region. INTRO was funded by the regional industry fund RDA, supported by the Ministry of Culture, and the municipality of Tromsø. The aim of the pilot was to provide new knowledge and experience about the cultural industries, culture-based business development in the region and the public approach to these. It was designed to identify challenges and coordinate knowledge within the field. The project also intended to develop knowledge that could be transferred to other municipalities.[3] In addition to building transferable competence, the programme aimed at developing a fund for cultural industries in the Tromsø region, where those working within art and culture sector could apply for financial support.

The programme was described as a signal project, a brave investment to increase innovation and release the commercial potential within the cultural activities of Tromsø – and thus strengthen the attractiveness of the city. In the project description, specific objects were set: to invest 150 million NOK over a five-year period, to create 25 new businesses, 150 workplaces and three international success stories, and to strengthen collaboration and new competences (Tromsø cultural industry fund, project description, 2009). After negotiations between the different partners, the project received 40 million NOK over a period of three years.

The municipality of Tromsø was delegated the decision-making authority of the INTRO fund. It set up an administration with three employees with the object of being a proactive unit. It also put together a board with members from the art and culture sector, businesses and academia. In addition, the administration unit of INTRO appointed more specific advisory panels. An important argument for establishing the programme was that the cultural industries differ from other industries, and that established support systems lack the necessary competence and ability to meet the special needs of actors within this sector. Still, the organizational model of the ordinary municipal business development fund became the organizing tool as the programme settled.

INTRO was divided into two funds: a main fund and a talent fund for young entrepreneurs. From 2010 to 2013, the main fund received 310 applications and the talent fund 217. A total of 90 businesses received financial support from INTRO, varying from 10,000 to 1.5 million NOK, but with an average of 260,000 NOK. INTRO did not support operating expenses, but did support development projects. Business potential, measured in value creation or employment, was a central criterion for allocation. The criteria changed during the project period, with a stronger emphasis on value creation, emphasizing the economic, marketing and business activities of creative industries.

The evaluation report concludes that the project has been successful; the employment rate within the funded enterprises has increased, while existing actors have become more robust and professional (Hauge et al., 2013). About half of the enterprises involved report that they have developed new products during the project period. INTRO is described as a low-threshold fund compared to other public support systems, and the evaluation concludes that it has contributed a first step in professionalizing the cultural industry enterprises. The decision of Troms county to close down this programme created some controversy. Some actors within the cultural industries feared that the proactive work would stop as the fund was enrolled into the established funding programmes of Innovation Norway and that the competence created would get lost. Others were critical of the decisions made and the criteria developed within the programme period, claiming that culture became invisible and was overruled by industry models. We are interested in the programme's work on intervening in innovation and creative projects. Further, we are concerned with the possibility of 'the x-factor' – the unpredictable and the unknown – to survive within a model of a conventional business development fund.

Creative practices and networks at work

We came together around a table, two researchers and a group of well-established actors from the cultural industry in Tromsø. In an open dialogue, the participants were invited to reflect upon 'the x-factor' in the cultural industry. In this process of reflection, they shared experiences from their own, specific creative projects: how ideas are developed into projects, how projects are organized and funded, and how innovation is achieved through expanding networks. The participants represented different artistic fields: film making, theatre, music and writing. All of these actors worked across such narrow categories. The writer worked with producers to develop performances, the film maker worked with musicians and all of them tied together multiple types of knowledge in the different phases of their projects. This complex and transboundary organization was an essential characteristic of the practices within the cultural industries.

The writer established a small company five years ago in order to offer writing labs for youngsters. The company Rulleramp produces writing labs for a range of lower secondary schools all around the region, as well as for prisoners and leader-groups at bigger companies. In the writer's latest project, she made a theatre performance highlighting the challenges of the everyday in the classroom. In order to produce a high-quality writing lab, the writer runs a one-day workshop for each class. She uses tools from theatre to organize playful writing events. Teachers, academics and students are invited to participate and analyse different situations and the writer's performance in specific classrooms. Her writing lab is included in the regional cultural portfolio, and in 2013 was nominated as the best performance in a national competition of educative cultural activities.

The writer needs others to perform well. She is part of the regional network called RadArt, where performing artists from different art scenes in Tromsø come together to learn from each other. The aim of RadArt is to stimulate productions and performances that cut across different artistic expressions. RadArt also serves as a mediator between established cultural institutions and the free art scene.

The music producer is well known both nationally and internationally. He has built his career through working as a technician, producer and songwriter. He has worked with a range of different artists and companies, including Stargate and international artists such as A-ha and Rihanna. Today he runs a small company in Tromsø, established by funding from INTRO. The aim of the company is to support and develop young talented musicians from the region, but also to attract leading national and international musicians to record and produce their music in his studio. In addition, he holds a position at the University of Tromsø, researching and teaching art music. This combination gives him economic stability and hence the liberty to explore new music. He does not consider himself an artist and explains that he produces commercial pop music – 'But sometimes it becomes art'.

The work of developing new music talents takes time – as an experienced producer he knows that. It comes with some talent, but even more with investment and hard work and the capacity to perform on stage. Talents need to travel from venue to venue and to keep up and not give up on the idea of becoming an artist who can make music and also make a living. His company wants to give young talents the possibility to perform internationally, for professional industry actors, to see if they can make it. The music industry is based on personal contracts, trust and relations. In this thorough work, he draws upon his many international contacts.

A relational network of connected elements is inherently unstable and fluid (Hillier, 2007). The presented cases show some of this fluidity and the need for flexibility in the cultural actors' planning processes. They must be able to put together the right competences, people and objects at the right time and in the right place. And they need a budget that is flexible enough to allow them to do so. In their creative work, the result of the innovative processes is unknown to them when they put a project together. It emerges gradually throughout the creative process. As Meyer (2007) argues, this is the essence of creativity and innovation.

Contested encounters

The cultural industry actors we met told us of both connections and disconnections as effects of the INTRO programme. Programmes like INTRO create distinctions that the actors consider to be artificial. The most important distinction is the one between culture and industry. A result of this distinction is the delimited definition of what the programmes are to support. As mentioned above, INTRO supported development work and infrastructure, not ordinary activity and operating expenses. For the RadArt members, this was challenging. They all expressed that what they need support for is to run creative processes. The writer said she needed money to develop the performance and the film maker needed funding to make a film. But the criteria of programmes like INTRO do not support these activities; they are considered as production of culture and thus as operating expenses. What the programme does support is the financing of infrastructure, marketing and business development. As the music producer expressed: 'In practice, it means that we can apply for money to travel, but not to do the studio work.' The writer adds: 'It's as if you can apply for everything around, but what I need is support to develop different performances.'

The cultural industry actors experience the application processes as decoupled from the projects they work on. They often do not consider the categories in the application forms as relevant to their realities and contexts. In order to fulfil the demands of the forms, they have to 'invent' numbers as well as the final outcomes of their projects. Experienced artists expressed that they rarely know whether a project will be a commercial success or not. INTRO introduced a request for business plans, to which the RadArt members tried to adapt. But such plans were of little relevance for their project-based companies. They say they have become 'extremely good at being creative in relation to releasing financial support', but that this takes the focus away from the creative process of developing the product they want to create. They also find it problematic that actors like them, representing very different artistic fields, have to adapt to the same models and categories. Paradoxically, the programme, although aiming to support innovation, seems to reduce the artists' conditions for creative work.

The programme's strong emphasis on commercial potential is contested by the cultural industry actors. The music producer stated that big international success companies like Stargate are often used as role models. But the conditions he works in are different. Situated in a small city in northern Norway, the local realities are not the same as in New York. The theatre producer addressed this issue in meeting with the public policy system: 'How are performing arts going to fit in to the cultural industry category?' Theatre is 'fresh produce', produced and consumed locally in real time. Even though some theatre plays are exported out of the region, it is difficult to prove the probabilities of commercial success for a local theatre in a small city. The same goes for the film producer, who meets distributors that 'only look for blockbusters'. The specific local realities that the cultural industry actors work with are something that programmes like INTRO need to acknowledge.

Culture and creativity

Our research shows that the work of actors within the cultural industries are project-based and network-oriented. They work to bring together relevant and different competences in different phases of their project development. Value is created through networks, and in these networks, connections and reconnections are made. Through these connections, knowledge, trust, work and objects flow. Networks can be connected to other networks and also to a market. As Oakley et al. (2008) have pointed out, the way in which this kind of art work is organized in project-based companies is becoming more widespread in the economy as a whole. We therefore need a better understanding of the complex crossovers that take place in the creative processes of cultural production.

The cultural industry actors often only have vague ideas about the final product of their creative processes when they start; the outcome emerges gradually. It is exactly within this uncertainty that the potential for innovation lies. As the music producer said: 'I don't look upon myself as an artist. But sometimes it becomes art.' When the writer was setting up the theatre performance built upon work she had done in different classrooms, the performance did not come from a ready-made script. It came into being on the theatre stage during the week when she, different youngsters, the director and other theatre workers rehearsed before the premiere. From their study of how artists in the UK understand innovation, Oakley et al. (2008) show similar findings: artists often use the term 'creativity' when describing their work. They use the term in a way that differs from that favoured by policy-makers. To art workers, creativity generally describes a process, not a product. They talk about being creative in their approach to work rather than as producing creative output.

When programmes are set to support creative business, these concerns are crucial. The question is how models can be created with sensitivity for the undefined and unknown outcomes. Oakley (2009) expresses concerns for programmes that attempt to link the cultural sector with innovation policy. The result, she argues, is that creativity becomes decoupled from culture. Traditional arts risk being downplayed and culture risks being 'thingified'. When the term 'creativity' is decoupled from specific cultural activities, we risk creative industries being non-political. Expressions that are marginal, radical and counter-cultural are at risk of being excluded. Creativity is being mainstreamed. In line with Adorno (1964), Oakley (2009) claims that the autonomy of the art workers is at stake. When an instrumental use of creativity is applied in many policy programmes and notions of fantasy and play diminish, this might result in a cultural industry that does not challenge social norms.

The new government in Norway has announced a stronger focus on cultural competitiveness and private financing of the cultural industry. When cultural value is enmeshed with commercial value, the cultural and creative industries are evaluated by economically measurable results. In recent years, we have seen a heated debate in Norway on the question of whether public investment in culture pays off and whether it actually creates attractive places and regions. In 2012, the Telemark Research Institute published a report concluding that there is no significant relationship between the level of cultural activity (the cultural index) in regions or municipalities and their ability to attract new inhabitants, and that investment in culture mainly creates just culture (Vareide and Korbo, 2012). Many contest the results and the parameters applied here. Such indexes lack sensitivity for the complex and long-term work of cultural industry actors. Building creative competence, networks and knowledge about, for instance, how the music industry works, how the film industry works and how artists can build an international career takes time. Indexes based upon economic models for value creation miss this work of creating competence. They also miss out on the influence of art and culture upon creating new horizons and imaginaries, and thus changing the city and making it a more interesting place. We argue that models that ignore the complexity and fluidity of cultural industries are counter-productive to their explicit aim of facilitating creativity and increasing the attractiveness of cities and regions.

Conclusion: the challenges of planning for the unknown

In this chapter we have critically investigated the cultural industries as a public policy arena for urban and regional development. We have asked what kind of models we need in order to facilitate creativity within the cultural and creative industries, and how policy programmes can support innovation. Through examples from specific encounters of cultural industry actors and policy programmes in Tromsø, we have shown how the concepts of creativity and innovation are used differently. Art workers talk of creativity related to their working processes rather than as producing creative outputs. The ongoing unknown, the appearance of the non-present, is a crucial part of their projects. The object of their work is to create outcomes that are unknown. This is what 'the x-factor' is all about: the undefined, the in-between – what lies beyond the horizon. Capranzano (2003) talks about the imaginative horizons as the blurry boundaries that separate the here and now from what lies beyond in time and space. These imaginative horizons are essential to how we experience the world. The cultural and creative industries offer such imaginative horizons.

We have argued that the cultural industry actors work in dynamic ways that demand improvisation and flexibility, but also planning. Their work is project-based, activating multiple networks and implies crossovers and creative experimentation. This flexible, project-based way of organizing work seems not to be fully recognized in policy programmes. INTRO was established as an experimental mode of policy-making. But, as we have demonstrated, in the implementation phase, more conventional models for industrial development are applied. As in other policy programmes, budgeting has been an important organizing tool. A challenge is to create a space in these programmes and budgets for the unknown or 'the x-factor'. When programmes like INTRO apply conventional business development models and request business plans, they also require that the art workers define the outcome of their projects from the outset. The result can be that policy programmes set up to facilitate creativity end up doing exactly the opposite. What characterizes creativity and innovation is that the result carries a possibility for something new, and thus is impossible to fully define from the start.

What are the implications for planning and development? Hillier (2007) problematizes the normative role of planning: the plan as a statement of what ought to be. She argues for planning that is performance-based rather than performance-measured and target-based – planning that is flexible and able to compromise; planning as becoming. This perspective is challenging for planning theory and practice. If planning is seen as creative experimentation, problems are not solved, but rather reformulated. Hillier urges us to give up the fantasy of controlling the future, without giving up the responsibility of facilitating a better future (Hillier, 2007: 20). Our argument is in line with that of Hillier; policy programmes for cultural and creative industries need openness, flexibility and experimentation. The cultural industry actors constantly find themselves in the tension between planning their projects, implying budgeting and financing as well as directing and performing, and at the same time ensuring the undefined and the unknown as an essential part of their work. The programmes need to acknowledge and take consideration of these tensions. Rather than programmes requiring project plans with predefined models and outcomes, based on conventional models and measurements for business development, we argue for more experimental cultural policy programmes. This implies changing the focus from products to creative processes, applying a more multifaceted concept of value and taking the risk of emphasizing what might be – the emerging and unknown aspects of creative projects.

Notes

1 Dagbladet, 11 August 2013.
2 RDA board, 8 October.
3 Letter of support from the Ministry of Culture, 29 October 2009.

References

Adorno, T. (1964) L'industrie culturelle. *Communications*, 3:12–18.
Alvesson, M. (2011) *Interpreting interviews*. London: Sage.
Capranzano, V. (2003) *Imaginative Horizons*. Chicago: University of Chicago Press.
DCMS (Department for Culture, Media and Sport), UK (1998) *Creative Industries Mapping Document*. London: DCMS.
Espelien, A. and Gran, A.B. (2011) Kulturnæringens betydning for norsk økonomi. Status og utvikling 2000–2009. Available at: www.menon.no/wp-content/uploads/23statistikkforkulturnringen2.pdf.
Florida, R. (2002) *The Rise of the Creative Class: And How it's Transforming Work, Leisure, Community and Everyday Life*. New York: Basic Books.
Haraldsen, T., Flygind, S.K., Overvåg, K. and Power. D. (2004) *Kartlegging av kulturnæringene i Norge – økonomisk betydning, vekst og utviklingspotensial*. Østlandsforskning report 10/2004.
Hauge, A., Hagen, S.E., Ericsson, B., Alnes, P.K., Aure, M., Kvidal, T., Nygård, V. and Power, D. (2013) *Evaluering av Intro – fond for kulturnæringer i Tromsø*. Østlandsforskning report 06/2013.
Hillier, J. (2007) *Stretching beyond the Horizon: A Multiplanar Theory of Spatial Planning and Governance*. Aldershot: Ashgate.
Hutton, T. (2009) Trajectories of the new economy: regeneration and dislocation in the inner city. *Urban Studies*, 46(5–6): 987–1001.
Ingold, T. and Hallam, E. (2007) Creativity and cultural improvisation: An introduction. In E. Hallam and T. Ingold (eds), *Creativity and Cultural Improvisation*. Oxford: Berg, pp. 1–24.
Lash, S. and Urry, J. (1994) *Economies of Signs and Space*. London: Sage.
Law, J. (2004) *After Method: Mess in Social Science Research*. Abingdon: Routledge.
—— (1992) Notes on the Theory of the Actor-Network: Ordering, strategy and heterogeneity. *Systems Practice*, 5: 379–93.
Meyer, S. (2007) *Det innovative menneske*. Oslo: Fagbokforlaget.
Ministry of Culture, Norway (2013) *Kulturløftet*. Available at: https://www.regjeringen.no/contentassets/778dc6de9d66490183e7131ccd08cffc/kulturloftet_august_b_nett3.pdf?id=2155465.
Ministry of Culture, Ministry of Industries and Trade and Ministry of Local Government and Regional Development, Norway (2013) *Fra gründer til kulturbedrift. Handlingsplan for kulturnæringer*. Available at: https://www.regjeringen.no/globalassets/upload/kud/samfunn_og_frivillighet/rapporter/fra_grunder_til_kulturbedrift_2013.pdf.

Mol, A.M. (2002) *The Body Multiple: Ontology in Medical Practice*. Durham, NC: Duke University Press.

Nyseth, T. (2011) The Tromsø experiment: Opening up for the unknown. *Town Planning Review*, 82(5): 573–93.

Oakley, K. (2004) Not so cool Britannia: The role of the creative industries in economic development. *International Journal of Cultural Studies*, 7(1): 67–77.

Oakley, K., Sperry, B. and Pratt, A. (2008) *The Art of Innovation*. London: NESTA.

Oakley, K. (2009) The disappearing arts: Creativity and innovation after the creative industries. *International Journal of Cultural Policy*, 15(4); 403–13.

Pine, J. and Gilmore, J. (1999) *The Experience Economy: Work is Theatre and Every Business a Stage*. Boston, MA: Harvard Business School Press.

Pløger, J. (2004) Strife – urban planning agonism. *Planning Theory*, 3(1): 71–92.

Vareide, K. and Korbo, L.U. (2012) *Skaper kultur attraktive steder?* Telemarksforskning, report 1/2012.

6 Innovative actions for local development in small and medium-sized towns

The case of the Centre-Val de Loire region in France

Christophe Demazière, Abdelillah Hamdouch and Ksenija Banovac

Introduction

In the European context, differences in population dynamics, economic and social opportunities, high unemployment, social exclusion, the degraded quality of the environment, etc. have contributed to the destabilization of a large part of the urban system, especially after the last economic and financial crisis (URBACT II, 2010). According to a survey on the impact of the economic crisis on European cities (URBACT II, 2010), more than 80 per cent of cities have been severely affected by the economic slowdown due to the drying-up of both private credit and private markets, with the most affected sectors being construction and industry.

During the period 2007–12, France lost more than 400,000 jobs (-1.5 per cent), which was relatively small compared to some other European countries. Nevertheless, it lost 800,000 jobs in the sole manufacturing sectors, and the French regions that suffered the most in terms of unemployment were industrial areas with a high degree of specialization. In geographical terms, the loss in industrial employment in small and medium-sized towns (SMSTs) has not been compensated for by the rise of advanced services, which tend to concentrate in large cities. As to the development of personal services (retail trade, sports and culture, education, etc.), it is linked to positive demographic dynamics and to significant flows of income that come from outside of the locality (pensions, social aid, etc.) (Davezies and Talandier, 2009). Between 1990 and 2006, and hence before the current economic crisis started, French SMSTs gained less population than large cities, but the average income and the number of jobs increased twice and three times faster respectively than in cities with over 100,000 inhabitants (Davezies and Talandier, 2009). Now the situation is more mixed because of the lagged effects of the economic crisis. Indeed, along with the direct local effects of the economic crisis in terms of job losses, social problems such as increased poverty, social exclusion, indebtedness, homelessness, health problems, crime, etc. have arisen as indirect consequences of the crisis in most SMSTs where the local economy was highly dependent on the manufacturing sectors.

However, and interestingly, many local governments in such SMSTs had engaged for a long time before the crisis in local policies related to social cohesion and cultural and creative activities, which could have contributed somehow to mitigating its effects (Demazière et al., 2014). Local initiatives for social cohesion address the issues of social order, civic culture, local identity and place attachment. Playing the role of social glue, social cohesion fosters socio-economic inclusion and diversity while improving institutions and strengthening solidarity (Ackert et al., 2011). For their part, cultural and creative activities contribute to both social and economic aspects of local development. On the one hand, they have the potential to include marginalized groups and improve communication between different groups of society through social regeneration projects. On the other hand, they generate revenues and employment through the organization of cultural events or through the development of cultural tourism, which captures revenues from tourists' spending on hotels, restaurants, museums, leisure activities or transportation (KEA, 2006; Selada et al., 2011).

The aim of this chapter is to analyse the influence of such local policies in French SMSTs.

Indeed, social cohesion and cultural and creative activities represent important but still largely neglected topics in development planning and policy-making in SMSTs. This is especially the case in times of global crises, when the main focus is on boosting industrial productivity, GDP growth and exports to large markets. In this chapter, we argue that a creative approach to development planning is needed in SMSTs whose policy-makers decide to address social issues such as exclusion and marginalization, and to look for new solutions by implementing the objectives of social cohesion, culture and creativity into their local strategies and plans.

This chapter explores innovative public policies and practices in SMSTs of the Centre-Val de Loire region in France, a region which has been badly hit by the current economic crisis. More precisely, we show how social cohesion and cultural and creative activities are planned in SMSTs and the way in which they contribute as innovative drivers to the local (re-)development.

Innovative drivers of the local economy

In this section, we define the concepts of social cohesion and cultural and creative activities, and we analyse their potential for (re-)activating the development processes in SMSTs.

Social cohesion

It is no coincidence that social cohesion has become an object of ever-increasing interest, given the consequences of multiple changes taking place in the global economy, production structure and in society overall (ECLAC/UNESCO, 2007). Even though social cohesion is a relatively new concept in the scientific literature, it soon became the research object for two groups of researchers (Chan et al., 2006). Some follow the sociological and psychological approach in order to study social cohesion as integration and social stability. Others, on the contrary, are policy-oriented and consider social cohesion to be a precondition for economic prosperity (Acket et al., 2011). Overall, social cohesion may be understood in two ways: as behaviours and value judgements of the members of society (i.e. trust in institutions, social capital, belonging and solidarity, acceptance of social rules and the willingness to participate in collective life), but also as the effectiveness of instituted social inclusion mechanisms (i.e. employment, the educational system, human rights and policies designed to encourage equity, well-being and social protection).

We argue that social cohesion may contribute to the local development of SMSTs through its three main aspects: economic (labour market insertion, equality in chances and equality in conditions), political (the legitimacy of public and private institutions, participation in public affairs and empowerment) and socio-cultural (acceptance of pluralism and tolerance, identity, the sharing of common values, the feeling of belonging to a same community) (Ackert et al., 2011).

Regarding the economic aspect, some economists highlight the positive relationship between social cohesion and economic benefits (Freeman, 2011). Places with high income polarization and inequality are more likely to have high levels of social conflict, which may, in short, reduce the overall competitiveness of the economy and stunt growth (Grynspan, 2011). In other words, communities with high levels of trust may have lower costs of economic cooperation and hence higher economic activity. Social cohesion may enhance growth by facilitating the provision and the access to public goods such as infrastructure, housing, education or health.

As the importance of social cohesion has become acknowledged, Kearns and Forrest (2000) observe policy developments in the field of social cohesion at different urban levels in Europe. Since SMSTs are part of urban systems, we argue that, directly or indirectly and explicitly or implicitly, many policies in the field of social cohesion affect the local development of SMSTs. Kearns and Forrest find that at the national level, policy aims at promoting a common set of values for citizens and at reducing disparities in wealth through de-urbanization, decentralization and inter-regional divergence. At the regional and city-regional scales, policy more closely addresses the issues of maintenance of social order through strategies of social control in city centres and public spaces; the improvement of the civic culture by fighting polarization between the inner city and the outer city; and the development of strong local identity and place attachment. Finally, social cohesion policies at the neighbourhood level have two key areas of focus: the role of social networks and social capital; and the fight against crime and antisocial behaviour in disadvantaged areas.

100 *Christophe Demazière et al.*

The final socio-cultural aspect of social cohesion that contributes to local development has not yet received much attention. The sparse scientific literature highlights that, regardless of its subjectivity, a sense of belonging to society forms an essential component of social cohesion as it consists of perceptions, value judgements and attitudes of the members of society (Knox and Mayer, 2009; Ackert et al., 2011). Indeed, unlike in polarized communities where members of certain social groups identify strongly with one another (due to their cultural, spatial or religious identity) and at the same time isolate themselves from other groups of the same community, in socially cohesive communities, members share common values as they accept and feel accepted the way they are by the whole community.

Cultural and creative activities

Whether the culture represents art, or a set of attitudes, beliefs and customs, or if it is a sector of activity that involves some form of creativity, it has gained scientific recognition as a factor of development (Bayliss, 2007). While for some authors, culture and its educational, traditional, democratic and social components enable social transformation, for others, culture also plays an important role in terms of competitiveness and market position (Scott, 1997; Cohendet et al., 2009).

The contribution of cultural and creative activities (CCAs) to the local development is multiple. First, CCAs have the potential to attract tourists, so their impact on the local economy may be direct (the creation of income and employment) and indirect (through tourist spending on hotels and restaurants, and the improvement of quality of life that attracts tourists and investors). Second, cultural goods and services produced at a local level can be exported and consumed outside the area of production. Besides, the economic function of CCAs is even more relevant considering the fact that culture and art benefit from operating in clusters. Finally, CCAs may also have a social impact through, for example, socio-cultural regeneration projects to include marginalized groups, cultural projects for better cohesion between rich and poor areas, creative projects with the objective of improving the communication between different ethnic groups, etc. (KEA, 2006).

When it comes to SMSTs, Knox and Mayer (2009) show through many cases in Europe and USA how CCAs may create opportunities for the greater engagement of citizens, visitors, neighbours, friends and families. Furthermore, CCAs may enhance the way in which citizens collaborate, as through new leadership a community may create new solutions for challenges it faces. Just as importantly, CCAs help to shape a community's identity and they contribute to the development of a new economy (Selada et al., 2011).

Besides the (re-)activation of local resources, CCAs provide SMSTs with the potential to attract new talents, namely those of the 'creative class', which may be a solution to their economic revitalization (Moulaert et al., 2013). Pushing the argument even further, creative industries are not limited to arts and culture, but, on the contrary, they have the potential to extend to fields where 'creative individuals, managers and technologists meet together (ICT, fashion, design, video, photography, cinema, computer games, architecture, visual arts, advanced services, etc.)' (URBACT Creative Clusters, 2011: 6). This study on creative industries and places shows how culture and creativity tend to go beyond the context of the main urban hubs and large cities. On the contrary, as sources of innovation, culture and creativity have a cross-spatial trajectory (URBACT Creative Clusters, 2011). In short, this enables SMSTs to rethink their local development and to look for new opportunities (Plaza et al., 2009).

For the aforementioned reasons, we distinguish four main potentials of CCAs for the local development of SMSTs. The first potential is a creative clustering that may induce changes that spur local development dynamics. As suggested previously, cities and SMSTs may pull benefits for their development from globalization processes. Thus, the size is not as crucial as the capacity to absorb global innovations (Knox and Mayer, 2009; URBACT Creative Clusters, 2011). A town may find its potential in creative clusters – spatial forms where talent and individual creativity are the key factors (McCarthy, 2006). Through the creation of conditions that are favourable for creative businesses (e.g. subsidies or tax incentives) and through improving the quality of life for the population (e.g. services, accessibility and infrastructure), a SMST may build on its resources/talents and attract new ones (new investments and new residents) (Montgomery, 2003).

The second potential for SMSTs is the presence of amenities that may become one of the key factors in attracting new population and tourists seeking an original atmosphere and experience. Such endogenous assets on which a town may rely are of various types: (i) natural amenities (warm climate, distinctive and picturesque countryside with topographical diversity such as valleys, rivers, lakes, mountains and forests); (ii) historical and cultural amenities (architectonic and archaeological heritage such as castles, churches, aqueducts and bridges, and intangible heritage such as memories, testimonies and legends); (iii) symbolic amenities (community spirit, neighbourliness and sociability, identity, authenticity and civic associations); and (iv) built amenities (health and social services, hotels, restaurants, bars, meeting spaces, museums, theatres, art galleries, studios, event halls, etc.) (Selada et al., 2011).

SMSTs may also attract new population by offering favourable conditions, infrastructures or support programmes (e.g. specific financing, land and services) that differ from those in large cities. Selada et al. (2011) argue that SMSTs traditionally attract young families, midlife career changers and active retired people. Nevertheless, young households increasingly seek SMSTs due to the cheaper cost of housing, better quality of life and the presence of quality schools, all of which are clearly facilitated by new

102 *Christophe Demazière et al.*

technologies. Furthermore, authors point at growing tendency for artistic and creative persons to look for smaller urban places for their work, which may be an opportunity for SMSTs to offer better conditions than those usually found in large cities.

Finally, one of the potentials for the local development of SMSTs lies in the embeddedness and connectedness of CCAs to the existing economic tissue. As some studies report, CCAs may provide innovative inputs for other sectors of activity, such as agriculture, handicrafts, furniture, textiles, tourism and gastronomy. For instance, architecture, design, advertising and software are strongly oriented businesses other businesses, regardless of whether they are traditional and creative ones (KEA, 2006; Quinn, 2006). Hence, through CCAs, SMSTs have the potential to achieve integrated development and prosperity that are attentive to the needs of population and businesses in a changing world.

Planning the development of SMSTs in France: from a hierarchical approach to multilevel governance

In the previous section, we reviewed potentials for new ways of organizing work in favour of social cohesion and creativity in SMSTs. From an institutionalist perspective (Nelson, 2007), such change requires new expectations, new government programmes and supporting institutions. We may argue that the 'successful territories' (SMSTs) are those with institutions already in place when they are needed or those which manage to build new institutions quickly and properly.

Over the three past decades, France has engaged in decentralization processes of its political and administrative structures, giving much more power to regional and local authorities for various economic and social issues such as employment, social affairs or culture.

Devolution and the creation of collaborative groupings of municipalities

France has long been a unitary state, but since the early 1980s, it has experienced an intense process of devolution. In 1982, the Decentralization Acts created 22 regions, transferred competences to sub-central territorial levels and introduced the principle of free administration. In terms of local governments, there are also 100 'departments' (counties) and 36,682 municipalities. With the constitutional reform of 2003 and the legislation following this, a further step was taken in terms of sharing revenue-raising powers between the state and local governments. Nowadays, the region has competences in economic development (management of direct and indirect subsidies to businesses), transport (management of the road and rail networks, development of seaports and airports), education (construction, maintenance and operation of second-level high schools) and vocational training. The main competences of departments are social action, education (construction, maintenance and equipment for first level secondary schools) and transport (the extension and maintenance of all roads that are not part of the national public domain).

Municipalities were legally created in 1790. Today there are still more than 36,000 municipalities over a territory of 550,000 square kilometres and for a population of 64 million. In comparison, Germany has 12,000 municipalities on an area of 360,000 square kilometres and a population of 82 million, and Italy has 8,000 municipalities on an area of 300,000 square kilometres and a population of 59 million. Since the Municipal Act in 1884, French municipalities have their own administrative organization, regardless of their size. Since the 1980s, their main competences are planning, economic development, housing, healthcare and the social sector, education and culture.

The expenditures of French local authorities represent 21 per cent of general government expenditure, which is far less than in federal countries like Belgium (42 per cent) or in Northern state countries like Sweden (45 per cent). Yet France is a country with a high level of financial autonomy: around half of the revenue of sub-national governments is comprised of local taxes. In order to levy taxes, many French municipalities (as well as the departments and the regions) have backed the setting-up of companies, job creation and housing development. But within a single conurbation, territorial competition to attract or to retain firms has proved to be unproductive.

Against this background, the state has fostered the creation of collaborative groupings of municipalities through which municipalities share resources, competences and tools. This policy rests on the free will of municipalities to unite, but the state has provided subsidies to the groupings and it has enabled them to levy their own taxes. At the beginning of 2012, 90 per cent of the French population and 96 per cent of municipalities were grouped together into collaborative groupings. Ten years earlier, both proportions were around 50 per cent. In some regions, the geographical extent of the cooperation is wide, covering the entire functional urban region, while in other places, medium-sized towns at the centre of city-regions bear the burden of financing services like social aid or culture, while some neighbour groupings of municipalities develop as job centres or as residential suburbs (Demazière and Serrano, forthcoming).

While respecting the autonomy of local authorities, the state also tried to launch joint territorial development policies with them. In the 1980s, France witnessed renewed territorial disparities which had a strong social and political impact. By subsidizing local initiatives, the state developed a policy towards deprived urban areas (*politique de la ville*) and helped rural areas to elaborate local development strategies (*politique des pays*). Such policies were expected to be multi-dimensional, based on context and 'partnership'. Overall, since their creation, the objective of territorial contracts

Regions and SMSTs

SMSTs are facing a range of conditions in terms of their demographics, productive or cultural influence at the international and national levels or within a regional area (Servillo et al., 2014). We illustrate this diversity through the example of the situation in the Centre-Val de Loire region. It is the fourth French region in area and the tenth in terms of population. It has a remarkable natural and built heritage characterized by the River Loire, which is listed as 'World Heritage cultural landscape' by UNESCO. The Loire Valley is also known for its castles that attract tourists from all over the world.

With a density of 66 inhabitants per square kilometre, the Centre-Val de Loire region is a sparsely populated region, but it is considered to be a fast-growing region; its population increased by 0.4 per cent per year on average between 1999 and 2009. Nevertheless, the region is heterogeneous. The northern part is under the influence of the Ile-de-France region, the Loire Valley is polarized between two large conurbations of over 300,000 inhabitants each (Orléans and Tours), and the southern part has suffered demographic and industrial decline for several decades. All over this wide territory, there are around 20 SMSTs, which are defined as conurbations between 5,000 and 50,000 inhabitants that also concentrate at least 2,000 jobs and services of the highest rank. Their potential role in the overall development of the region is important, but it has been acknowledged only recently.

Throughout the 1990s, in order to organize a fundamentally heterogeneous regional territory, the Regional Council created segmented contracts, first for rural areas, later on for the largest conurbations and only recently for medium-sized towns.

In the early 1980s, the region launched a policy to encourage the development of rural areas by creating inter-municipal cooperation through an inter-sectoral approach and on the initiative of local actors. Since 1994, sub-regional contracts (*contrats de pays*) kept the same bottom-up approach. Such contracts are based on the elaboration of a development chart with diagnosis and long-term projects (10–15 years) and the implementation of a four-year action plan. Such an approach was successful since 30 sub-regional areas that cover the region were identified between 1995 and 2000. In the early 2000s, the Regional Council devoted €185 million to the sub-regional contracts, over a period of five years. Nevertheless, the analysis at the level of individual cases reveals a frequent lack of a structured development plan as well as action objectives that lack originality (opening up the territory, promoting employment and integration, preserving the environment, etc.). There is also an absence of spatial coherence of sub-regional areas that are formed around large cities.

In 2000, the region initiated a reflection on 'poles of centrality' which led to creation of the medium-sized town contracts (*contrats de villes moyennes*). In order to be eligible, medium-sized towns had to satisfy several conditions: having at least 3,000 inhabitants, being outside any conurbation and having at least 2,000 jobs. The contract is signed with the town centre (its central municipality). In order to benefit from this policy, a town that is considered to be medium-sized needs to draft an urban project and to propose a clearly defined development strategy that enables it to carry out the centrality functions and to enhance its attractiveness. The financial support of projects is related in many cases to the construction of cultural and sports facilities. Out of 40 potential towns, 20 towns have signed a contract. The total funding offered of these contracts was €14 million.

Despite several positive effects, it seems that the policy for medium-sized towns needs to be improved. The relationship between policies for sub-regional areas (*pays*) and medium-sized towns can be complex. In fact, in some cases it may even cause some tensions.

The reflections on territorial development have continued to spread since the Council of the Centre-Val de Loire region adopted the 'Regional Plan for Sustainable Development and Planning' (SRADDT) in 2011. This followed a period of consultation and work that involved more than 4,000 people across 23 territorial forums, six thematic forums and three citizen panels. The plan gives a vision of the future development of the region based on three key priorities: knowledge society, networked territories and mobility. In the 'Geographic positioning and structure of the territory' part, the emphasis was put on the dialogue among actors and on balanced urban structure, in particular between the large cities and the SMSTs.

Following the objectives of the SRADDT to maximize the development potential of each territory and to reduce disparities in the living conditions of its inhabitants, in 2012 the Centre-Val de Loire region re-introduced a new territorial scale of action: living areas (*bassin de vie*). Living areas are defined as territories of 'everyday life' and are based on job commuting or on accessibility to services and facilities (consuming). Thus, the 23 living areas in the Centre-Val de Loire region are seen as the most suitable for addressing the key issues of economic, social and environmental development of a territory (including employment, housing, transportation and services). Since 2012, the region has been encouraging dialogue between local actors, including representatives of groups of municipalities (communities of agglomeration, communities of municipalities, unions of countries, medium-sized towns, etc.), important social and economic actors, and institutional partners.

Innovative practices from selected French SMSTs

As we demonstrated in the previous section, concrete action in relation to towns was realized in the 1970s when the state initiated the decentralization

106 *Christophe Demazière et al.*

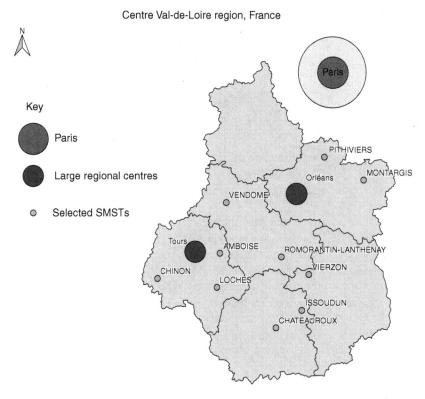

Figure 6.1 Case studies situated in the proximity of the large cities of Paris, Orléans and Tours

process that aimed at improving the quality of life and public infrastructure in those particular areas. Furthermore, since the 1990s, regional authorities provided different contracts to tackle development challenges first in rural areas, and later in large conurbations and medium-sized towns. As a result, local actors had to be mobilized and new sustainable strategies, plans, actions and projects had to be defined. In this section, we observe the choices that were made by local policy-makers in order to creatively address the issues of social cohesion, culture and creativity. More precisely, we observe projects, activities and plans related to social cohesion and CCAs in four SMSTs of the Centre-Val de Loire region (Figure 6.1).

Châteauroux (47,600 inhabitants) is the capital of the Indre department (county) that is located in a remarkable natural environment, including the Brenne regional natural park, the valley of the River Creuse and the Champagne Berrichonne natural region. Due to de-industrialization and demographic decline, the town has faced social challenges such as poverty, exclusion and lack of opportunities. In that sense, one of the valuable public institutions of Châteauroux is the Community Centre for Social Action (CCSA), which has the mission of promoting social inclusion and coordinating social policy in the town. It has a wide range of competences: management of housing of young workers, services to the elderly (residential homes, perennial housing and retirement homes) and reception of the Roma population when they arrive in the area. One of the innovative activities of the CCSA has been the creation of the University of Citizens, which trains people how to speak out in public and participate in public policy debates alongside policy-makers and professionals. For the elderly, the CCSA has established an office that seeks to fight against the isolation of old people by offering various activities. In addition, Châteauroux has created a status form for people aged over 70 that contains all their health information (the name of their general practitioner, health problems, allergies, etc.). The town's department for public health also organizes a healthcare workshop that aims to support disease prevention by coordinating health action in the territory in partnership with professionals and local community in order to tackle social and territorial inequalities in healthcare.

When it comes to transportation, the whole town's bus network, including in its suburbs, is free of charge, which makes Châteauroux a unique case in France. The goal of the local authority was to allow mobility for all, to facilitate commuting and exchange among people, and to improve the ability to participate in the town's events.

In addition, a rare innovation for a town of this size has been the establishment of the Councils of Large Districts. More precisely, the town was divided into seven sectors, which have been led by community representatives, associations and elected officials. The idea behind the establishment of these Councils was to improve neighbourhood life by empowering people at the district level.

Vendôme (17,024 inhabitants) is located only 40 minutes from Paris thanks to the high-speed train. The town has a strong industrial basis and it has particularly thrived after the arrival of multinational companies such as Thales, Avionics and Bosch. However, despite stable employment and a stable population, the town faces challenges such as the outmigration of the young population and the ambiguous effects of being linked to Paris. As a response, an existing dense and well-developed network of associations has been encouraged in Vendôme by the local authority. Employment and social cohesion have been identified as key challenges. Within this field, the town adopted the Local Plan of Inclusion and Employment and founded several institutions such as the Solidarity and Health Centre, the Medical-Educational Institute and a home for the elderly. At the same time, a large number of the town's associations have been devoted to helping people in difficulty to find a job and training them to make a career change if necessary. Some of these associations offer professional orientation and training services.

Culture is also one of the major tools of local policy in attracting and retaining population. The local authority has proposed a special cultural offer to residents with low revenue in order to ensure their access to culture. In order to encourage cultural education and sensibility, Vendôme has supported the work of the Wish Theatre Association, which offers acting classes at low prices. Furthermore, there are several venues that contribute to the cultural offerings of the town: the event hall (which hosts various cultural and music events), the music school, libraries, cinemas, a museum and a youth centre.

Finally, in order to improve accessibility to public services, the town's authority has harmonized all administrative procedures. There is an information point for the most common services used by families (canteens, childcare, etc.), a single registration process for services (i.e. special registration for entire families) and charging for services according to a household's income (i.e. the poorest families get the same services at lower prices).

Vierzon (39,715 inhabitants) is a medium-sized town situated on the banks of the River Cher and some 33 km from the city of Bourges. In the late eighteenth century, the town became industrialized, with iron and steel farming tools, glasswork and ceramics, and agricultural machinery being the main products. With the demise of many factories during the 1970s and 1980s, Vierzon had to face high unemployment and a brain drain.

As Vierzon has an important industrial heritage and numerous old production sites, an important goal of the local authorities has been to improve the town's image through its urban renewal policy. A programme of urban renewal has been developed and funded jointly by the municipality, the department, the Regional Council and the National Agency for Urban Renewal. The programme focuses on the densification of neighbourhoods, the renewal of social housing, the rehabilitation of existing housing, the construction of new roads, parking areas and residential areas, and the delimitation of green areas.

To enable residents to participate in the decision-making process, the local authority established a Junior Council and five Neighbourhood Councils. The representatives of the Junior Council, who are elected by pupils and students of the town's schools, address their demands directly to the town's council. Some of their demands have already been accepted, such as funding of the movement 'Lets clean the nature' and several sports tournaments between schools. The Neighbourhood Councils, which were established in 2009, are composed of elected representatives, associations, businessmen and real estate professionals.

Furthermore, the Disability and Autonomy Centre (DAC) (*Pôle Handicap et Autonomie*) was founded in 2007, the aim of which is also to promote the implementation of new projects in that field. Emphasis is put on technological projects and innovative services in the domain of accessibility, tele-health and disability. In partnership with other organizations, the DAC created a cluster that has united users with disabilities, associations representing beneficiaries, caregivers and professionals, medical and social personnel (doctors, therapists, nurses, teachers, coaches, paramedical staff, etc.) and existing networks in gerontology and home care in order to develop and to promote innovative projects and research in the fields of gerontology, disability, accessibility and mobility.

Issoudun (12,931 inhabitants) is located in an area of milk production, manufacturing and cheese ripening. Its industry is composed of a large number of SMEs and of few large companies such as Sicma (Zodiac Aerospace Group), Vivarte, Louis Vuitton Moët Hennessy (LVMH) and Cemex. Issoudun has had a long-standing and well-connected mayor who has been in office since 1977. During the municipal elections in 2008, the mayor won again by introducing a programme called the 'New Issoudun'. This contains 75 economic, social, educational, cultural and environmental proposals to boost dynamism in the town.

Culture is perceived as the creator of social cohesion and it is strongly used to attract and maintain population in the territory. Issoudun hosts various cultural events, such as the Guitar Festival, the Youth Book Fair, a gliding championship, national competitions of the country dance, the Fairs of All and Curiosity, the Fair of Saints, the motorcycle market and the antiques fair. There are also various sports and cultural facilities in the town, such as the Albert Camus Media Library, the Albert Camus Cultural Centre, the Congress Centre, the Music Box, the Conservatory of Music, cinemas, the art studio, the Hall of Exhibitions and Sports, etc. In addition, public transport within the larger area is free of charge; as such, residents have access to all cultural and sport activities and facilities.

In the social field, there are several associations and organizations whose mission is social assistance and solidarity. For example, the Day Care Centre and the Municipal Public Health Centre provide care to people with multiple disabilities. The Municipal Centre for Social Action offers associative gardens, activities for retired people, meal delivery, a night shelter and emergency assistance. The Agenda 21 of Issoudun is also strongly focused on solidarity. One of its measures is the social microcredit scheme to assist new households in settling into the area. This measure was funded by the local authority in partnership with the county authorities and the Municipal Centre for Social Action.

Finally, Issoudun proposes some interesting training, such as a vocational high school with a special 'Leather clothing' section related to the presence of the LVMH production site. There is also a special training in music and TV production in connection with the Music Box and the town's Bip-TV channel. In fact, Issoudun is the first town in the region whose university offers degrees in music management. Other departments of the university are marketing, transportation and logistics, and communication and marketing of cultural products with a specialization in musical and performing art industry.

Discussion on creative lessons from French towns

As we can observe from French SMSTs and their approach to the implementation of plans and actions relating to social cohesion and CCAs, we find a variety of creative solutions that address local socio-economic challenges. The first and most frequently used instrument is to boost the work of the CCSAs, which are institutions that exist in all of our case studies. According to the French national Act on Social Action and Families (L. 123–4–L. 123–8), the CCSAs are public institutions operating in different areas such as day care centres and nurseries, assistance to the elderly and disabled, social inclusion and quality of life at the neighbourhood level. Nevertheless, even though the operational area of CCSAs is strictly social cohesion, the CCSA in Châteauroux made a breakthrough with some innovative initiatives such as the creation of the University of Citizens.

Besides the CCSAs, several SMSTs founded specific professional institutions that offer very specific services to different groups within the population: for example, the Solidarity and Health Centre and the Medical-Educational Institute in Vendôme, the Disability and Autonomy Centre and the Geriatric Centre in Vierzon, etc.

Another important instrument concerns creative policy-making. Among our case studies, some created and implemented special local strategies and plans that directly tackle social cohesion. We mentioned in the previous section the Local Plan of Inclusion and Employment in Vendôme. Alongside policy-making, towns such as Châteauroux and Vierzon have created Neighbourhood Councils, the Children's Municipal Council and the Council of the Rights and Duties of Families that aim to improve life in the towns by empowering people to participate in decision-making and learn about citizenship.

Indeed, encouraging the population to take part in local associations has been a traditional means of promoting social inclusion and cohesion. We described in the previous section the particular role of associations in SMSTs. For example, in Châteauroux, an association representing the elderly succeeded in creating (in cooperation with the local authorities and the CCSA) a special status form for people aged over 70 containing their detailed health information. In Vendôme, associations focused on unemployment and professional orientation and training.

When it comes to cultural and creative activities, the majority of our case studies recognized the (touristic) development potential of cultural events. The foundation of facilities and events which would serve to assist in cultural education and sensibility were various and innovative. Indeed, the Wish Theatre in Vendôme, a training in music and TV production, a university degree in the marketing of cultural products and a university degree in the musical and performing art industry in Issoudun are surely among the most creative local initiatives that go beyond the 'usual' cultural facilities and events in the region. Nevertheless, the cultural offers (music festivals, shows, fairs, etc.) that exist in other towns and that engage the local population to think and act creatively should not be underestimated in terms of their contribution to cohesion and economic development.

Conclusion

Local policies and initiatives are important for the socio-economic development of territories, especially those that are far from (and not easily connected to) large cities. Such policies and initiatives are not restricted to the public sector, but attempt to mobilize a broad array of actors in order to address the real needs of local communities.

At first, the vision of France as a hierarchical and balanced territory has guided public investment towards SMSTs with the aim of improving the quality of life and boosting economic development. This approach resulted in the implementation of different territorial contracts, in the provision of technical expertise and in the coordination of regional and local authorities for the realization of projects considered as priorities. We gave some examples of the national policy targeting deprived urban areas (*politique de la ville*) and the elaboration of local development strategies in rural areas (*politique des pays*) as responses to the growing public concerns over territorial disparities. The standpoint of these particular contracts has been the need for a synergy among actors in the fields of urban planning, housing, employment, education, recreation, public services, etc. Within this context, the contracts have enabled a broad mobilization of actors and resources to deal with the challenges of social exclusion, unemployment and spatial polarization.

In a subsequent step, as emphasized in the case of some SMSTs in the Centre-Val de Loire region, municipalities have succeeded in implementing creative and innovative policies related to social cohesion and cultural and creative activities, in spite of a complex administrative system and the challenging socio-economic situation. The local authorities in our case studies seemed to have sufficient knowledge, capabilities and experience to identify new opportunities, and to design and implement strategies for long term sustainable (re-)development. Indeed, some SMSTs have had more opportunities to benefit from some key economic, social and academic actors than others. In other words, they seemed not to have underestimated or ignored the potentials that could be valorized through the identification and mobilization of actors and through their networking in implementing new shared economic and social projects.

References

Acket, S., Borsenberger, M., Dickes, P. and Sarracino, F. (2011) Measuring and validating social cohesion: a bottom-up approach. Paper for the International Conference on Social Cohesion and Development, 20–21 January, Paris.

Bayliss, D. (2007) The rise of the creative city: Culture and creativity in Copenhagen. *European Planning Studies*, 15(7): 889–902.
Béhar, D. and Estebe, P. (2004) Aménagement du territoire: une mise en perspective. In *L'état des régions françaises*. Paris: La Découverte.
Carrier, M. and Demazière, C. (2012) La socio-économie des villes petites et moyennes: questions théoriques et implications pour l'aménagement du territoire, *Revue d'Economie Régionale et Urbaine*, 2: 135–49.
Chan, J., To, H. and Chan, E. (2006) Reconsidering social cohesion: Developing a definition and analytical framework for empirical research. *Social Indicators Research*, 75: 273–302.
Cohendet, P., Grandadam, D. and Simon, L. (2009) Economics and the ecology of creativity: Evidence from the popular music industry. *International Review of Applied Economics*, 23(6): 709–22.
Davezies, L. and Talandier, M. (2009) *Repenser le développement territorial*. Paris: La documentation française.
Demazière, C., Hamdouch, A., Banovac, K. and Daviot, L. (2014) *Observation des dynamiques économiques et stratégies des villes petites et moyennes en région Centre (ODES), Volume 1: analyse des dynamiques de développement de 16 villes petites et moyennes*. Final Research Report for the Région Centre, Tours.
Demazière, C. and Serrano, J. (forthcoming) Does strategic spatial planning practice help territorial sustainability? The case of France. In L. Albrechts A. Balducci and J. Hillier (eds), *Situated Practices of Strategic Planning*. Abingdon: Routledge.
ECLAC/UNESCO (Economic Commission for Latin America and the Caribbean Educational, Scientific and Cultural Organization) (2007) *Social Cohesion: Inclusion and a Sense of Belonging in Latin America and the Caribbean*. New York: United Nations Publications. Available at: www.eclac.org/cgi-bin/getProd.asp?xml=/publicaciones/xml/0/29030/P29030.xml&xsl=/tpl-i/p9f.xsl&base=/tpl/top-bottom.xsl.
Foa, R. (2011) The economic rationale for social cohesion – The cross-country evidence. Paper presented on the International Conference on Social Cohesion and Development, 20–21 January, Paris.
Freeman, R. (2011) Can competitive labour markets produce social cohesion: Lessons from advanced and developing countries? Plenary session/keynote speeches for the International Conference on Social Cohesion and Development, 20–21 January, Paris.
Grynspan, R. (2011) Advancing human development: Towards policies that build social cohesion. Plenary Session/Keynote Speeches for the International Conference on Social Cohesion and Development, 20–21 January, Paris.
KEA European Affairs, Media Group, MKW Wirtschaftsforschung GmbH (2006) *The Economy of Culture in Europe*. Available at: http://ec.europa.eu/culture/library/studies/cultural-economy_en.pdf.
Kearns, A. and Forrest, R. (2000) Social cohesion and multilevel urban governance. *Urban Studies*, 37(5–6): 995–1017.
Knox, P. and Mayer, H. (2009) *Small Town Sustainability: Economic, Social and Environmental Innovation*. Basel: Birkhauser.
McCarthy, J. (2006) The application of policy for cultural clustering: Current practice in Scotland. *European Planning Studies*, 14(3): 397–408.
Montgomery, J. (2003) Cultural quarters as mechanisms for urban regeneration. Part 1: Conceptualising cultural quarters. *Planning, Practice & Research*, 18(4): 293–306.

Moulaert, F., MacCallum, D., Mehmood, A. and Hamdouch, A. (eds) (2013) *The International Handbook on Social Innovation: Collective Action, Social Learning and Transdisciplinary Research*. Cheltenham: Edward Elgar Publishing.

Nelson, R.R. (2007) Institutions and economic growth: Sharpening the research agenda. *Journal of Economic Issues*, XLI(2): 313–23.

Plaza, B., Tironi, M. and Haarich, S.N. (2009) Bilbao's art scene and the Guggenheim effect revisited. *European Planning Studies*, 17(11): 1711–29.

Quinn, B. (2006) Problematising 'festival tourism': Arts festivals and sustainable development in Ireland. *Journal of Sustainable Tourism*, 14(3): 288–306.

Selada, C., da Cuhna, I.V. and Tomas, E. (2011) Creative clusters in low density urban areas: A case study approach. Lisbon, Portugal: INTELI.

Servillo, L., Atkinson, R., Smith, I., Russo, A., Sýkora, L., Demazière, C. and Hamdouch, A. (2014) *TOWN – Small and Medium-Sized Towns in their Functional Territorial Context*. Final Report, Luxembourg: ESPON.

Scott, A.J. (1997) The cultural economy of cities. *International Journal of Urban and Regional Research*, 21(2): 323–39.

URBACT Creative Clusters (2011) *From Creative Industries to the Creative Place: Refreshing the Local Development Agenda in Small and Medium-Sized Towns*. Brussels: European Programme for Sustainable Urban Development.

URBACT II (2010) Cities and the economic crisis, a survey on the impact of the economic crisis and the responses of URBACT II cities. Available at: http://urbact.eu/survey-impact-economic-crisis-and-responses-urbact-cities.

7 Inter-municipal cooperation as a means of creative territorial planning

José Serrano and Abdelillah Hamdouch

Introduction

Small and medium-sized towns (SMSTs) play a major role in structuring space and hosting inhabitants. They constitute a dense seedling of towns distributed in a homogeneous way across the French territory. Some of them are included in spaces dominated by built-up areas and they contribute to the organization and animation of the activities and relationships of the metropolized areas. By contrast, some others are more or less spatially isolated. However, their autonomy is variable depending on their ability to cope with the influence of major built-up areas (including rather distant ones) or even to play an active role in the organization of the space at a larger territorial scale. Between these extremes, small and medium-sized towns certainly have a peculiar structuring and connecting role to play in the inter-territorial combination of various urban, peripheral and rural spaces (Santamaria, 1999).

Still, as peri-urbanization is rapidly expanding, more and more SMSTs are becoming (with varied intensity) dependent on the urban core. Does this mean that SMSTs structure space only at the lower level of the urban system? Do they become passive as mere appendices of (or 'territorial gap fillers' between) urban cores? Moreover, as their economic base is narrower than those of larger cities, are they able to develop specific strategies for coping with a sharp inter-territorial competitive context?

We present the case of two SMSTs located in the peri-urban areas of Marseille and Rennes in France, and we analyse the economic projects elaborated at the scale of the urban region and by the two municipalities chosen. In the first section, we explain the creative approach concept and the kind of relationships assumed by this approach. The second section presents the methodology. We justify the choice of peri-urban areas and present the cases studied. The third section presents the results. We will see how municipalities design their economic strategy at the urban regional level and at the local level. We focus on the implementation strategy of business parks. The final section will discuss the results while looking at the creative approach concept.

The multiscalar-creative approach, economic development and inter-municipal cooperation

The creative approach as a process of space specification

The links between innovation, economy and territory have been conceptualized by the territorial economic theory. According to this theory, innovation in not only a break with the past; it must also be considered according to a wider approach and considering environment and space. The theory began with the concept of industrial districts. It introduced the idea that competitiveness also depends on relationships between firms. Small firms connected and sharing a common culture and complementary knowledge and skills can be more efficient than bigger companies. Economies of scale can be efficiently counterbalanced by the complementarity and strong cooperation among small and medium-sized companies co-located in a specific local area (Crevoisier and Jeannerrat, 2009).

Spatial analyses of the relationships between economic agents focus on the distances between them. This distance is physical, but it is also social. According to values given to space, agents are more or less close among them in terms of institutional and cognitive proximity (versus distance), i.e. with reference to shared social norms, patterns of behaviour, territorial identity, etc. This social proximity is very important because it determines the kind of relationships between the actors: cooperation, competition or even ignorance of each other. Actors try to control this distance (versus proximity) and to establish the kind of relationships that are suitable for them. But space is not just a result of these relationships; it also acts on the actors who design their projects and strategies according to spatial values (Lussault, 2007). Thus, economic agents act *within* space and not only *on* space; hence, space can be considered as constituting a genuine economic asset or resource.

Therefore, the links between space and economy are complex. Courlet (2008) and Pecqueur (2007) consider space not to be neutral. It is not just a container where economic dynamics take place. Courlet and Pecqueur argue that each territory is the product of a specific social and historical building process of space, and as such it can constitute a resource for economic agents. These agents can use it and, in turn, the territory acts on them (Fache and Hamdouch, 2014). Space can then be considered as an economic asset.

This approach is another paradigm and it changes the concept of innovation. Territorial economics highlight the transformation of local resources. It describes bottom-up processes where local economic agents establish close relationships. These networks allow actors to produce original resources. The economic strategies of actors are considered in a wide and competitive context. The strength of local actors and clusters is specialization. However, researchers now consider more differentiated processes of clustering and networking, especially around innovative and creative activities (Depret and

Hamdouch, 2009; Crevoisier and Jeannerat, 2009). In this context, actors are at the same time connected with close milieu and build relationships with distant actors. This is not merely a process of propagation and integration of outside knowledge or experiences. Local actors are able to exchange with distant actors and at the same time elaborate their own projects at the local scale (Hamdouch, 2010). As a consequence, in a global context where everybody can easily connect to everybody (whatever the respective location of each of them), actors need to be able to distinguish themselves from other players in terms of knowledge, competences, capabilities or resources (Hamdouch, 2010). Thus, innovation in a multiscalar collaborative process produces differentiation (Crevoisier and Jeannerat, 2009).

This multiscalar approach of the spatial and social organization of actors' relationships within innovation-creativity dynamics highlights both the impact of globalization (i.e. the need for developing diversified connections at various geographical scales) and the specific role that SMSTs could play as local anchors of innovative actors.

The multiscalar-creative dimensions of spatial organization in the context of globalization

Halbert (2013) describes the effects of globalization on territories and especially on territorial development policies at the metropolitan level. Globalization is presented as a process of economic agents' disembeddedness in relation to local resources (Michalet, 2007). Leader firms prefer mobility to territorial commitment. These firms organize a large share of industrial and financial activities and flows from their headquarters and decision centres concentrated in a few global cities (Sassen, 2001). According to this approach, the mobility of production factors breaks traditional solidarities and places territories with varying levels of endowments into an unfair competition.

But globalization can also be seen in another way. Production tasks are increasingly divided according to vertical and horizontal organization. Jobs are becoming more and more specialized. For example, industrial firms can share production lines among several plants spread over different countries (Saxenian, 2002). So, lying between competition and complementary situations, the relationships among territories can, in a better way, be qualified as *interdependence*.

Halbert (2013) suggests that globalization gives advantage to metropolitan areas and favours generic development factors. Metropolises offer a wide range of production factors and develop long-range connections with other places in the world. They are in tune with the key characteristics of globalization: a combination of diversified and complementary factors, and openness to the world. Hence, metropolises are seen as the engine of economic growth and development (Scott, 1996; Halbert, 2005). Their expansion rate is above average and they are able to spread the resulting wealth to their surroundings. According to this vision, metropolises are considered to be the spearhead of territorial development by most public policy and decision-makers at the national and regional levels.

As a consequence of this priority given to metropolises, SMSTs are placed in an unfavourable position in terms of territorial and creative development. Hence, there is a vital need for them to orient their economic development in a way that allows them to play as advantageously as possible in the 'market of territories'. Territories are in competition for attracting foreign firms, creative people and investors. The challenge for SMSTs is therefore to attract exogenous agents who handle the territory in the globalized exchanges network and spread growth at the local level. For many SMSTs, coping with this challenge often translates into policy development strategies based on the improvement of infrastructures, re-specialization of manpower skills and capabilities, and aggressive territorial marketing through, for example, subsidies and tax cuts offered to investors (Demazière, Hamdouch and Banovac, 2014). However, this approach is hazardous because public actors need to invest money (sometimes large amounts based on debt) and they cannot be sure of the success of the investments. In addition, economic agents are very mobile and they can move to another territory as soon as the latter proposes better infrastructures or financial-fiscal conditions.

Halbert (2013) highlights the fact that there is another option for metropolitan development. This option joins the creative approach described above, but does not solve the problem of the autonomy of SMSTs in relation to metropolises. He calls the second option 'sweet territorial engineering', which combines 'cross-fertilization' and 'open innovation'. It is based on the ability to be connected and to exchange in order to create synergies, but also on the ability to be open to the outside in order to find and combine resources which are not available locally. Both abilities are necessary. Moreover, the ability of a territory to combine continuously generic and specific resources is crucial (Colletis-Wahl et al., 2008). Coordination is the core of this approach and it is reflexive. This means that when economic agents cooperate in order to combine their own resources and create new ones, they develop a collective ability to think about a common future (Halbert, 2012).

Metropolises are seen as being well equipped to operate this double combination: they have a highly diversified productive web and they have the infrastructures enabling the creation of long-range connections. What about SMSTs? Obviously these do not have the strengths of the metropolises, their productive base is narrower and their influence is more localized. Therefore, they need to engage their development strategies in alternative patterns of territorial organization, primarily through a better valorization of their local resources, but also by finding new channels of cooperation and enhanced complementarity with other territories, with other SMSTs, and with larger urban areas and metropolises.

Which place for SMSTs in new urban hierarchies?

Some researchers suggest that the negative evaluation of SMSTs is closely related to the way they are considered (i.e. as marginal, poorly endowed or declining territories). By contrast, a more attentive analysis shows that they are not devoid of advantages and that they can even offer unique resources, amenities and opportunities, both for residents and economic activity.

Most urban studies focus on metropolises because they are considered as good laboratories to investigate the consequences of globalization on territories (Demazière et al., 2012). The results of globalization are supposed to spread later on to the lower layers of the urban hierarchy. Metropolises are seen as the starting point of the general transformation of the urban system (Bell and Jayne, 2009). Small and medium-sized towns have not been considered as a specific class for investigation. The general conclusions learnt from the study of metropolises are transposed to smaller cities and towns. This places SMSTs in a subordinate position, which in turn suggests that they are passive.

In the French context, the designation 'small and medium-sized town' reinforces the perception of subordination (Santamaria, 2012). In France, the urban system is described as a very hierarchical and stable system. In the context of globalization and competition between territories, large cities and metropolises are considered to be the best model. SMSTs are not supposed to be able to catch up because the urban system is considered as very stable and the rank of towns in the territorial hierarchy is not modified even after a long period. However, positive and specific qualities are attributed to SMSTs. They offer a good living environment and quite good job opportunities. These qualities confine such towns to the middle of the urban hierarchy as quiet and sweet places to live, but without sufficient infrastructure to face intensive economic competition (Santamaria, 2012).

This vision is biased because it does not consider the role that SMSTs can play in spatial planning and the territorial organization at the larger scale of urban regions. Indeed, many SMSTs are in a good position to attract growth and residential incomes and to distribute them to their surroundings. They avoid wealth being concentrated only in big cities. They cover the territory more evenly as they allow for a more balanced spread of demographic and economic growth. Moreover, they are seen as 'relaying spaces' from metropolises to the surroundings. They avoid metropolises being cut from their surroundings (Santamaria, 2012). The category 'small and medium-sized town' makes it possible to move beyond a polarized vision of the territorial organization restrained to big cities on the one hand and low-density spaces on the other. It introduces an intermediate scale allowing for a more even distribution of development over the whole territory (Aubert et al., 2011).

Therefore, the key issue facing SMSTs is not primarily economic development per se, but planning. Once SMSTs are seen as relays or go-betweens in the urban hierarchy, it is easier to link their role to the multiscalar-creative approach of territorial development defined above. While SMSTs are in close relation to local surrounding spaces, they can also develop larger-scale relationships through the metropolises they are connected to. But immediately the question of spatial governance rises. Indeed, existing institutional spatial structures ignore the singularity of SMSTs while standard planning systems do not really allow for their integration as concrete components of the territorial organization.

How can we escape this problematic situation? Building on the considerations above regarding the pertinence of the multiscalar-creative approach to territorial development on the one hand and the go-between role that SMSTs can play in the urban hierarchy on the other, we suggest that *inter-municipal cooperation* between large cities and SMSTs at the urban region scale can be a creative solution for a more comprehensive planning approach encompassing all categories of interrelated spaces. Cooperation means both that SMSTs contribute to elaborate the planning project with the main cities of the urban area and that they are not dominated or subjected by these larger urban areas. At the scale of the urban region, cooperation makes it possible to go over opposition and extreme competition. It can produce a spatial quality which SMSTs are able to use as a specific resource while large cities may benefit from the functional complementarity offered by SMSTs.

Methodology

Peri-urban areas as a laboratory of inter-municipal cooperation

The examples chosen for this research involve two major French cities (Rennes and Marseille) and two SMSTs located in their respective peri-urban areas: La Mézière (4,426 inhabitants) and Marignane (34,405 inhabitants).

We privileged the urban region scale to observe the coordination between major cities and SMSTs because it assembles two kinds of spaces in a functional area. Major cities are included in built-up areas. They concentrate inhabitants and jobs. SMSTs are usually in less densely inhabited countryside. These two kinds of spaces are linked by an economic relationship. The peri-urban areas send commuters to the urban core where jobs are concentrated. Urbanized areas and countryside can be considered either antagonist or complementary.

Dichotomous approaches consider urbanized areas and countryside to be opposite in nature. Urban sprawl is then interpreted as conflict of land use and it is a feature of peri-urban areas (Mora, 2008).

The relation to nature is important to define the town–countryside pair (Vanier, 2005). Instead of considering that nature is different in essence inside towns and in the countryside, nature can be considered along a gradient across towns/cities and their countryside. Usually, urban nature is aesthetic and hygienic, whereas countryside nature is dedicated to food production. These considerations are obsolete because there are also allotments and wild animals and plants within cities, while in the countryside intensive food production is no longer considered as so 'natural'. Therefore, nature is not cut off or separated between the urban space and countryside, but shapes a continuum (Vanier, 2005). This approach is not just an abstract interpretation. It is supported by the mobility of peri-urban inhabitants. Due to the high level of mobility, people practise and use in parallel several kinds of spaces, urban cores as well as peri-urban areas and countryside. Time to spend moving across these discontinuous spaces is so important that it becomes a life space itself. The mixture of urban and rural spaces creates a new class of space called the 'third space' (Viard, 1990; Vanier, 2008). The relationships to nature considered as a continuum and the generalized mobility of inhabitants make peri-urban areas an 'interface' (Vanier, 2008). Therefore, the key feature of these spaces can be coordinated relationships. Vanier calls it 'interterritoriality'.

Peri-urban SMSTs are within an interface space. This means that the relationships of SMSTs with other spaces are structuring. Taking the viewpoint that natural spaces abolish a dichotomous approach of the relationships between urban spaces and the countryside, it opens up new perspectives for the relationships set up by SMSTs. They are no longer repressed between two antagonist spaces, but they are in a more balanced place inside a natural space which shapes at the same time densely inhabited spaces and low-density spaces.

In concrete terms, we propose analysing the business parks strategy planned by municipalities in order to interpret the relationships between SMSTs and their neighbouring large cities. Business parks are an important economic tool used by municipalities for their economic development. The implementation of business parks also has an important environmental footprint because they use green spaces. This angle of analysis can therefore help us to understand how municipalities place themselves in a globalized-competitive context, how this translates into economic development strategies and infrastructures, and how the latter affect the consumption of rural/natural space and the environment. Moreover, as the case studies examined below will show, inter-municipal cooperation can potentially (but not systematically, as the case of Marseille demonstrates) play a key role in designing and implementing more coherent development dynamics while the impacts on the environment and natural space are better taken into account.

Presentation of the case studies

The urban areas studied have been selected from a sample of the four most dynamic French urban areas.[1] This sample was designed for a research work which studied the articulation between sustainability and municipal cooperation (Demazière et al., 2013). The sample was constituted of the

Table 7.1 Demographic and job data of urban areas selected

Urban area	Marseille/Aix-en-Provence	Rennes
Number of inhabitants (2009)	1,714,828	663,214
Evolution of population (1990–2006)	12.1%	26.5%
Total number of jobs (2009)	683,421	306,289
Increase in the number of jobs (1999–2009)	13%	24%

Source: DARES-DATAR-INSEE (2011)

Table 7.2 Institutional context

Urban area	Marseille-Aix-en-Provence	Rennes
Number of municipalities in the urban area/number of local municipality associations	90/10	189/20
Kind of urban shape	Polycentric	Monocentric
Number of SCoTs in the urban area	1	6
Quality of intercommunal cooperation	Contentious	Fixed

Source: Demazière et al. (2012)

urban areas that have the highest demographic and economic growth (see Table 7.1), which puts renewable resources in tension between economic development and natural conservation. Therefore, the case studies are also appropriate for assessing the effects of inter-municipal cooperation as a creative planning approach to mitigating such tension while favouring local economic development and job creation.

We focus more specifically on the role of SMSTs in inter-municipal cooperation. Therefore, among the sample areas, we chose the most contrasting cases in terms of the relationships between the 'urban pole' (urban core or central city) and the peripheral SMSTs (see Table 7.2).

Also, the urban areas have been selected more on growth criteria than on similarity. This is why the urban area of Marseille has three times more inhabitants or jobs than the urban area of Rennes. Marseille can be considered an international metropolis, whereas Rennes has more of a regional influence. However, both the urban areas of Marseille and Rennes benefit from a good road network which connects them to national and European economic spaces. Rennes is at the centre of a radial network while Marseille's network has no privileged directions. But in both cases, these networks connect the built-up areas with their regional space and with national or international economic catchment areas. In addition, Marseille benefits from a high-speed train network and a major port.

Both urban areas also differ in terms of their urban shape and the quality of inter-municipal cooperation. The urban area of Marseille is polycentric. It is made up of two urban centres (Marseille and Aix-en-Provence) to which several important towns of more than 20,000 inhabitants are added. Marseille is not recognized by the other municipalities as being the leader of the urban region. For a long time, it has developed despite ignoring its hinterland. During this time, the other towns could benefit from Marseille's important industrial centres and a good transport network. The polycentrism of Marseille's urban area favours competition between local authorities. Antagonism is increased by very strong identities, strong political rivalries and the fear of having to share the wealth with Marseille – which is declining. The development of municipal cooperation is very slow, despite strong national incentives. The relationships between local authorities are marked by permanent rivalries.

The situation in Rennes is quite the opposite. The urban network is monocentric. The dichotomy between Rennes and its hinterland is strong. Rennes has the best location at the centre of the radius transport network. But municipal cooperation is old and rooted. It began in 1970 with the creation of a district. The elected authorities of Rennes became aware of the scarcity of land inside the municipal area. Inter-municipal cooperation makes it possible to build a collective and voluntarist policy in order to orientate economic development and at the same time save land consumption. Interestingly, the local authorities of the peri-urban fringe, which pioneered and pushed for more intensive inter-municipal cooperation, are involved in the design of strategic planning documents initiated by Rennes.

The quality of inter-municipal cooperation has been tested through the implementation of business parks. Business parks are a major issue for municipalities because of the local taxes they yield (Serrano and Demazière, 2009). Municipalities can decide on their own to implement business parks, but they work together to elaborate a strategic planning document called 'SCoT' (*Schéma de Cohérence Territoriale* or territorial coherence scheme). This planning document (which has a legal basis defined at the national level) has been precisely designed to coordinate the municipal projects on the one hand and to harmonize sector-specific approaches on the other hand.

The implementation of business parks at the urban region level and the relationships between municipalities have been studied in three ways.

The analysis combines the study of land use and the content of planning documents. The land use is analysed using a geographic information system. For both urban regions, it compiles land use data from the Corine Land Cover and Sitadel2[2] databases. We aggregated to this data the perimeters of the protected areas for wildlife and the location of business parks. We then calculated the land consumption for new business parks and the overlap of business parks on protected areas.[3] This spatial analysis is completed by the study of the content of planning documents at the scale of the urban region, and also of detailed documents about a specific economic project such as a new business park). Interviews with elected representatives or planners were

Table 7.3 Features of the studied business parks implemented by SMSTs

Name of the business park (town, urban region)	La Bourdonnais (La Mézière, Rennes)	Les Florides (Marignane, Marseille/Aix-en-Provence)
Economic content of the project	Renewable (20 ha) and growth (10 ha) Establishment of green activities	Creation of 87 ha, 53,000 m² Eurocopter 17,000 m² companies village
Kind of inter-municipal cooperation	Strong custom Shared development and complementarity	Rivalries between municipalities or between their associations
Environmental obligations	Weak	Strong Remarkable wildlife Environment under state protection

Source: Demazière et al. (2012)

added to better understanding the economic development strategy. The subject matter of interviews was as follows: the strategy of economic development, the appearance of environmental concerns in local economic policies, and the strategic planning of economic development and environmental issues. Taking account of environmental issues requires the sharing of a global and common vision of the urban region. This necessarily involves inter-municipal cooperation. By contrast, unilateral visions of the urban region exacerbate the rivalries and competition among municipalities and prevent them from replacing places chosen for economic development concerned by environmental issues with other potential locations.

Finally, two projects have been selected for the two urban regions. We focused on economic projects that are significant in size in relation to the scale of the urban region considered. The projects also have a dominant economic aim (offices, warehouses, industries, etc.) (see Table 7.3). The projects considered were also designed after the production of the planning document at the regional scale in order to highlight the influence of the inter-municipal cooperation at the local level.

Key findings

Arbitrage processes in the location of business parks at the urban region level

We consider three levels of protection of wildlife. The strongest level forbids any buildings inside the area. The lowest level of protection is just information about the presence of interesting habitats or protected species. Areas with strong protection are quite rare even in the case of the urban

Table 7.4 Wildlife protected areas overlapped by business parks

Urban region	Part of the urban area concerned by a strong protection	Part of the urban area concerned by a medium protection	Part of the urban area concerned by a weak protection	Number of business parks overlapping protected areas (% of all business parks)
Marseille	3%	Unknown	9%	36 (19%)
Rennes	0%	0%	1%	8 (4%)

Source: Demazière et al. (2012)

region of Marseille, which accommodates remarkable species. Most of the supposed 'protected areas' are in fact just meant to inform the public. As a result, planners and elected representatives are the real decision-makers as to whether to protect or not an area.

In the case of the urban region of Marseille, we can see that 19 per cent of the business parks overlap protected areas (see Table 7.4). But most of the business parks were implemented before the protected areas. In the case of Marseille, the protected areas with a high level of protection (the MAB biosphere reserve of Camargue) were decided in 1977, but the other areas with a weak level of protection were delimited at the beginning of the 2000s after most of the large business parks had been implemented. So the high level of overlapping in the case of the urban area of Marseille must be understood as a high level of richness of wildlife. What we saw is the difficulty in escaping the modernization of business parks that are considered as being of major importance for the urban region. Likewise, the industrial harbour of Étang de Berre, located in the reserve of Camargue, continues to be developed despite the exceptional value of the biodiversity identified on this site.

In the case of the urban region of Rennes, there are very few areas listed as containing outstanding or even notable species. The wildlife is ordinary. There are very few business parks overlapping natural protected areas (see Table 7.4 and appendix).

But the main lesson drawn from the comparison between the Rennes and Marseille urban regions comes from the study of the business parks decided by the selected SMSTs in these areas. We will see that, surprisingly, it is the municipality which has fewer notable natural areas which will better protect them and even integrate them into the development of economic projects.

The role of strategic spatial planning

The contents of the SCoTs of Marseille and Rennes have been analysed. The analysis focused on the spatialization of economic development and

Table 7.5 Summary of strategic trends of SCoT and connections between economic development and environmental issues

	Marseille Provence Métropole	Rennes Métropole
Quantitative approach of economic development	Identification of places with no quantitative objectives	Quantified estimation of land needs (short and medium term)
Reluctance to control economic land	Medium Knowledge of scarcity of land	Weak
Concrete definition of economic aims	Medium	Strong Quantitative objectives
Economic sprawl control	Medium Limited to industrial sites and logistic activities	Strong Identification and mapping of strategic sites
Landscape and urban account	Medium Just formulated	Strong Multifunctionnal areas
Brownfield reuse	Poorly formulated	Aim assured with quantitative targets

Source: Demazière et al. (2012)

on economic sprawl. We also looked for the directions formulated in the planning documents attached to the SCoT. The results are summarized in Table 7.5.

The mitigation of land consumption and the protection of natural or agricultural spaces appear to be justified aims and they are placed at the core of the SCoT. The aims are formulated in both SCoTs, but the real will of reducing the economic sprawl is not convincing in both cases. Marseille has not really achieved its strategy, whereas Rennes proposes a SCoT with more precise regulations.

Because of the topography and the strong concentration of inhabitants and companies in the central area of the city of Marseille, land is scarce. The situation is exacerbated by demographic growth. Due to the availability of many brownfields along the port area, the main urban transformation of the city is the Euromediterannée project (which is mainly concentrated on housing and offices) located in that area. By contrast, the solutions for economic development are orientated towards peripheral areas of the city. The design of the SCoT helps elected people and planners take awareness of the seriousness of the situation and the need to strongly regulate land use. But two limits appear in relation to this objective: the limited spatial perimeter of the SCoT of Marseille and the decisions taken in the case of a new business park (Les Florides). The SCoT of the Marseille Provence Métropole covers only the inter-municipal cooperation structure comprising Marseille

126 *José Serrano and Abdelillah Hamdouch*

and its neighbouring municipalities. It facilitates cooperation between the municipalities within the SCoT, but it concerns only a small part of the urban area of Marseille and there is no real coordination with the other inter-municipal cooperation structure of the Pays d'Aix-en-Provence. This association has not yet finished its planning documents and orients its economic development according to the opportunities coming from outside of the area. Likewise, the location of activities is not thought of according to environmental criteria. The strong attractiveness of the area induces high negative externalities (rise of real estate prices, traffic congestion, etc.). Another reason is demonstrated by the new business park decision. Les Florides business park is located in a constrained natural area (identified as containing interesting species and being at risk of flooding). Compensatory actions were decided in order to enable the implementation of the business park. In reality, planning documents were mainly used to rationalize and justify the change of use of land.

In the case of Rennes, maps and figures indicate the stock of land which will be used for economic activities over the next ten years. The prospective areas are managed in a hierarchical system according to the kind of activity expected, and the number of hectares assigned to urbanization has been fixed. The new business parks are designed according to landscape issues and to a global diagnosis for the economic development at the urban area scale. Business parks have also been located according to the ecological structure and connections between the various types of natural spaces (greenbelts and areas, water corridors, wetlands, etc.) within the SCoT perimeter. The trends exposed in the SCoT are clearly defined in order to limit economic sprawl.

Table 7.5 shows how economic development and environmental issues are coordinated in the two cases. Marseille and Rennes are aware of environmental issues. These are presented in the SCoTs of both areas. In the case of Marseille, elected people face a context with strong environmental restraints. But as their ambition is to push Marseille to become a European metropolis, large economic projects are privileged over other considerations. Marked by its economic decline in the 1980s and 1990s, Marseille plans to shine again at the international level and has identified strategic activities (like logistics and other professional tertiary activities) that will be implemented in the area. Even if Rennes is not concerned with strong environmental constraints, it has nonetheless aggregated environmental issues like landscape into new business parks and has a strong level of control over economic sprawl. But even in the case of Rennes, the aim is not to undermine the economic opportunities from which it can take advantage.

Rennes and its surroundings define themselves as an archipelago city. It is not a geographical concept because the urban region of Rennes is not a polycentric urban area. Rennes' urban area is monocentric. But Rennes and its surrounding towns consider themselves as a fragmented but a whole city. The farmlands between Rennes and the secondary towns are not considered as an empty space, but as a part of the urban space. The importance of farmland and natural land for the identity of the Rennes urban area and for the welfare of its inhabitants is recognized in all strategic planning documents. In Rennes, the concept is operationalized by the definition of what they call 'urban agricultural fields' and 'visibility cones' (open landscape view areas). 'Urban agricultural fields' and 'visibility cones' should be protected from construction and from urban sprawl. They have been designed and situated in order to preserve interesting landscapes and to avoid the joining of urban settlements. Thanks to 'urban fields' and 'visibility cones', the municipalities are able to decide where and how much open space should be preserved from construction

Which features of the economic projects are implemented at the local scale?

Business parks have been chosen in order to demonstrate the capacity of SMSTs to articulate environmental issues and local economic development. Beyond these issues, it is the ability of SMSTs to combine local resources with external resources, and more precisely their ability to coordinate their own resources with immaterial resources built at the urban region scale, which explains why their local economic development is coherent with environmental considerations.

Still, in the case of the Les Florides business park, the environment is seen as an impediment to the achievement of the economic project. Instead of adapting the project to the environmental constraints, it is the environmental constraints which are transformed. Thus, it is the environment which becomes compatible with the economic project and not the opposite.

In the urban region of Marseille-Aix-en-Provence, the elected representatives of Marignane (a medium-sized town nearby Marseille) are faced with the high natural value of a site that they want to dedicate to business parks. Wildlife is given strong protection. A Territorial Planning Regulation[4] has been implemented before the launching of the new Les Florides business park project. Then the spatial separation between environmental and economic issues cannot be the solved by an arrangement between the local authorities. The French Ministry of Environment must agree on any land use change. Local authorities will only get this agreement if they offer sufficient compensatory actions.

Les Florides business park is presented as a high environmental quality park dedicated to aeronautics. It spreads over 87 hectares and is close to two motorways (A7 and A55). The most important point is that this park adjoins other business parks dedicated to aeronautics. But these parks belong to rival municipal associations. This rivalry is exacerbated because these activities are looking for additional free land to develop their operations.

The very constrained environmental context is known and is presented in the planning documents. The Bolmon small lake is identified as a remarkable space for wildlife which is threatened by anthropogenic pressure. The

Table 7.6 Features of business parks implemented by the SMSTs chosen

Name of the business park (town, urban region)	Les Florides (Marignane, Marseille-Aix-en-Provence)	La Bourdonnais (La Mézière, Rennes)
Economic content of the project	Creation of 87 ha, 53,000 m² for Eurocopter, 17,000 m² for other companies	Renewable (20 ha) and growth (10 ha) Establishment of green activities
Environmental processing	Preservation of small river Large green spaces and large views to natural landscapes Compensatory actions Energy production buildings	Preservation of *in situ* tree lines and ponds Economic sprawl limited Electricity produce *in situ*
Kind of inter-municipal cooperation	Rivalries between municipalities or between their associations	Strong custom Shared development and complementarities
Environmental obligations	Strong Very high value of wildlife environment under state protection	Weak
Economic strategy	Competition among municipal associations Consolidation and valorization of own comparative advantages Economic analysis oriented to land supply and public subsidies	Analysis of supply and demand of land
Links between the economy and the environment	Environmental issues are considered as constraints which make it harder to benefit from comparative advantages. These advantages are usually due to the capture of economic rent	Environmental issues are internalized to the project of development

Source: Demazière et al. (2012)

planning territorial instruction advice is to find a balance between urban and economic development and the protection of natural environments, and to keep large open spaces.

The Eurocopter Company, which is based in Marignane, planned to move to the neighbouring municipality. Thanks to compensatory actions, the Mayor of Marignane got the Ministry of Environment to give up its veto on the implementation of the business park and could then retain Eurocopter in its municipal area. The new building designed for Eurocopter covers 45,000 m². It has been built in a very short amount of time and it is regarded as an ideal building in relation to its technical and energy-saving performance. The regional environmental protection office has considered the potential environmental impact as being rather weak.

However, the impact study found two protected plants – *Ononis mitissima* L. and *Phalaris paradoxa* L. – which are restricted to cultivated lands and fallow lands. The Ministry of Environment allowed their destruction if Marignane bought and gave 20 hectares to the Coast protection agency and the Marseille Provence Métropole accepted to pay the management costs of these natural spaces for ten years. These spaces are close to the Les Florides business park. As a result, all environmental issues related to the business park project have been moved outside the space dedicated to economic activities.

The treatment of the environment within the La Bourdonnais business park is completely different. The business park was implemented in the 1970s. It is well connected to major roads and a motorway, and it accommodates several companies. Nowadays, the park is considered to be in a dilapidated state. In 2008, the 'Bocage en Bourdonnais' municipal community decided to refurbish and extend the park by 10 hectares. Several environmental targets were decided: to increase the density of the park (up to 50 per cent of the area would be built upon), to conserve boscages and ponds *in situ* and to orientate the park to 'green' activities.

This positioning was not a simple wish but the real will of the elected people. The actions of land consumption control and of wetlands and wood landscape preservation were strong, all the more so as the geographical and regulation context did not require it. At the urban region level, land is available and nature is common. There were very few protected areas. The regional environmental protection office was satisfied by the treatment of natural areas. It had no doubt as to the capacity of the elected representatives to conserve biodiversity inside the park. It also appreciated the efforts proposed to save energy. Nevertheless, it was circumspect on the priority given to 'green' companies.

The environmental preservation actions are not merely for show. They are coherent with the green activities direction given to the La Bourdonnais business park. The elected representatives adopted an experimental approach. On the one hand, they refurbished an existing zone and on the other hand they targeted green activities without any clear definition of what these were. They expected to forge an experience basis and also that companies interested in environmental processes or environmental image would wish to locate themselves in an exemplary business park. Thus, at the same time, they could improve their credibility and the work conditions for their employees.

This approach seemed coherent because the inter-municipal partnership of La Bourdonnais was quite demanding both in relation to the characteristics of the business park and the companies it should host. In comparison with Les Florides, environmental and economic issues were not spatially separated and they were even considered as compatible. The engagement of elected people in an environmentally friendly approach was used as a means to attract a specific segment of economic activities.

Discussion and conclusion

In the case of Marignane, the municipality adopted a strategic approach of competing within 'the market of territories' (see above). The economic issue was not to attract new firms but to avoid local implemented firms moving to another municipality or association of municipalities. Municipalities or their inter-municipal associations are clearly in competition. Being attractive means offering more ready-to-use land or doing it before the competing territories. Motorways provide good connections throughout the entire urban region. Under such conditions, available land to firms is a generic resource because no municipality can distinguish its advantages from those of its competitors.

Because of the constraints due to the protection of wildlife, land comprising protected areas can be seen less attractive to firms. Wildlife protected areas are seen as a threat which can reduce the attractiveness of a location. Municipalities prefer to move the environmental constraints elsewhere rather than imposing them on firms.

In the case of la Mézière, the nature of the wildlife is very ordinary and yet it is there where municipalities have succeeded in cooperating and in turning environmental issues into a specific resource.

Although the urban area of Rennes is monocentric, it is there that the concept of archipelago town has been elaborated as an identity concept (Dormois, 2007). The archipelago town is an approach which grasps the history of urban development and the identity of the territory. The history aims to demonstrate that public authorities make better use of the available land in the area than private agents would do because the latter are interested only in the most promising sites. It is used to legitimate collective planning decisions and also to convince public authorities to make good use of planning.

The archipelago city introduces the idea of a multifunctional space. It defines an urban shape: urban nuclei dispersed in a sea of farmland or natural land. It aims to prevent connections between towns due to urban sprawl. It organizes the localization of urban or economic growth and it also gives a landscape function to farmland or natural land. This role is assumed by local elected representatives.

The analysis of the contents of the territorial coherence scheme of Rennes (see Table 7.5) shows that the archipelago town concept is credible. The 'urban fields', the 'visibility cones' and the 'green and blue network' operationalize it. These elements give form to a green belt. With these elements, municipalities said which spaces are necessarily conserved, i.e. they demonstrate how to conserve the existing urban landscape.

The analysis of the strategic planning documents reveals the value given to space by municipalities, but these documents are also a means for expressing this value. It is a cognitive resource which can be used by SMSTs to implement business parks.

The creation of a cognitive resource is an example of 'sweet territorial engineering'. Municipalities collaborate in order to share a common vision of the territory. With the concept of the archipelago town, they share a spatial concept which helps them to imagine a common future. This concept provides a specific urban shape which helps to orientate the urban development.

SMSTs are not totally or systematically under the direct domination of the urban core of the urban region. Of course, they cannot implement the concept of the archipelago city, but, on the other hand, the main city which is usually the political leader in the urban region needs SMSTs. These have enough green space to substantiate the archipelago model. Using natural spaces to organize the future of a territory balances relationships and stimulates cooperation. Green spaces are localized and they cannot be replaced by external resources, which is why when the municipalities build a concept of archipelago town, they territorialize their development. They unify space at the scale of the urban region as a specific resource.

Notes

1 These urban areas are Marseille-Aix-en-Provence, Nantes, Rennes and Tours.
2 Sitadel2 is a database created by the French Statistics Institute (INSEE) based on the surface area (m^2) of non-residential buildings developed during a period.
3 For details on the method, see Serrano et al. (2014).
4 Directive territoriale d'aménagement.

References

Aubert, F., Georges-Marcelpoil, E. and Larmagnac, C. (2011) Les villes intermédiaires et leurs espaces de proximité – processus et scénarios. *Territoires 2040*(4): 107–27.

Bell, D. and Jayne, M. (2009) Small cities? Towards a research agenda. *International Journal of Urban and Regional Research*, 33(3): 683–99.

Colletis-Wahl, K., Corpataux, J., Crevoisier, O., Kebir, L., Pecqueur, B. and Peyrache-Gadeau, V. (2008) *The Territorial Economy: A General Approach in Order to Understand and Deal with Globalization*. Cheltenham: Edward Elgar.

Courlet, C. (2008) *L'économie territoriale*. Grenoble: Presses Universitaires de Grenoble.

Crevoisier, O. and Jeannerat, H. (2009) Les dynamiques territoriales de connaissance: relations multilocales et ancrage régional. *Revue d'Économie Industrielle*, 128: 77–99.

Demazière, C., Hamdouch, A. and Banovac, K. (2014) The changing profiles of small and medium-sized towns in the European context: Between residential economy, competitiveness and innovation. In A. Kwiatek-Sołtys, H. Mainet, K. Wiedermann and J.-C. Edouard (eds), *Small and Medium Towns' Attractiveness at the Beginning of the 21st Century*. Clermont-Ferrand: CERAMAC-PUBP, pp. 29–40.

Demazière, C., Hinfray, N., Nadou, F., Serrano, J., Servain, S., Lerousseau, N., Manson, C., Farthing, S., Hall, S., Smith, I., Douay, N., Bouba-Olga, O., Ferru, M. and Guimond, B. (2012) *Viabilité de l'économie productive des régions* urbaines: investigation à partir de la planification stratégique. *Une comparaison entre la France et l'Angleterre.* Tours: Citères.

Demazière, C., Serrano, J., Servain, S. and Nadou, F. (2013) *Between Innovation and Resistance: How Does Strategic Spatial Planning Balance Ecological Viability and Economic Development?* Dublin: University College Dublin.

Demazière, C., Serrano, J. and Vye, D. (2012) Les villes petites et moyennes et leurs acteurs: regards de chercheurs. *Norois*, 223: 7–13.

Depret, M.-H. and Hamdouch, A. (2009) Clusters, réseaux d'innovation et dynamiques de proximité dans les secteurs high-tech: une revue critique. *Revue d'Économie Industrielle*, 128: 21–52.

Dormois, R. (2007) Pour une analyse dynamique des ressources dans la conduite de l'action publique. In H. Gumuchian and B. Pecqueur (eds), *La ressource territoriale*. Paris: Economica-Anthropos, pp. 49–65.

Fache, J. and Hamdouch, A. (2014) Quand l'innovation forge les territoires, et vice-versa. *Bulletin de la Société Géographique de Liège*, 62: 25–33.

Halbert, L. (2005) Les métropoles, moteurs de la dématérialisation du système productif urbain français: une lecture sectorielle et fonctionnelle. *Bulletin de l'Association des Géographes Français*, 82: 277–99.

—— (2012) Collective and collaborative. Reflexive coordination and the dynamics of open innovation in clusters. *Urban Studies*, 49: 2357–76.

—— (2013) Les deux options métropolitaines de politiques de développement. *Annales de Géographie*, 689: 108–21.

Hamdouch, A. (2010) Conceptualizing innovation clusters and networks. In B. Laperche, P. Sommers and D. Uzunidis (eds), *Innovation Networks and Clusters: The Knowledge Backbone*. Brussels: Peter Lang, pp. 21–63.

Lussault, M. (2007) *L'homme spatial, la construction sociale de l'espace humain.* Paris: Seuil.

Michalet, C.A. (2007) *Mondialisation, la grande rupture.* Paris: La Découverte.

Mora, O. (2008) *Les nouvelles ruralités à l'horizon 2030.* Paris: Editions Quae.

Pecqueur, B. (2007) L'économie territoriale: une autre analyse de la globalisation. *Alternatives Économiques*, 33(1): 41–52.

Santamaria, F. (1999) *Les villes moyennes françaises: entre hiérarchie et réseaux (étude comparée avec l'Espagne et le Royaume-Uni).* Lille: Presses Universitaires du Septentrion.

—— (2012) Les villes moyennes françaises et leur rôle en matière d'aménagement du territoire: vers de nouvelles perspectives?. *Norois*, 223: 13–31.

Sassen, S. (2001) *The Global City: New York, London, Tokyo.* Princeton: Princeton University Press.

Saxenian, A.L. (2002) Transnational communities and the evolution of global production networks: The cases of Taiwan, China and India. *Industry and Innovation*, 9: 183–202.

Scott, A.J. (1996) Regional motors of the global economy. *Futures*, 28: 391–411.

Serrano, J. and Demazière, C. (2009) Développement économique et gestion de l'espace agricole et naturel, Les tensions au niveau local, le cas de l'agglomération de Tours (France). *Territoires Wallons*, 3: 123–34.

Serrano, J., Demazière, C., Nadou, F. and Servain, S. (2014) La planification stratégique spatialisée contribue-t-elle à la durabilité territoriale? La limitation des consommations foncières dans les schémas de cohérence territoriale à Marseille-Aix, Nantes-Saint-Nazaire, Rennes et Tours. *Développement Durable et Territoires*, 5(2): 18.

Vanier, M. (2005) La relation 'ville/campagne' ré-interrogée par la périurbanisation. *Les Cahiers Français*, 328: 13–17.
—— (2008) *Le pouvoir des territoires. Essai sur l'interterritorialité.* Paris: Economica, Anthropos.
Viard, J. (1990) *Le tiers espace, essai sur la nature.* Paris: Méridiens Lincksieck.

8 Potential and obstacles to creative planning in a crisis context

The case of the city of Patras in western Greece

Pavlos Marinos Delladetsima and John Loukakis

Introduction

During the 1990s, culture and creativity have emerged as key concepts of the spatial development and planning agenda (Kunzmann, 2004: 383–4). This evolution has partly occurred in response to increasing budgetary uncertainty imposed by the dominant austerity doctrines, forcing a search for alternative policy realms. Culture and subsequently creativity have turned out to be inherent policy dimensions – if not objectives – of the urban development and planning processes. The cultural parameters of spatial development have thus become a main policy thread of the local-regional administrations, expressed with the promotion of mega-events, flagship cultural investment initiatives and the overall emphasis placed on the cultural sector as economic activity, the establishment of cultural clusters (Chapain et al., 2010) and the designation of cultural neighbourhoods in the context of city branding and redevelopment strategies. The cultural thread has also 'internally' influenced planning itself, stipulating a problematic around 'planning cultures' related to their adaptability and their efficacy in introducing change in policy-making (Knieling and Otengrasen, 2009; Reimer, 2013). The notion of planning culture inhibits a wider perception of the process, which involves institutional-governance structures, formal and informal patterns of action, collaborative-participatory structures and sustainable development considerations. The cultural approach formed the basis for the development of the complementary notion of creativity (Andersson, 1985), which was also introduced into spatial development with the adoption of various perceptions such as 'creative industries', 'creative city' (Landry, 2008), 'creative capital' and 'creative classes' (Florida, 2002, 2008; Florida et al., 2008). These perceptions have had effective repercussions at the policy level and thus many cities in Europe (and internationally) introduced strategies to support creative initiatives, fostering a boost to innovation, entrepreneurship and economic growth. Cities today increasingly seek to be distinguished as 'creative cities' and to promote initiatives to sustain 'creative classes' as nested parts of a broader cultural policy domain. As to spatial planning, the influence of 'creativity' in theoretical evolution and practice is not yet highly pronounced – and here lies a central contribution of this book – although it has been expanding as a notion in various domains, sectors and at many distinct levels of the urban milieu. Obviously, creativity has been subject to different interpretations according to the specific scientific discipline, historical context or socio-economic cultural setting. A main trend on the research concerning creativity was based on individual behaviour vis-à-vis physiological approaches (Arieti, 1976). Based on the confluence theory of creativity (Lubart and Guignard, 2004), creativity has been approached as an outcome of both individual and societal potential. It has been argued, for instance, that in many cases, the creative potential of individuals is suppressed by a society that in principle stipulates intellectual conformity (Sternberg and Williams, 1996). Csikszentmihalyi (1999) added additional components (both cultural and social) to a systemic approach that gradually also included environmental considerations.

Among many approaches of creativity with valuable insinuations for spatial planning are those that place emphasis on socio-economic and cultural networks (Williams and Yang, 1999) and even more on socio-economic and institutional dynamics. Creative planning implies an overcoming of the conventional planning rationale and the rigidities of the prevailing planning culture, the understanding of the potentials and obstacles to change. It also implies the ability to mobilize socio-economic and governance-institutional assets in a proactive urban development strategy for servicing sustainable development and innovation objectives. Hence, the purpose of this chapter is to elaborate on the role of planning and its creative potential in contributing to local sustainable development and innovation in a distinct urban context. Understanding the role of creative planning policy actions and their dynamics in various contexts is strongly linked to the different urban development trajectories, planning traditions and associated governance structures. For this, a case study from Greece is examined: the port city of Patras (western Greece), which has assumed an essential role in the development of the new urbanization and developmental pattern in Greece throughout the last two decades (Delladetsima, 2012). The chapter focuses on the identification of factors determining the developmental potential of the city in question, together with factors that act as obstacles to it, and finally highlights the creative role of spatial planning in alleviating negative factors or encouraging positive factors in order to enhance the creation of a sustainable and innovative growth trajectory. In particular, it elaborates on the context of the current crisis and the extent to (and/or the preconditions under) which creative planning could assist in overcoming the prevailing negative trends.

Some key considerations about the development of the agglomeration

The city of Patras incorporates a long-standing historical pathway that is reflected as blueprints in its current urban structure (hence, the city embodies in continuity traces from the Prehistoric, Mycenaean, Classical Greek and Hellenistic era, while its most important historical period appears to be the Roman age, which was consecutively followed by periods of Byzantine, Venetian and Ottoman rule). In its modern history (especially since 1828), it became the second-biggest city in Greece and gradually throughout the nineteenth century established itself as the major exporting port of the country. During the twentieth century, it consolidated its role as a gateway to Western economies and as an important credit and industrial centre (Frangakis-Syrret, 1994). The contemporary spatial organization of the city maintains a linear structure along the sea front with a high-density development concentrated in the north and lower density in the south. The urban fabric is composed of the old city and the grid-planned centre (Despiniadou, 2000), which are surrounded by suburban growth areas (coastal and the high zones) generated by consecutive waves of urban sprawl.

The city of Patras is a medium-sized urban agglomeration in the European context and the third biggest in terms of population in Greece. Since the late 1960s, it has performed an up-and-coming role – as have other medium-sized cities in Greece – and to a certain extent has managed to resist the overpowering dominance (demographic, economic and political) of the two major agglomerations of the country: Athens and Thessaloniki. In the following decades, the city's economy re-emerged from an acute de-industrialization process by intensifying and diversifying its developmental pattern and absorbing the new waves of inter-regional migration flows. The city has acted as a primary factor in sustaining regional population outflows by strengthening its role as a service economy and as an international port. Seen in this context, Patras seems to be one of few cases of a medium-sized city able to benefit from opportunities derived from the changing economic conditions and to adjust positively to them. On the whole, the agglomeration – albeit in a disjointed manner and in the absence of any strategic component – has dynamically developed as a major regional-national centre and has sustained a relatively autonomous developmental path in relation to the Athens agglomeration. Administratively, the municipality of Patras is part of the Peripheral Unit (formerly the Prefecture of Achaia) belonging to the broader Periphery of Western Greece (see Figure 8.1).

The municipality (as determined by the amalgamation of the Patras former municipality and four adjacent municipalities) amounts to 213,984 permanent inhabitants, manifesting a tangible metropolitanization potential (2011

Figure 8.1 Location of the city of Patras
Source: Harokopio University (HUA)

census, EETAA 2012). The region increased its population by 7.46 per cent between 1991 and 2001, while it decreased by 2.62 per cent between 2001 and 2011. The population decreases experienced by the agglomeration partly reflects suburbanization dynamics and the expanding role of other adjacent minor urban centres of the periphery. Patras therefore plays a focal role within an accentuated urbanization – if not a metropolization process – that embraces the entire regional setting. As a matter of fact, approximately 30 per cent of the regional population is located in rural areas, three per cent in semi-rural areas (most of them adjacent to urban concentrations) and 66 per cent in urban areas (predominately in the city of Patras and the second-biggest regional urban centre, Aigio). On the whole, the urbanization process has focused on the north-western coastal area as a key geographical reference, while the mountain hinterland is faced with conditions of abandonment and decline (see Figure 8.2). In this context, 80 per cent

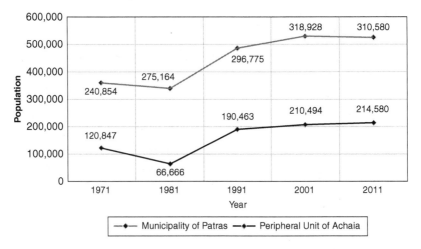

Figure 8.2 Population growth in the Peripheral Unit of Achaia and the city of Patras
Source: ELSTAT (1971, 1981, 1991, 2001, 2011), authors' elaboration

of the total population is concentrated in 14 per cent of its total surface; Patras, together with the city of Aigio, make up 58 per cent of the total population along a linear coastal strip.

Evidently, all the aforementioned imply agglomeration advantages, urbanization economies and other inherent factors that are embedded into the urban-structure which have sustained its development and can likely determine opportunities for innovative and sustainable future growth. Whereas this could become a feasible proposition, a lot will depend on the creativity of the governance system and decision-making process. In this respect, the next section tries to identify the major factors that currently determine the potential and developmental dynamics of the urban concentration.

Positive factors shaping the developmental dynamics of the agglomeration

The wider factors that in essence define the potential and positive potential of the city are the port and its economy, the Rio-Antirio Bridge, the presence of a strong knowledge infrastructure, the location of the city and the accessibility conditions, the labour market characteristics, the persistent industrial base, the agricultural hinterland, the role of the city as a core administrative pole, and the growth of service economy and its potential.

Table 8.1 Evaluation of the international importance of ports (western Greece)

	Ports	Commodities		Containers	Costal Shipping	Cruise	Yachts	Fishery
		General merchandise	Bulk shipments					
1	Patras (Peloponnese)	+	−	+	+	+	+	+
2	Igoumenitsa (NW Greece)	+	−	−	+	−	+	−
Ports of national importance W. Greece)								
1	Kyllini (Peloponnese)	+	−	−	+	−	+	+
2	Katakolo (Peloponnese)	+	−	−	+	+	+	+
3	Astakos (W Greece)	+	+	+	−	−	−	−
4	Mesolocggi (W Greece)	+	−	−	−	−	+	+

Source: National Strategy of Ports, Greek Ministry of Shipping & Aegean 2013–2018

The port and its economy

As stated above, the role of the port and its associated economy has historically acted as a critical factor in the development of the agglomeration. Nonetheless, there is always the impression that although the city did not benefit to the maximum from the port, the port's role has been undervalued. At the present time, however, expectations have risen due to the expansion/construction of a new port, which was intended to provide a new boost to trade and to the maritime and regional economy. The conversion of the former 'Patras Port Fund' into 'Patras Port Authority Ltd' also marks a trend towards privatization and it thus becomes difficult to evaluate the impact of the new port on the urban-regional economy, since the anticipated activities are bound to be both labour-intensive and export-oriented.

The impact of the old port (Pasgialis, 2008) on the regional economy (in terms of employment and income) has been rather limited. It provides approximately 100 direct and 1,100 indirect jobs in firms engaged in port-related sectors (auxiliary to transport activities, ship supplies, repair activities, logistics, food supplies and catering, crew recruitment, legal maritime firms, ticketing and freight brokers). On the whole, direct and indirect employment associated with the port amounts to 2.5 per cent of the periphery's total. It could thus be argued that two main factors have been impeding the growth of the port economy: first, the proximity of the harbour to the Athens agglomeration, as a result of which some port-related activities bypass the local market and are taken over by firms in the Greek capital; and, second, most commercial activity takes place via ferry boats including passengers, vehicles and cargo – two-thirds of the freight is carried by commercial lorries and trucks. All these manifest a reduced economic role of the port as a transport hub, competing predominately with the 'mainland routes' and not directly with other international ports. However, much can be expected from the new port, especially with the anticipated growth of sectors such as cargo services and international transport, acting a major transport integrated node in the national and international markets.

At the same time, Patras harbour is losing its commercial importance in relation to the other major port of Igoumenitsa in north-west Greece (see Table 8.1), while regional passenger ferry connections are shifting to the port of Kyllini (Peloponnese) and cargo containers to the Playtigialiou-Astakos port in mainland central-west Greece. The latter also includes a shipping-industrial area and is in a position to provide support for all cargo types (container shipment cargo, roll-on/roll-off, car terminal, general cargo, bulk and dangerous cargo). With the prospect of expanding its functional area and the improvement of highway connections (which are in progress), the port of Astakos may well become a major integrated node and an industrial shipping centre (see Table 8.1).

As regards passenger and private-commercial traffic (see Figures 8.3 and 8.4) during the period 2000–2008, the port of Patras, although still the

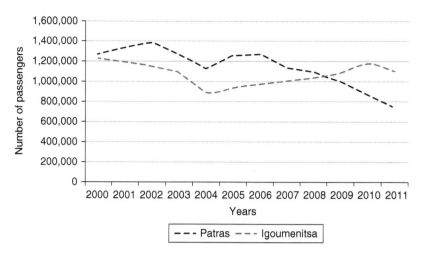

Figure 8.3 Transportation activity of the ports of Patras and Igoumenitsa (passengers)
Source: ELSTAT (2011), authors' elaboration

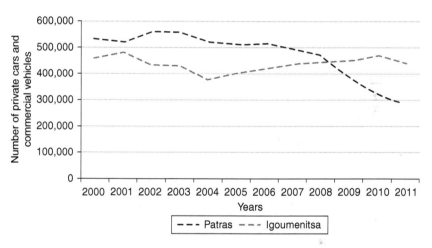

Figure 8.4 Transportation activity of the ports of Patras and Igoumenitsa (private cars and commercial vehicles)
Source: ELSTAT (2011), authors' elaboration

leading port in western Greece, experienced declining trends for the first time. Its role was utterly contracted in 2009, which was followed by an impressive loss of traffic during 2010–11 in favour of the port of Igoumenitsa. This was due to transport intensification generated by the functioning of the Egnatia international highway (connecting Igoumenitsa to north-east Greece and the

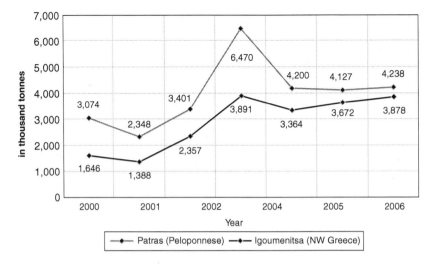

Figure 8.5 Transportation freight activity of the main ports of western Greece (commodities)
Source: Eurostat (2105), authors' elaboration

Balkan countries) to port improvements and lower shipping-transport costs. In particular, since 2008, Igoumenitsa became the most fast-growing port (in terms of passengers and vehicles) in western Greece. The port of Patras had sustained a positive performance in relation to the transport of commercial vehicles, due to its proximity to the Atheninan market, but in 2010–11, this was counterbalanced by the port of Igoumenitsa growth trends in the respective cargo categories.

In relation to cargo transport (see Figure 8.5), the port of Patras sustained a relative prevalence in relation to Igoumenitsa, which was significantly reduced in 2006 (360,000 tonnes). Thus, Patras harbour, under the competition it faced from the the ports of Igoumenitsa and Astakos, might well reduce its growth potential and in turn its role in the hinterland economy, affecting the development of links and networks with local sectors. In this respect, it may well be claimed that the weakened position of the old port and the anticipated turnover and added value increase that the new port will generate make the functioning of the latter an absolute priority (University of Patras, 2010: 12). Capturing value benefits for new port functioning and redistributing them to the local economy and society falls within the objectives of a creative planning agenda.

The Rio–Antirio Bridge

The Rio–Antirio Bridge (also known as the Charilaos Trikoupis Bridge) was completed in 2004 and became an international landmark. It is the world's

Potential and obstacles to creative planning 143

Figure 8.6 The Rio–Antirio Bridge
Source: P.M. Delladetsima (2013)

longest multi-span cable-stayed bridge (with a suspended deck of 2,250 m) connecting the Peloponnese with mainland Greece (see Figure 8.6). In combination with new transport infrastructure, the bridge has had an extensive impact by restructuring the geography of western Greece and of the region itself. At the national level, the bridge connects the two major highways of the country (Kalamata-Patras-Korinthos-Athens-Thessaloniki with Antirio-Ioannina and the port of Igoumenitsa) – the latter will in the future be replaced by the new Western highway, which is currently under construction. At the regional level, it has extended the catchment area of Patras by further incorporating, as part of a wider metropolitan economy, other agglomerations on the opposite coast of mainland Greece. This stipulates further economic integration involving many sub-markets like second home ownership, tourism and regional businesses.

There still remains a necessity to creatively approach the impact of the bridge in order to maximize (Pappas, 2005) locally embedded benefits by promoting employment and income generation initiatives (in logistics, retail/entertainment, conference and cultural initiatives); in essence, capturing benefits for the agglomeration from the exceptional opportunities (locational advantages, population and traffic flows) generated from the operation of the bridge. Of particular relevance in this case could be a proposed project (still in the consultation phase and presumably as a Public-Private Partnership concession scheme) concerning the redevelopment of a vacant former construction site (comprising a 223,000 square metre area and a 60,000 square metre built-up area) for new uses, such as hotels, a conference centre, an exhibition centre, marinas and a maritime industry centre.

The knowledge infrastructure

The city hosts three of the most important higher education institutions (HEIs) in the country: the University of Patras, the Technological Educational Institute (TEI) and the Open University of Greece, together with the Institute of Chemical Engineering and High Temperature Chemical Processes (ICE-HT) and a leading Science Park. The University of Patras offers higher education studies and research in all academic schools and scientific disciplines (natural sciences, engineering, health sciences, humanities and social sciences, economics and business administration). The second, the TEI, focuses on skill provision and on applied research technology directly associated with the labour market demands. The third is the Hellenic Open University, which provides long-distance tertiary education and lifelong learning via the elaborate technological-educational systems.

As part of this HEI knowledge potential of the area of relevance is the Patras Science Park (established as a technological/innovation hub), which promotes the development of innovative firms through spin-off/spin-out processes and cooperation between HEIs and research centres and industry. Nowadays, it contains a number of innovative enterprises in Information and Communication Technology (ICT), biotechnology, green energy and industrial technologies. Furthermore, the city hosts the ICE-HT academic institute, which became the first founding institute in the country of a national research network. Also of relevance is the Patras InnoHub, which aims to provide small and medium-sized companies of the region with office facilities, qualified labour support and access to regional, national and international markets (RUnUP Thematic Network, 2005).

There is therefore an unquestionable strong knowledge infrastructure (KI) that has not at the same time managed to foster effective capacity building (CB) in the regional setting. The KI maintains a rather confined role and has not contributed substantially to the generation of an innovative environment (involving spillovers and added-value products and services) not becoming an integral part of the local and regional socio-economic structure (Tsekouras et al., 2005). Moreover, in the absence of a systematic KI and CB strategy, the knowledge transfer process by HEI and research-driven actions is not translated into any integral outcome in the regional economy. As a matter of fact, this is partly revealed when examining information related to research and development (R&D) and innovation. At the peripheral level, total expenditure for R&D and innovation reached €72,146 milion

(Eurostat, 2011); the area is ranked fourth (5.2 per cent of the national expenditure) in the hierarchy among the 13 administrative peripheries of the country. It is also ranked (4th) among all peripheries in the country in relation to R&D share of GDP (0.75 per cent), which is higher than the national average (0.67 per cent), but lower than the EU average and evidently far lower than the eurozone (2.12 per cent). Nevertheless, when we come to employment, 86.1 per cent of employees in R&D is absorbed by HEIs, 9 per cent by the private sector and 4.9 per cent by the public administration (Eurostat, 2011), indicating the confined character of KI and its impact on the regional economy. In view of a more creative approach, the strong KI basis constitutes a major potential for innovative development and sustainable growth, which is responsive to both the commercial and social needs of the urban region.

Accessibility improvements: highway and railway connections

The agglomeration is situated in a privileged geographical location which could have been decisively improved in terms of accessibility had the highway and railway connections been completed (the upgrading/construction of the Patras–Athens highway and the respective new railway). On the whole, the region is experiencing many delays in terms of benefiting from the new transport infrastructure due to administrative bottlenecks and the effects of the crisis environment that directly influenced financing. This is particularly prominent in all major works concerned with the development of trans-European, inter- and intra-regional networks, which in turn affected the viability and operation of other main infrastructure projects such as the port and the Rio-Antirio Bridge. At the same time, the agglomeration lacks a hierarchically structured road network allowing for effective connections between international-national and regional transportation routes. In this respect, a key area of a creative planning approach in relation to accessibility conditions could include the integration of transportation and land use plans, and the timely and coordinated provision of urban infrastructure, which for the time being does not form part of the regional-local policy agenda.

The labour market

Irrespective of the conditions and problems experienced by the urban region and exacerbated by the current crisis conditions, the labour market of the area still inhibits a considerable level of potential that could form a critical component in structuring a creative approach. This is primarily defined by the variety of employment sectors operating in the economy and by the presence of a young qualified labour force. The regional economy – as conditioned principally by the Patras agglomeration – shows considerable divergences when compared to the national breakdown of sectors of economic activity.

In 1991–2001, the labour market started to exhibit its foremost negative features that were manifested in the following periods (Tsekouras et al., 2002) and as a matter of fact in 2010–13, the area experienced, among other adverse effects, sharp unemployment increases (Ergani – Information System, 2013). The labour market is also determined by its relatively small size and the prevalence of family-owned and run SMEs, which together shape an inward-looking entrepreneurship with a low export orientation. Moreover, the small and fragmented business structure develops in the absence of associative institutions and collaborative actions that could in turn result in more effective access to EU and other forms of funding (Chalari and Kaminioti, 2005). The situation is further aggravated by the absence of effective vocational training and re-skilling institutions, and by the lack of information dissemination mechanisms and knowledge support for local enterprises.

Changes in the local economy and labour market, in the last decades, produced a discrepancy between the supply of skills-expertise and local labour market demand (Data RC, 2010, 2012). The intermediate and high-ranking employees are in principle absorbed by external markets, especially the main metropolitan areas of the country. Although the average employment age in the region is relatively low compared to national levels and the periphery (< 35.4 years), there is an accentuated mismatch between skills availability and employment demand (Chalari and Kaminioti, 2005). It is thus increasingly difficult for young qualified people to gain access to the more advanced employment sectors (the manufacturing sector, the port economy and knowledge-based industries), since the local labour market tends to gravitate increasingly towards conventional service sector activities (see Figure 8.7). An imperative outcome of this situation is the predominant role of those 'customer-facing skills' mostly demanded in retail and leisure, which increase the level of competition for youth labour for the same job types.

The persistent industrial base

The agglomeration of Patras has a long-standing industrial tradition, being historically one of the main manufacturing centres of Greece. Confirmation of this is given by the presence of two organized industrial infrastructures: the industrial zone and the industrial park. However, the participation of the secondary sector in the peripheral employment structure underwent significant decline during recent years, reaching 13 per cent in 2013 (compared to 15.8 per cent nationally). The same trends can be seen both regionally and in the agglomeration.

Since the late 1980s and 1990s, the urban region has experienced an acute de-industrialization process, critically affecting its economic structure and causing widespread unemployment. The manufacturing sector in the area faced significant recession, experiencing a decline of 7.5 per cent between 1995 and 2001. The losses of the manufacturing sector have been counterbalanced by the growth of the construction sector (accounting for

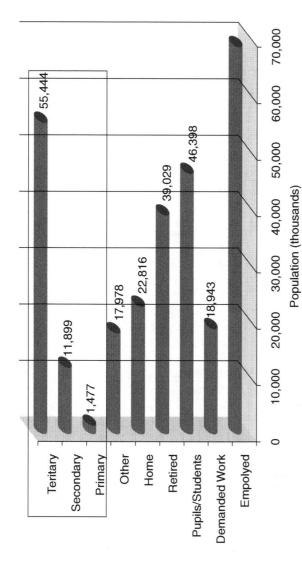

Figure 8.7 Workers and population by sector of economic activity, city of Patras, 2011
Source: ELSTAT (2011), authors' elaboration

8.7 per cent of gross added value) and related industrial activities (building material and equipment). Despite the de-industrialization process, the sector remains the third largest in Greece (comprising 3.4 per cent of GNP) and is composed mainly of sub-sectors such as food and drink, textiles, clothing, non-metallic minerals, machinery and equipment. Moreover, 17.4 per cent of the manufacturing businesses have experienced a relative positive growth during the last five years; interestingly enough, 40 per cent of these are concentrated in sectors that perform negatively at the national level. However, the main trend governing the sector is the constant reduction of bigger units (> 10 employees) and the growing share of SMEs in the regional economy (Data RC, 2010, 2012). This trend is further accentuated by existing crisis conditions and the lack of investment initiatives. Nevertheless, the sector still maintains a gravitational significance, thus constituting a strategic parameter in search of a more creative planning strategy for the conurbation.

The agricultural sector and the hinterland

Overall, primary sector activities still comprise an important share of income and employment as compared with other areas in the periphery and in Greece as a whole. The primary sector in the region absorbs 20 per cent of the economically active population and contributes 11.6 per cent to the Regional Gross Product. Also of relative significance is the fisheries sector, which comprises a professional fishing fleet and a fish-pier. Nevertheless, the participation of the primary sector in the employment structure has increased substantially since 2012, presumably due to the growing crisis and the attempts by some strata to seek alternative employment solutions in agriculture. Overall, economic activity in the primary sector between 1995–2001 and 2001–11 has on average declined by 2 per cent.

Agriculture is particularly strong along the coastal zones and in the western territories, producing a number of export-oriented but also local market products (e.g. olive oil, viniculture, citrus fruits, horticultural products, greenhouse potatoes, currants, industrial tomato farming, cotton, animal farming and dairy products). A conflicting situation results in the sense that high-productivity land is located in the coastal areas, where at the same time the most intense suburbanization-urban sprawl and second home-ownership trends are concentrated. In addition, the sector is faced with problems of property fragmentation, lack of entrepreneurship and training, poor commercialization-distribution networks and the overall crisis in cooperative institutions of the last decade. Yet, irrespective all the aforementioned problems, there are unquestionable relative advantages of the agricultural sector for the region (arable areas, water resources, mild climatic conditions, agricultural traditions and skills, the existence of agro-food complexes, etc.) which embody a potential towards conventional agriculture growth and alternative initiatives in bio-food farming.

The city as a core administrative pole

The city accumulates other than the conventional administrative institutions that is the headquarters of the municipality, the Sub-peripheral Unit, the Periphery and a range of other public, semi-public institutions, economic and professional chambers, associations and non-governmental organizations (NGOs). To these could be added the headquarters of the peripheral administration of Western Greece and the Ionian Islands, a central entity in charge of controlling finances of the peripheral and local institutions. Eventually, the municipality has become the most active institution in fostering local development and planning initiatives. Until recently, the municipal administrations have promoted initiatives such as the development of a small industry and handicraft park, a cooperative bank (jointly with the Chamber of Achaia), the Patras InnoHub (mentioned above), the Enterprise for Touristic Development and the Centre of E-commerce.

The growth of the service economy

At the level of the periphery, the tertiary sector seems to be the leading one in terms of employment generation and income. On average, tertiary sector employment in (2013 amounted to 61.3 per cent of the workforce, which is significantly lower than the national average (70.6 per cent). Interestingly, this difference appears to have increased further during 2014–15, presumably due to the economic crisis and the tendency that has indirectly stimulated employment growth in agriculture and service activities. Conventional services are still the leading ones in the sector, however, international sea transportation, health services and education have gained an increased share that in a way differentiates the economy of the Patras agglomeration from others in the country. In many respects, the city – taking into account the presence of HEIs, a young educated labour market, research centres, the port economy enterprises and architectural studios – embodies the potential to act as a niche (UNCTAD, 2010; Scheffel and Thomas, 2011) for knowledge exchange (Marrocu and Paci, 2012), specialized production and creative job growth.

Obstacles to innovative and sustainable development of the agglomeration

Contrary to all the aforementioned points, there are other socio-economic and cultural factors that hinder innovation and sustainable development in the agglomeration. The first – as stated already – concerns the inherent characteristics deriving from the small and fragmented market, which poses severe obstacles to innovative development. Irrespective of the existing strong KI basis, CB is hampered by the peculiarities of a market characterized by the coexistence of both economically advanced and underdeveloped sectors. This polarization creates pressing difficulties for HEIs – and related knowledge infrastructure – interaction with local socio-economic systems. In conjunction, there is also a prevailing weak entrepreneurial culture that does not make it possible to foster local collaborative actions. Consequently, the region is characterized by an overall lack of drive for innovation from the local communities and businesses, together with a low local awareness of the KI potential existing within the regional setting. Evidently, all these have detrimental effects on the employment structure and unemployment rates. As a result, most initiatives between HEIs, local institutions and business tend to trickle down, as in occasional collaboration and ad hoc partnerships, or 'forcefully' emerge as a precondition to gain access to financing, especially from EU institutions. For this reason, many innovative initiatives seem to have a very confined or even negligible impact on the local economy and society, irrespective of the resources and the high costs involved.

Second, a key problem affecting the agglomeration is the exacerbated increase in unemployment as a direct effect of the current economic crisis and disinvestment, Unemployment rates in the periphery experienced dramatic increases during the last three years, reflecting general trends at the national level (nearly double the EU average). More specifically, unemployment reached 28.5 per cent in 2013 and 29.9 per cent in 2014, which was higher than the national average. Even in the past and especially during the period 1998–2003, unemployment in Achaia was higher compared the national average and since then it has predominately affected the 20–24 age group. Unemployment rates experienced striking increases from 2009 to 2013, with far higher rates than the national average, mostly affecting the young, female workers and the long-term unemployed generated throughout this whole time. On the whole unemployment appears as a core developmental obstacle. As such, this raises an urgent need to promote job provision schemes, especially among the most vulnerable groups, and to actively engage the governance system and employers' organizations in both the policy process and in the labour market itself.

Third, another factor negatively affecting the process concerns physical development patterns and the scarcity in development control vis-à-vis land use planning policy (Pappas, 2005). Thus, the agglomeration is experiencing a twofold negative trend: an increase in population and building densities and uncontrolled sprawl. Set in this context, the planning process in the conurbation has proved unable to systematically enforce a regulative environment, thus perpetuating a worsening situation in the central areas (high densities, real estate prices, traffic congestion and pollution) and in the peripheral areas (affected by acute sprawl trends consuming landed assets from agricultural, forest and coastal areas). In other words, the city is confronted with agglomeration disadvantages that are in principle encountered in the biggest metropolitan areas of the country and in many respects are not easily justifiable, taking into account its medium size, available resources and governance structures.

Fourth, the operation of many local economic circuits (entertainment, commerce, recreation/retail, food businesses, transport and housing) targeting predominately the young student population appear as the leading and expanding economic activities and absorb most of the local investment capital. This to a certain extent constitutes an obstacle to new investment, diverting valuable resources away from innovative and productive initiatives.

Fifth, the governance system is based on a fragmented structure involving central state departments and institutions (such as the peripheral administrations and centrally controlled regional institutions), the periphery (democratically elected regional and sub-regional institutions) and the municipality at the local level. The array of institutions normally involved in planning and spatial development is indicative of a complex decision-making process. The situation is further complicated by scarcities resulting from the 1994 and 2010 administrative reforms (Law 2218/1994 and Law 3852/07/07/2010), which did not provide sufficient transparency in terms of the allocation of new competencies and funds. The planning process is thus hindered by overlapping and contradictory competences causing significant delays or even inertia. This disjointed framework is reflected in an inherent inability to formulate an effective spatial strategy. Spatial planning thus becomes a compartmentalized practice, dealing mostly with land-owning interests (Delladetsima, 2006, 2012) and, in the absence of collective social negotiative mechanisms, involving the state and the urban communities.

A role for creative planning

Spatial planning in the agglomeration – and hence its weak planning culture – relies heavily on a physical deterministic blueprint rationale, simple land use plans and development control practices. This rationale has remained practically unaltered as determined by the philosophy (Act 947/1979, Law 1337/82 and Law 2508/97) paying negligible attention to a strategic component (something that was only introduced by the recent Law 4269/2014, which has not yet been implemented). A major strategic leading objective as the compact city (higher densities, mixed uses, intensification of the urban fabric, sprawl containment) was introduced in the Master Plan of Patras (*Ryrthmistico Sxedio*, in compliance with Law 2508/97) The Master Plan constituted the first systematic attempt to regulate the wider metropolization process in the region. However, the Plan was not implemented and proved to be in conflict with conventional economic, social and physical developmental patterns.

Broadly speaking, in the current state of affairs, spatial planning is detached from other economic, social, environmental and cultural policies, and, as a result, developmental and innovation initiatives assume an ad hoc character. This has also been revealed by the inability of the city to systematically benefit from the organization of such mega-events such as venues of the Olympic Games in 2004 and being designated the Cultural Capital of Europe in 2006.

Both experiences were rather unsuccessful with respect to the benefits generated for the local/regional economy and society (EU-CE, 2010). The same applies to long-term projects and programmes related to big infrastructure projects such as the Rio-Antirio Bridge, the new rail and suburban rail connections, the new western Ionian highway axis, the construction of the new harbour, the expansion of the port installations and the reuse of the old port area (Argyriadou, 2008; Kordos, 2009; Dimas et al., 2010). Moreover, the local governance system and especially the local authorities have no active development role in strategic economic development through networking with key local partners such as HEIs, the science park, the port and the business centre. At a lower level, the system further contributes to this inertia with a scarcity of policies concerning the land-use plan implementation process, development control, sprawl trends management, traffic and parking issues, and protection of the peri-urban space and the coastal front.

Thus, the case of Patras clearly constitutes an example of a city that embeds most important developmental potential (in terms of its geography, economy, social capital, knowledge-based infrastructure and cultural assets) that proves to be unable to valorize by mobilizing its creative milieu, deriving from multivariate social, economic and cultural assets. As a consequence, what emanates from this situation is a need for a more 'creative planning' approach, which can combine physical planning, social, economic, cultural and environmental policies, and valorize many features of the previously described potentialities. Set in this context, what is required is the harmonization of 'big investments' (the new port, the Rio-Antirio Bridge, the anticipated improvements in the highway and railway networks) with the economic, social and environmental dynamics of the urban region. In addition, other priorities that emerge are: the generation of synergy networks between the port economy and local enterprises; the provision of innovative services to local SMEs by the existing KI; the provision vocational training schemes by local institutions for distinct social population groups (the young population, female workers and the long-term unemployed) of the local labour market; and the support of conventional sectors of the economy (agriculture, manufacturing) in the local and national markets.

References

Andersson, A. (1985) Creativity and regional development. *Papers of the Regional Science Association*, 56: 5–20.

Argyriadou, E.S. (2008) *Study for Potential Land Use Development, Valorization of the Road Axis Adjacent to the Port of Patras, Determination of Alternative Recommendations and Contribution to Sustainable Development*. Summary Report, Prefecture Development Agency. Patras: Prefecture of Achaia (in Greek).

Arieti, S. (1976) *Creativity: The Magic Synthesis*. New York: Basic Books.

Chapain, C., Cooke, P., De Propris, L., MacNeill L.S. and Mateos-Garcia, J. (2010) *Creative Clusters and Innovation*. London: NESTA.

Charari, A. and Kaminioti, O. (2005) *Demand for Specialties and Skills in the Private Sector of Achaia Prefecture*. Research Report Summary. Patras: Employment Observatory IT Research Ltd (in Greek).

Csikszentmihalyi, M. (1999) Implications of a systems perspective for the study of creativity. In R. J. Sternberg (ed.), *Handbook of Creativity*. New York: Cambridge University Press, pp. 313–35.

Data RC (2010) *Annual Report on the Economy and Labour Market of the Periphery of W. Greece*. Patras: Data RC (in Greek).

—— (2012) *Labour Market Analysis*. Patras: Data RC (in Greek).

—— (2014) *Report on the Labour Market-Investment and Development of the Periphery of Western Greece, Proceedings: 2nd International Conference: Development Prospects for W. Greece*. Patras, Greece, 12–13 April (in Greek).

Delladetisma, P.M. (2006) The emerging property development pattern in Greece and its impact on spatial Development. *European Urban and Regional Studies*, 13(3): 245–78.

—— (2012) Sustainable development and spatial planning: Some considerations arising from the Greek case. *European Journal of Spatial Development*, 46(12): 11–17.

Despiniadou, V. (2000) Property, plan and use transformations of a block in the historical centre of Patras. *Technica Chronica*, II(1–2): 9–29.

Dimas, A., Pappas, V. and Tsekouras, K. (2010) *Patras Sea Front-Port-City, Research Programme*, vols 1–7. Patras: University of Patras (in Greek).

Ergani – Information System (2013) *Salaried Labour Employment in the Private Sector*. Athens: Ministry of Labour-Social Security and Welfare (in Greek).

EU-CE (2010) *Patras: Results of the Intercultural Cities Index*, Intercultural Cities programme (ICC), Joint Action of the Council of Europe and the European Commission.

Eurostat (2011) http://ec.europa.eu/eurostat/web/science-technology-innovation/data/database.

Florida, R. (2002) *The Rise of the Creative Class*. New York: Basic Books.

—— (2008) *Who's Your City? How the Creative Economy is Making Where to Live the Most Important Decision of Your Life*. New York: Basic Books.

Florida, R., Mellander, C. and Stolarick, K. (2008) Inside the black box of regional development – Human capital, the creative class and tolerance. *Journal of Economic Geography*, 8: 615–49.

Frangakis-Syrret, E. (1994) Monoculture in nineteenth-century Greece and the port-city of Patras. *Journal of the Hellenic Diaspora*, 20(2): 9–34.

Hellenic Enterprise for Local Government and Development (EETAA) (2012) *Comparison of Population Censuses 2001–2011*. Athens: EETAA (in Greek).

—— (2012) *Population and Housing Census for Permanent Population*. Piraeus: ELSTAT (in Greek).

Hellenic Statistical Authority (ELSTAT) (2013) *Research on Labour Market Potential*. Piraeus: ELSTAT (in Greek).

Knieling, J. and Otengrasen, F. (2009) *Planning Cultures in Europe*. Farnham: Ashgate.

Kordos, N. (2009) Planning facets for the Patras port zone. NTUA Thesis. Athens: NTUA.

Kunzmann, K.R. (2004) Culture, creativity and spatial planning. *TPR*, 75(4): 383–404.

Landry, C. (2008) *The Creative City: A Toolkit for Urban Innovators*. London: Earthscan.

Lubart, T.I. and Guignard, J.H. (2004) The generality-specificity of creativity: A multivariate approach. In R.J. Sternberg, E.L. Grigorenko and J.L. Singer (ed.), *Creativity: From Potential to Realization*. Washington, DC: American Psychological Association, pp. 43–56.

Marrocu, E. and Paci, R. (2012) Education or creativity: What matters most for economic performance? *Economic Geography*, 88: 369–401.

Müller, K., Rammer, C. and Trüby, J. (2009) The role of creative industries in industrial innovation. *Innovation: Management, Policy & Practice*, 11(2): 148–68.

Municipality of Patras Working Group, (2013) *Appraisal Reorganization of Structures of Patras Municipality*. Patras: Municipality of Patras.

Observatory for Employment IT Research (2008) *Demand for Specialties and Skills in the Sub-peripheral Unit of Achaia: Summary of Research Results in Private Enterprises*. Patras: IT Research (in Greek).

Pappas, V. (2005) The Rio-Antirio connection: From the continuity to the discontinuity of a metropolitan phenomenon. *Conference Proceedings: Metropolis Geography: Facets of the Phenomenon*, Thessaloniki, Greece, 21–22 October (in Greek).

Pasgialis, A. (2008) IT-Port – Innovative harbour technologies improvement and local development. INTEREGG III, Greece-Italy 2006–2010. Patras: Port Authority of Patras (in Greek).

Reimer, M. (2013) Planning cultures in transition: Sustainability management and institutional change in spatial planning. *Sustainability*, 5: 4653–73.

RUnUP Thematic Network (2005) *Conclusions and Recommendations*. Final Report, Project URBACT II. Brussels: EU.

Scheffel, E. and Thomas, A. (2011) Employment and intangible spending in the UK's creative industries. *Economic and Labour Review*, January.

Sternberg, R.J. and Williams, W.M. (1996) *How to Develop Student Creativity*. Alexandria, VA: Association for Supervision and Curriculum Development.

Tsekouras, C., Skouras, D. and Tsegenidi, K. (2002) *Employees Study for the Periphery of W. Greece, WISE: Western Greece Region Integrated Strategy for Employment Stimulation*. Patras: University of Patras.

—— (2005) *Analysis and Findings from Recent Studies on Achaia, Restructuring by Innovations in Achaia*. Patras: University of Patras, Department of Economic Sciences (in Greek).

United Nations Conference on Trade and Development (UNCTAD) (2010) *Creative Economy a Feasible Development Option*. New York: UNDP Special Unit for South-South Cooperation.

University of Patras (2010) *Patras Waterfront, Port, City: Research Programme. Economic Impact Form on the Functioning of the Port, 07*. Patras: University of Patras (in Greek).

Williams, W.M. and Yang, L.T. (1999) Organizational creativity. In R. J. Sternberg (ed.), *Handbook of Creativity*. New York: Cambridge University Press, pp. 373–91.

9 Territory vs. function
Ambitions and tensions in the creation of a new urban neighbourhood

Nils Aarsæther and Halvard Vike

Introduction

The purpose of this study is to analyze a unique process of planning and constructing a completely new urban neighborhood in the Norwegian capital region. In particular, the aim is to show how an outright territorial approach in this respect challenged the modernist principle of functional organization of governance and public service provisions. As very few planning efforts today have the privilege of starting from scratch, the learning potentials from this process may at first sight seem modest. However, the motivations of the planners and, most significantly, the challenges they encountered in the phase of implementation make this case relevant to the discussion on how to develop sustainable urban neighborhoods.

In this study, we discuss the preconditions for and barriers to creating a territorial order in an environment that offers exceptional conditions for deploying such an order and its further development. By "territorial order," we refer to institutions that are sensitive to people's needs in their local context. The Fornebu case, we argue, is of special interest not only because its scope and ambitions were in line with a critique of excessive functional specialization (Friedmann and Weaver, 1979: 7; Healey, 1997: 292), but also because the planners were able to start from scratch, as in the "New Towns" tradition (Stein, 1951, Healey, 1997). With the former airport area cleared, the planners had a unique opportunity to form the new neighborhood according to their ideas, without having to adapt to barriers created by an existing built environment or a bureaucratic service provision system operating on functionalist principles.

The empirical basis of the study is the Fornebu area, i.e. the site of the former national airport in Norway which was closed down in 1995 when the new national airport at Gardermoen was opened. The Fornebu area is located in the Bærum municipality, adjacent to Oslo. From its inception, the municipal planning efforts for the "liberated" area were based on "territorialist" ideas. The ultimate goal was to create a dwelling environment in which inhabitants were offered easy access to public and private services, to nature and leisure, and to employment possibilities in service sectors and high-tech firms, all within walking/bicycling distance, for a prospective population of about 14,000 inhabitants. Due to the long-lasting period of national airport functions in the area, several leading firms, which together employed 10,000 people, had their offices located close to the airport.

The potentials of linking a bourgeoning private sector job market to a new dwelling area spurred the planners of the Bærum municipality to embark on a process to create an ecologically and socially sustainable new neighborhood. Guided by what can be called an integrationist, territorial principle, the municipality's planning approach was to be reflected in the development of public services in the area. New service functions were planned to be offered from a small number of integrated "village centers" with at least a partial breakdown of professional and institutional boundaries between education, childcare, libraries, sports facilities and welfare services. In the following, we will tell the story of the Fornebu experiment and will then provide some analytical reflections on what it may take to pursue a territorially oriented, integrationalist planning approach that may survive confrontations with conventional forms of administrative control.

This study began with an invitation from the Development Unit of the Bærum municipality to individual researchers representing various institutions to participate in an evaluation of the Fornebu experiment in providing integrated municipal services. The purpose was to finance a larger evaluation project, but due to problems related to obtaining external financing, a downscaled evaluation project was carried out. In 2008 and 2010, the municipality financed the work of research assistants who conducted interviews, administered surveys and performed on-site observations in the "village centers." Two project reports from the fieldwork periods were submitted to the municipality (Dyrkorn, 2008; Sverdrup et al., 2011). In addition, the present study is based on municipal documents and the authors' participation in a series of meetings with the Development Unit from 2007 to 2011.

Theory: territory and function

The tension between territory and function acts as a theoretical point of departure for the analysis of the Fornebu case. Roughly speaking, the process of modernization has led to increasing levels of differentiation and specialization in society. It entails the dissolution of multi-purpose (traditional) institutions, which served to integrate local populations according to a social logic in which social roles were not clearly separated (Offe, 1996: 6, Castells, 1997: 60). As such, the modernization may be interpreted as a response to what came to be seen as the deficiencies of traditional society's "unproductive" mixing of activities and social spheres. In modern society, progress in numerous areas of life has been grounded in economic and professional specialization, and institutions are formed (and reformed) on the basis of specialized scientific knowledge and its practical applications.

Indeed, modern society may express itself as a conglomerate of a broad range of specialized functions, both private and public, that organize various aspects of citizens' lives. However, the logic behind functional specialization generates vertical patterns of power and communication, and forms of service provision which may correspond poorly to people's needs. Most people's lives and needs are embedded in social relations that are to a large extent locally based. Needs may be better satisfied if the organization of service provision promotes sensitivity to identities and social relations, which are specific to localities rather than to the functional requirements of a professional environment and to the New Public Management dictum of making services cost-efficient.

Modern, specialized society is geared toward producing economic growth and an array of tangible products and in-person services. In the European context, this dynamic is clearly expressed in the role of the welfare state. However, the specialization or "functional" logic inherent to the process of modernization has undermined the ability of individuals, families and communities to reproduce solutions that are essential to their well-being. In the era of globalization, advanced specialization is dissolving geographical barriers due to the principle of comparative advantages. Hence, the idea of a geographically delineated local community has been rendered outdated (Castells, 1997: 61). However, the functional specialization of the productive system does not necessarily coincide with the way most people live their lives. Dysfunctions generated by the logic of specialization have emerged in the form of a lack of coordination and connections between multiple specialized services and activities. At the micro level, this problem may produce a sense of estrangement for citizens because each service only affects specific elements of a person's total life situation. At the level of the local community, excessive functional specialization and the centralization processes which tend to go with it may entail a loss of local identity due to the absence of institutions and arenas that formerly brought people together.

Urban planning, which in Norway is the task of elected local government institutions, has been performed for over a century and involves applying advanced knowledge to counter or modify the externalities produced by excessive specialization (Jacobs, 1974; Tyler and Ward, 2011). When urban planning has preceded and guided private investments, government institutions have indeed been able to manage emerging or expanding cities. However, the underlying principle of urban planning has been to adhere to a "functional" worldview by allocating certain areas to specialized activities using zoning mechanisms. Under this worldview, housing, industry, traffic, trade and leisure activities should be segregated and connected by transport corridors. During recent decades, however, urban planning activities seem to have been overtaken by the swift actions of private developers. Technological innovations, industrial restructuring needs, the sheer speed of private and public sector venture growth, and neo-liberal policies of non-interference in urban development have, in many cases, left planning institutions hopelessly behind (Beauregard, 1989). This state of affairs is exacerbated by the fact that the planning profession failed to include cultural and social competencies for quite some time, a shortcoming that has rendered planners unable to come up with solutions in the face of increasingly heterogeneous urban populations (Young, 2008).

The need for the coordination of activities and services in a territorial setting can be responded to by both inter-sectoral top-down solutions and by measures such as "bottom-up" local organizational strategies (Friedmann, 1987: Chapter 9). Bottom-up approaches differ from intersectoral approaches by taking the local communities or areas as their point of departure. Such approaches are normally anchored politically in the system of micro-democratic organizations, i.e. municipal, community, or neighborhood councils. In general, territorial approaches to public service organization resonate well with people's everyday experiences in the cities or communities where they live (MacCallum et al., 2009) Therefore, citizens' well-being and the attractiveness of urban localities are positively influenced by territorial approaches to the extent that services offered are user-directed and interconnected. However, within the material framework that is shaped by current ideas about management, and in the contexts of insufficient legal and economic resources available to local authorities and organizations, it is a demanding task to create and sustain local environments in which the various amenities are coordinated by bottom-up strategies.

Prerequisites for achieving territorial reason

Municipalities may be organized with geographical borders that coincide with the local community area and with a local commitment to place, but most often municipalities comprise several local communities. In the case of Bærum, with a population of more than 100,000, the relations between the community/neighborhood level and the municipal level will be a critical factor. There are hardly any reasons to assume that the process of creating integrated services in a new neighborhood as a smooth, linear process in which the decision-making powers of the municipality itself is sufficient to achieve this aim. On the contrary, many types of actors will be involved, in particular organized civil society actors, and not least the citizens/users in the new neighborhood. The relations between these actors and the planners are important, but so too is the "ideological" work to be carried out in order to translate what the territorial idea is about and to anchor this idea in relevant centers of power, i.e. among actors that normally will think and operate in a functionalist-modernist manner:

A. *Bureaucratic commitment to integrated public services*: the first prerequisite is to establish some kind of mutual understanding and achieve support for the territorial scheme at the level of public service providers. This means that the service personnel and leaders recruited must be informed about, and motivated for, working in an inter-services organization, sharing the same roof. The planners themselves may be easily committed to the territorial idea, but other types of personnel will not have received this form of training from previous or educational experiences. T. Veblen's classical statement of "trained incapacity" (Merton, 1940) is a useful reminder in this context.

B. *Public–civil society partnerships*: the second precondition is the linking of voluntary organizations to the new public service system. Although such partnerships are functional and task-specific, they contribute to territorialization by displaying a mode of problem solving that draws on local community resources. According to Putnam's (2000: 22) analysis of *bridging* social capital, the existence of overlapping memberships in voluntary associations has a profound and positive effect on territorial integration, and a successful municipal/voluntary nexus is expected to enhance local creativity and to lubricate cross-sectoral agency.

C. *Citizen empowerment*: as a third component of territorial organization, we propose a focus on micro-democratic structures in the form of e.g. informal neighborhood organizations, formal community councils, and housing cooperatives. Such boards or councils may be initiated by the municipality, but may even be formed autonomously, without formal relationships with the municipality. They can empower the inhabitants of an area to voice their suggestions and demands vis-à-vis the municipality and can produce local solutions on their own or in interaction with other actors whose presence affects the well-being of the inhabitants (Friedmann, 1987: 360 ff.)

D. *Translation and anchoring*: the fourth precondition involves the translation of the territorial planning vision into political and administrative terms. Clearly, any type of administrative organization challenging a system of classical bureaucratic departmentalism is likely to encounter problems, and thus there will be a need to anchor and legitimize the experiment, in particular among elected politicians and administrative leaders of the municipality.

Following this reasoning, we hypothesize that successful territorial organization will depend on the ability of the municipality to organize cross-sectoral service production, to build connections with voluntary organizations that can form the basis for public–civil society partnerships (including business sector partnerships), to create or recognize channels for the recognition of citizens' demands based on democratic principles, to translate its significance in political terms, and to communicate its potentials and merits to a wider audience.

From national airport to a new neighborhood

At the local level, the territorial institution *par excellence* is the municipality. The legal powers vested in the municipal institution by the Planning and

Building Act (1966, 2008) have enabled the municipality of Bærum to take control over planning in the Fornebu area, an area that was partly owned by outside actors (the Norwegian government and the municipality of Oslo) at the time when the Norwegian Parliament decided to close the national airport (Jensen, 2005). The municipality of Bærum, together with its co-owners, the Ministry of the Environment and the municipality of Oslo, saw the potential to develop a new town in the area of the former airport. Through the planning of low-rise apartment buildings, it would be possible to create 6,000 dwellings in the area, which would mean 10,000–14,000 new inhabitants. Within walking distance, a number of recently built office buildings already had provided a similar number of jobs. In 1993, the municipality decided to start the planning process (Lingsom, 2005). The municipality would be responsible for the detailed area planning, for providing physical infrastructure for the area, and for providing in-person public services to the incoming population.

By observing the approaches that the municipal Development Unit used to plan the new neighborhood, we noticed that planners displayed a strong commitment to ideas of local participation and partnerships, and because the new neighborhood was at that time unpopulated, they worked to mobilize the participation of nearby partners in the form of voluntary organizations in the local community adjacent to Fornebu. In terms of steering, the planners operated not in the classical "governmental" mode, but by applying strategies that are captured by the "governance" term (Stoker, 2006: 67). The territorial ethos was remarkably strong in the first phase of service development in Fornebu. Key people in the top administrative and planning staff were committed to the Fornebu project; they developed plans for a service system that was not only well horizontally integrated, but also one that could be marketed as economically efficient. This last point was important given the preferences of the conservative political majority that controlled the municipal council. To start the planning process, a spectacular event was initiated, called "The Wild Night" event (2006), which was an open session designed to generate ideas and mobilize enthusiasm for and commitment to the Fornebu project. On this occasion, citizens were asked to share their suggestions of how to make the new area into an attractive place to live and work. A total of 2,000 people were reported to have participated in the event and, as a result of the enthusiastic discussions, a declaration was drafted. The Fornebu declaration is a rather general and abstract statement, and, translated into English, the key sentences of the declaration are as follows:

> Fornebu shall inspire people to bring out the best in themselves and in each other, and will provide a range of activities that is broad enough to elicit the contribution of all residents. At Fornebu, we will be brave enough to show that we care. The unique natural resources and wildlife will provide enjoyment now and in the future. Fornebu is to be a

place where new knowledge meets old wisdom and a good community because people will live, think, believe, and love differently here.

"The Wild Night" was an important event (perhaps despite the somewhat opaque formulations in the declaration) because the response to the invitation to participate was tremendous. The people from the neighboring areas, business leaders, future inhabitants, and people from the municipal administration who attended seemed to have been carried away by their enthusiasm for this grand project. It is interesting, however, to observe that this single event did not lead to the creation of a network or organization to function as a forum for the future inhabitants of the Fornebu area.

The provision of *employment* and *dwellings* are market-based processes. A sufficient number of jobs were already available in the area, and the municipality expected that the construction of flats in planned residential areas would tempt many of the employees who already worked in the area to change their current commuting practices to move to Fornebu. From the beginning of the planning process, the municipality and the Ministry of Environment had strong ambitions to develop the area into more than a traditional residential area. First, the natural environment was unique and to be protected, and the municipality wanted to include the natural resources in the residential area through parks and recreational facilities. In addition, the municipality saw a unique opportunity to create a service system that differed from the standard mode of organization and created a positive image of the area. However, all of these goals had to be reflected in the site costs, so the private developers had to pay a rather high price for the residential areas, a price that in its turn would be passed on to the new homeowners.

A model for integrated services: the village centers

In a report on Fornebu, the former Chief Administrative Officer (CAO) of the municipality of Bærum suggested using the term "village center" (*grendesenter*) for the planned public service organization in the new residential area. Instead of constructing schools, childcare centers, sport facilities, and other such services in separate buildings, the CAO argued that a small number of village centers, each containing several public service functions, should be built and that the services administered in each of these should be led by "center leaders." It was argued that the community center would produce various benefits. First, it would reduce building expenditure through the co-localization of services that could utilize common facilities. Second, locating several services together would make accessing diverse functions easier for users. Third, it implied the possibility of improving services by bringing people together from different professions. In terms of scale, the citizens and inhabitants of the Fornebu area were not to be served by one large center, but by three (with an option of two more) village centers located in their immediate neighborhood.

Each of the three village centers was planned to have a distinct profile related to "technology," "environment," and "culture," respectively. The first center was opened in 2008, the second in 2010, and the third, the old airport control tower, in 2011.

Another aspect of the vision for Fornebu is worth mentioning because it may indicate how the territorial and "integrationalist" ideas not only seemed reasonable and interesting, but also how it inspired policy extensions. Village centers were, as indicated above, supposed to constitute a "natural," seamless environment for the inhabitants due to their multifunctional character; inhabitants' needs would be met regardless of their specific nature. The planners' vision, as we encountered it during the planning process, was extended by the realization that such an arrangement could eliminate the barriers which prevented smooth interaction between the system of service provision on the one hand and the inhabitants on the other. Families and children with particular needs were especially "targeted" by this extension. Planners started to realize that well-integrated services provided at the community centers could not only be easily accessible and adequate for those visiting them, and for the children attending pre-, primary, and secondary school there, but that these services could also be used as a platform for greater ambitions. They envisioned a community that, with the assistance of a wide spectrum of municipal services and strategies, could develop a radically preventive orientation toward children's health and the well-being of families and communities. A well-known psychologist who is an expert on the so-called "attachment" approach was brought into the Fornebu project. She held a series of courses for personnel at the Hundsund village center. These courses promoted the idea that if parents and professionals (teachers and health workers primarily) were sufficiently sensitive to children's needs, and if cooperation occurred across professional-administrative boundaries, several social and health-related problems could be prevented.

This vision of anticipating and preventing social problems was intimately related to the "territorial" idea behind the village centers. The first two centers were staffed by personnel who went through a special recruitment process that emphasized not only professional competence and experience, but also personal motivation for involvement in an exceptionally strong multi-disciplinary environment. This orientation was to be promoted by the village center leader, who was not only a primary school principal, but also took charge of all of the functions that were localized in the center. However, a major concern among the municipal planners and administrators throughout the planning process and the first part of the implementation phase was that the professionals and their unions might fail to understand the benefits of integration and might undermine it by a lukewarm attitude. Indeed, the strategy encountered some serious problems. To some extent, teachers and preschool personnel failed to internalize the conviction that they had much to learn from each other and to gain from "integrating" their activities. Even though they made some attempts at integration, these personnel encountered problems that many of them had predicted in previous phases of the process, including a lack of time, insufficient professional competence among the preschool staff, and a lack of adequate supervision on the part of the leader – who was, unsurprisingly, extremely overworked. However, as we shall see, these problems were not seen as insurmountable and they were not the main reasons for the ultimate abandonment of the vision of integrated services.

A partnership strategy was essential to the vision that the municipality of Bærum tried to realize by establishing the village centers. The municipality encouraged public/private partnerships at Fornebu, and the planners, in close cooperation with the village center leaders, sought to realize this ambition.

At Storøya village center, partnership agreements were made with two voluntary organizations, the (national) Table Tennis Association and the Lilløyplassen Nature House. Preceded by shrewd networking activities, the National Table Tennis organization decided to select the village center as a national venue for the sport, thereby bringing forth economic support from the Ministry of Culture. The venue is used by the school and hosts students from the Sports High School and the local table tennis club. Notably, through the table tennis club (and the curling club, which is located in an adjacent curling hall), connections were established between the village center and some of the businesses that were located at Fornebu. A follow-up of this was the idea to jointly invite various employees' sports clubs and to develop and host conferences and events.

As an environmental organization seeking to protect the unique natural environment at Fornebu, the Nature House organization's green profile corresponds well with the village center's commitment to nature. Fornebu's natural environment includes various ecosystems including wetlands, beach moors, swamp forest, pine forest, and a variety of marine environments – each of which is fairly small and vulnerable. In summary, the combination of the small scale and great diversity of the region, which includes 12 separate protected areas, makes Fornebu a favorable location to observe a rich variety of plants, birds, and insects. The enthusiasts running the Nature House engaged in various pedagogical projects with the preschool children and students. They emphasized in interviews that they appreciate the cooperation with the community center and that it works smoothly, not least because the village center leader has the necessary enthusiasm and authority.

At Hundsund village center, three organizations have established partnerships with the center to provide services. The *Snarøya Sports Club* is responsible for operating the outdoor sports facilities, the *Snarøya Women's and Family Association* runs the school restaurant, and *Bærum Swimmers* runs the swimming hall. The partnership agreements are all different. *Bærum Swimmers* institutionalized its activity in the form of a business that formally hires personnel and rents the hall to its customers. The *Snarøya Sports Club* had owned a part of the property at Hundsund for some time and has contributed to the improvement of the sports facilities. Running the facilities is a complex matter that involves icing the skating rink and tending to the artificial grass on the football field. During peak periods, three paid employees were needed to complete these tasks. The *Women's and Family Association* had been involved in the planning of the village center from the beginning and had been especially influential in the planning of the restaurant area. The association also ran the preschool. The *Women's and Family Association*'s restaurant was entirely based on voluntary efforts, but had been able to cover the costs of two part-time cooks, who were assisted by one volunteer. In addition, the association had invested 1.6 million NOK in kitchen appliances.

The partnerships described here are unique in a Norwegian context. In interviews, the municipality's partners emphasized that the partnerships worked very well. In particular, they found it much easier to deal with the village center leaders than with the municipal administration. The transactions costs were thus lower because far less time was wasted in the process of gaining access, waiting for decisions to be made, and ensuring that mutual interests were attended to in harmony with the specificities of local knowledge. Another vital factor here is that because the partnerships tended to generate ideas and innovations, the sense of local ownership and the ability to make the necessary decisions were highly dependent on the relative autonomy of the village center leaders. The structural position of the village center leaders in the midst of cross-cutting networks, combined with their easy access to relevant knowledge, and the decision-making power delegated to them, made them very important and seemingly extremely efficient.

At Fornebu, corporate investment providing jobs, and the high-class municipal provision of infrastructure and public services were expected to attract a large number of people to the area. The plan for housing at Fornebu was completed on time and by 2007, several developers began to market the apartment building projects. In the journal *PLAN*, this part of the Fornebu project was described as "the largest housing project in the Nordic countries" (Nysted, 2005: 32). Through a special arrangement, about 4,700 out of a total of 6,050 planned dwellings were marketed by inviting families and investors to buy individual apartment options at a price of NOK 100,000 per flat. These initial payments were intended to provide a financial base for developers to progress with detailed planning and construction. However, the response was unsatisfactory because only 1,300 shares were sold by 2005 and the developers consequently decided to delay the construction (Nysted, 2005: 32). Dissatisfied representatives of the initial buyers then took the developers to court and, during this prolonged process, the financial crisis ended the demand for apartments at Fornebu. A standstill in the construction process followed, and by 2010, only about 5 percent of the 6,000 planned apartments had been built.

The obvious consequence of this delay was a lack of local inhabitant activities. Thus, the two village centers that are currently in operation lack a vibrant local community in their immediate environment. Additionally, organized citizens were not present to articulate their viewpoints and to negotiate and seek solutions with the leaders of the village centers. The partnerships that were formed involved participants living in the adjacent neighborhood (Snarøya), in other parts of the Bærum municipality, and in the capital region, but for obvious reasons, not in the Fornebu area.

In light of the enthusiasm created by "The Wild Night" activity, one may wonder why so few people responded positively to the idea of living in the Fornebu area. One obvious reason was the high price of housing, because the development costs relating to high-quality infrastructure, nature preservation measures, leisure activity facilities, and other expensive requirements would be passed on to the individual apartment buyers. Additionally, the delay caused by the weak initial response resulted in the coincidence of the implementation with the onset of the financial crisis in 2008, which had a profound negative impact on the already ailing construction projects. Even today, the area is far less populous than intended. So far, the centers primarily serve people who live outside Fornebu, and the majority of the children who attend the preschool and primary school there are bussed in from nearby areas. But given the location and the natural qualities of the area, the planners expected that housing sales would increase with time.

The fall of the integrated services model

The Fornebu project and its village center model may be viewed as a spectacular experiment in territorial organization and definitely as a social innovation (Moulaert et al., 2013). As pointed out, the devolution of administrative authority and the horizontal integration, both of which are symbolized by the role of the village center leader, made the public services at Fornebu both radically autonomous and structurally different from the way in which services were provided in other parts of the municipality. Researchers followed the experiment for more than two years and, throughout this period, spirits remained high. No actor we encountered was against it, no one voiced serious criticisms of the project, and no one raised the possibility of ending it. However, most of the users who we talked to at the centers did not have a clear understanding of the municipal ambition to achieve integrated services. They generally regarded the facilities as extremely useful and, in addition to its high-quality architectural design, they appreciated having a place where several of their key concerns could be addressed by professionals who seemed to take them seriously. Indeed, a vital element of the municipal vision for the community centers was that the personnel would become "local." By working in a multifunctional arena, sharing information and extending their professional concerns by focusing on individual children rather than on separate functions, they were expected to not only be competent but also relevant, affable, and a part of the local milieu.

In the spring of 2010, two years after the first village center was opened, we learned that only a few members of the municipal council in Bærum had substantial knowledge of the Fornebu experiment. This observation strengthened our initial suspicion that to a large extent, the Fornebu experiment was a result of the kind of creativity that tends to be associated with a high degree of planner autonomy. At the same time that we came to this realization, the CAO of the Bærum municipality left her position and a new chief administrative officer was appointed. While the previous leader seemed comfortable with the development at Fornebu, the new top leader did not. During the spring of 2010, a municipal decision was made to fully incorporate the activities in the village centers into the vertical logic of the municipal organization, and thus to terminate the integrated-services experiment, largely ignoring the achievements of the territorial and horizontal organization. A concrete manifestation of this change was the abolition of the role of the village center leader. The two center leaders were offered other positions in the municipal staff. The reason for this abrupt reorganization was not that the centers failed to function properly. To our knowledge, the model was neither regarded as too expensive nor was it a victim of informal sabotage within the municipal administration. The official reason for the termination of the experiment was that it was, first, the slowing down of the development process at Fornebu due to housing market failure and, second, the strengthening of the principle of vertical organization in the Bærum municipality.

The question of why the territorial, "integrationist" strategy was abandoned in the Fornebu service system still remains unanswered. As pointed out above, the administrative decision to "re-verticalize" the services provided at Fornebu can be seen as less surprising than the fact that it encountered very little opposition. In the first part of this chapter, we emphasized that for various reasons, functional considerations tend to gain primacy when several, often conflicting forms of rational action are brought to bear on complex forms of organizational action. Clearly, insofar as functional specialization organized vertically into administrative sectors may secure hierarchical control, one main reason for the primacy of the functional approach is that it serves managerial needs. At Fornebu, the municipality of Bærum had successfully implemented a territorially oriented form of organization that seemed to serve the users well and that clearly inspired innovation and partnerships, which added value to the experiment. It is difficult to understand how the integration of the various services, partnerships, and favorable conditions for further innovation, which were supported by the key position held by the village center leaders, could be so easily reproduced within the context of a more traditional, vertically oriented form of organization.

From the top of the administrative pyramid in the large Bærum municipal organization, with a new chief administrative officer in place, the relationship between means and ends in the Fornebu experiment was considered to be irregular, and thus nothing could prevent a classical, bureaucratic reaction to what appeared to be administrative disorder.

Most actors who participated in the planning process and the implementation phase were clearly enchanted with the experiment. There was considerable and widespread enthusiasm concerning what the territorial model could achieve in terms of realizing substantive goals. Indeed, the village centers were seen by some as "a new beginning," and the horizontal integrated-services vision inspired bureaucrats and professionals to envision a more balanced system of social relations, rather than as a set of parallel sectors based on hierarchical and asymmetrical relations.

Moreover, during the process, the planners were engrossed in learning from their experiences as the experiment progressed. Observing this process, we were struck by the great interest they took in achieving outcomes as opposed to output; they were seriously dialogical and open about what they were trying to do and about how the effects of their planning were experienced by others. "Reflexive planning" (Howe and Langdon, 2002) became a buzzword among the planners in Bærum, and it reflects their attempt to avoid the classical tendency to celebrate the desired results as effects of the planning strategy and attribute undesired results to external factors.

At Fornebu, the conditions were favorable for a realization of the territorial principle. Notably, when the chief planner introduced us to the model, he argued that in this unique context, it was the only reasonable alternative. The Bærum municipality declares itself to be innovative and ambitious, and tries to inspire solutions that make sense. The problem of territorial integration, however, is that even though it may improve services, it may also stimulate autonomy at the lower levels of the hierarchical system and threaten not only functional differentiation but also vertical control. However, the exact cost in terms of the loss of vertical control, that is, in terms of whether the village centers became unruly, never became clear. With the partnership arrangements, the highly motivated professional staff, and the positive feedbacks from users, it is reasonable to assume that the centers were never directly regarded as a problem. Beyond the small group of planners themselves, however, the principles behind the village center models were never articulated as the generator of the very special type of organizational forms which were emerging at Fornebu.

In its practical manifestations in public sector organizational processes, the tensions between territorial and functional principles are always multifaceted and involve complex forms of interplay with other administrative tensions such as those subsumed by devolution/centralization, liberalization/ bureaucratic control, political control/professional autonomy, and discretion and deliberation in owner/provider relations. Following the post-war development of the Norwegian welfare state and in the municipalities in particular, the territorial principle seems to have been weakened during a process of post-war modernization, but at several times during recent decades, it has nevertheless had a certain momentum. What seems to have triggered these reactions to the functionalist hegemony are popular, most often highly local experiences of vital welfare services becoming more inaccessible and less sensitive to user needs – or the experience of how the search for efficiency (which typically generates some form of vertical integration) can hurt the functioning of local communities. The territory/function distinction resonates strongly with the distinction between central steering and local autonomy. As Friedmann and Weaver state:

> Given inequalities at the start, a functional order is always hierarchical, accumulating power at the top. Territorial relationships, on the other hand, though they will also be characterized by inequalities of power, are tempered by mutual rights and obligations which the members of a territorial group claim from each other. (Friedmann and Weaver, 1979: 7)

Thus, political ambitions to expand the scope of the welfare state, improve services of all kinds, and reach more people who are in need of them may easily be taken literally by grassroots bureaucrats and leave "too" much to local discretion. The most problematic version of this dilemma seems to appear when it becomes clear that local (and perhaps professional) autonomy both results in better services and more unambiguously reflects political will, although at times it may be too costly. At Fornebu, planners, administrative leaders, and grassroots bureaucrats were quite inspired by the experiment, and they saw new possibilities in the creative partnership arrangements that were established. To our knowledge, problems of swelling budgets and the loss of vertical control never materialized. In the 2010 annual report issued by the Bærum municipality, it is stated that *running costs* of the Fornebu infrastructure programme amounted to 33 million NOK *less* than what was originally budgeted, and the Fornebu investment programme was by 2010 running 83 million NOK under the budgeted level (Bærum kommune, 2011: 78).

Returning to the four conditions for the institutionalization of territorial governance, the Fornebu experiment scores very highly on the first condition, at least until the termination of the most ambitious aspect of services integration, the role of the center leader. Second, the partnership strategy paid off, both literally and figuratively, by relieving the municipalities of direct responsibility for running a school restaurant, several sports facilities, and environmental education. The third element, the empowerment of the local population to be served by the village centers, is perhaps the weakest element. To a large extent, the absence of the citizens' voice can be explained by the low number of inhabitants moving in, due to a stalemate in house construction.

As for the anchoring of the experiment at the municipal leadership level, the Fornebu planners could not stop the reorganization initiative from the new CAO, entailing the re-enforcement of the functional principle in the service system. Perhaps a well-organized local public could have protested against this, informed a wider audience, and forged alliances that could contribute to the unique territorial experiment's survival. But the lack of a political anchoring of the experiment became conspicuous as the process of termination went ahead without causing much friction. In our view, it seems reasonable to conclude that the main reason why the ambitious attempt to adapt municipal services to people's needs was that politicians never seemed to become fully aware of what was at stake. They seemed to believe that the questions related to planning and organization were primarily technical, a belief that the planners themselves did very little to influence. Thus, the necessary alliances never materialized.

In more abstract terms, what happened to the Fornebu experiment can be seen as a form of administrative appropriation. The argument applied by the administrative leadership was not that the experiment had failed, but that the services at Fornebu should adhere to the overall vertical structure, which the administrative leadership wanted to strengthen (Bærum commune, 2011: 1). At the same time, the Bærum municipality's focus on innovation remains strong, and in the future this will demand that "all administrative sector managers must establish and commit themselves to projects and initiatives which demand shared efforts and priorities and make sure that the leaders of service providing units actively follow them up" (Bærum commune, 2011: 1). As was pointed out earlier in the chapter, there is no indication that the administrative (or political) leaders in the Bærum municipality linked the achievements at Fornebu with the specific form of organization that was implemented there – the link was, as indicated above, essentially seen as arbitrary. Ironically, on the basis of the Fornebu experience, the municipal leadership signed a partnership contract with the Association of Norwegian Municipalities granting Bærum a special status as a "case municipality" in the Association's innovation program. There is a double irony here, as the administrative appropriation of the Fornebu model almost surely prevented the organization from learning from its own failure.

References

Bauman, Z. (2000) *Liquid Modernity*. Cambridge: Polity Press.
Beauregard, R. (1989) Between modernity and postmodernity: The ambiguous position of U.S. planning. *Environment and Planning D: Society and Space*, 7: 381–95.
Bærum kommune (2011) *Årsrapport [Annual Report] 2010*.
Castells, M. (1997) *The Power of Identity*. Oxford: Blackwell.
Christensen, T. and Lægreid, P. (2003) *New Public Management: The Transformation of Ideas and Practice*. Aldershot: Ashgate.

—— (2007) *Transcending New Public Management: The Transformation of Public Sector Reforms*. Aldershot: Ashgate.
Crook, S. (1991) *Modernist Radicalism and its Aftermath*. London: Routledge.
Douglas, M. (1986) *How Institutions Think*. New York: Syracuse University Press.
Dyrkorn, K. (2008) *Offentlig innovasjon på Fornebu: En kvalitativ studie av Hundsund grendesenter*. Report, Utviklingsenheten, Bærum commune (in Norwegian).
Friedmann, J. (1987) *Planning in the Public Domain: From Knowledge to Action*. Princeton: Princeton University Press.
Friedmann, J. and Weaver, C. (1979) *Territory and Function: The Evolution of Regional Planning*. London: Edward Arnold.
Gregory, R. (2007) New public management and the ghost of Max Weber: Exorcized or still haunting? In T. Christensen and P. Lægreid (eds), *Transcending New Public Management: The Transformation of Public Sector Reforms*. Aldershot: Ashgate, pp. 221–45.
Healey, P. (1997) *Collaborative Planning: Shaping Places in Fragmented Societies*. Basingstoke: Macmillan.
Herzfeld, M. (1992) *The Social Production of Indifference: Exploring the Symbolic Roots of Western Bureaucracy*. Chicago: University of Chicago Press.
Howe, J. and Langdon, C. (2002) Towards a reflexive planning theory. *Planning Theory*, 1(3): 209–25.
Jacobs, J. (1974) *The Life and Death of Great American Cities*. Harmondsworth: Penguin.
Jensen, R.H. (2005) Makt og avmakt i fysisk planlegging og gjennomføring – refleksjoner fra etterbruk av Fornebu. *PLAN*, 1: 9–17.
Lingsom, H.K. (2005) Aktørene på Fornebu: flere hoder – mange roller. *PLAN*, 1.
MacCallum, D., Moulart, F., Hillier, J., and Vicari Haddock, S. (eds) (2009) *Social Innovation and Territorial Development*. Farnham: Ashgate.
Merton, R.K. (1940) Bureaucratic structure and personality. *Social Forces*, 18(4): 560–8.
Moulaert, F., MacCallum, D. Mehmood, A., and Hamdouch, A. (eds) (2013) *The International Handbook on Social Innovation: Collective Action, Social Learning and Transdisciplinary Research*. Cheltenham: Edward Elgar.
Nystad, J.F. (2005) Fra Fornebu til Forneby. *PLAN*, 1.
Offe, C. (1996) *Modernity and the State: East, West*. Cambridge: Polity Press.
Putnam, R.D. (2000) *Bowling Alone*. New York: Simon & Schuster.
Sverdrup, T., Aarsæther, N., and Vike, H. (2011) *Tjenester og partnerskap på Fornebu*. Sandvika: Bærum kommune.
Stein, C. (1951) *Toward New Towns for America*. Boston, MA: MIT Press.
Stoker, G. (2006) *Why Politics Matter: Making Democracy Work*. Basingstoke: Palgrave Macmillan.
Tyler, N. and Ward R.M. (2011) *Planning and Community Development: A Guide for the 21st Century*. New York: W.W. Norton.
Weber, M. (1969) *The Theory of Social and Economic Organization*. New York: Free Press.
Young, G. (2008) *Reshaping Planning with Culture*. Aldershot: Ashgate.

Part III
Social innovation, participatory governance and collective learning as levers of creative planning

10 Envisioning dialogues of new urban landscapes in Nuuk

Kjerstin Uhre and Knut Eirik Dahl

Introduction

In the autumn of 2009, the Greenlandic architect office *tegnestuen tnt nuuk* contacted us, Dahl & Uhre Architects, in the Norwegian Arctic city of Tromsø. This was the beginning of two years of north-to-north cooperation and dialogue-based co-design. In this chapter we share experiences from the making of the project *Nunarsuup Qeqqani Nuup Qeccani/In the Middle of the World in the Middle of Nuuk*.[1] Through evidence drawn from two comparable citizen participatory processes in Tromsø, we present ways to think creatively about city dialogues. We will show and discuss examples of how broad and inclusive dialogues at the city level combined with visual representations of the ideas that are conceived in such dialogues can open up opportunities to address a broad spectrum of questions related to planning under rapidly changing conditions.

Being a capital, Nuuk contains metropolitan qualities and given the vast distance to the nearest towns and its close ties to Denmark, the city also displays some characteristics of a satellite city. The global searchlight on climate change and Arctic resources placed Greenland in the middle of the world. At the climate summit in Copenhagen (COP 15), the Prime Minister of Greenland argued for Greenland's right to build up its extractive industry sector in order to sustain an independent national economy. In return, he promised that 'we are going to reduce the emissions from the civil society. We will be restoring houses and we will build new houses with the best technology available'.[2] The Home Rule under Danish administration had left behind a building mass worn down and suffering from systemic neglect. Amongst the first votes of Naalakkersuisut, the Government of Greenland, on the path to independence was the decision to demolish the infamous Blok P built in 1969 that had become the iconic representation of Danish rule, and Tuujuk, the adjacent neighbourhood of 11 rows of houses constructed between 1962 and 1964. In addition, the Department of Housing, Environment and Infrastructure had designated 1,250 potentially dilapidated buildings in Nuuk, which with its 15,470 inhabitants (as of 2010) was experiencing a critical shortage of housing for a growing population. Following this vote, Naalakkersuisut and Sermersooq Municipality commissioned a comprehensive plan (referred to as 'the strategy plan' hereinafter) of these central areas with the aim of staging a broad democratic dialogue about the future city of Nuuk. The political and administrative authorities wanted to discover the core questions and concerns that affected citizens' lives, to gather knowledge about citizens' thoughts on these questions and to articulate public concerns spatially in the new strategy plan for the city centre.

Dialogue as a basis for planning has been discussed in planning theory since John Friedmann explored the relationship of knowledge to action through the concept of *transactive planning* in 1973: 'The broad aim is the collective self-production of life, and the knowledge we bring to its realization, one step at a time, is obtained through mutual learning' (Friedmann, 2011: 60). Dialogical practices have become more centred in planning literature, as democratic hearings have now been embedded in legislation and have challenged how one can engage citizens in participation and as to how the voices are heard. 'Participation has to be in a form that is relevant to the particular context, to the particular policy problem, and to those interests that are affected' (Nyseth et al., 2010: 225). In exploring creative approaches to dialogue-based planning from the architect's point of view, we regard the act of drawing drawings and modelling models as ways of understanding, processing and mediating complex and sometimes contradictory knowledges and desires in the becoming of spatial futures. Hillier draws attention 'to Foucault's ideas of immanence, and to Deleuze and Guattari's ideas of becoming, or moving beyond as notions that allow unexpected elements to come into play and things not to quite work out as expected ... where outcomes are volatile, where problems are not "solved" once and for all but are rather constantly recast, reformulated in new perspectives' (Hillier, 2007: 189). Our contribution to theories of urban dialogues is to emphasize the importance of and the opportunities that arise as a result of producing visual and material arguments during participatory processes. To creatively utilize visual methods to sustain a dialogical planning culture goes beyond the instrumental scope of representing political visions or realizing a building project.

In the next two sections we discuss concepts of city dialogues based on two examples of participatory planning in Tromsø. Then we introduce the challenges appearing on-site, in the middle of Nuuk. Our approach to the citizen participation process in Greenland was: 'They shall see what we hear.' The city dialogues informed and shaped the design of the spatial structure of the strategy plan, which in turn informed further dialogues. This dialectics of mapping and remapping, designing and redesigning that was based on the city dialogues is described in the section entitled: 'Who are you and what is your desire?' The main findings that were articulated as architectural concepts are described in the 'Learning as catalyst' section below. Revisiting the public exhibition of the strategy plan, we ask if it is possible to construct a political dialogue in such a way that ideas and concepts about inclusion and city development remain ambitious. The chapter concludes with reflections on the transformative potential of open public discourse at the city level. We reflect on what the aftermath of a citizen participation process might be and what can be learned from our experience. To contextualize the chapter intuitively, we invite the reader to travel back in time and arrive with us in Nuuk on 4 January 2010 by using a short piece of creative writing:

> Suspended in a perfect landing curve, the Air Greenland Dash-8 extends its wing flaps and sinks through the arctic winter night. Cabin lights are dimmed as the plane circumscribes Nuuk. Through the cabin windows we take in the modernist urban pattern that has become an inventory to our thinking by our interpretation of maps, plans, and transatlantic Skype conversations with the architects from tnt nuuk. From a distance we see the Colony Harbor. Further along the plane's trajectory we pass the silhouettes of the housing structures at the Radio Mountain. The plane continue at low altitude over the city center and there, perpendicular to the Bloks One to Ten, stands Blok P. We pass it very close, hesitantly realizing that its presence soon belong to the past. That night the concrete giant radiated with homely interior lighting and Danish Design Christmas stars. Colored lights flashed in multiple pulses along the two hundred meter long facade and the Greenlandic flag was displayed at every single terrace.

Legacies of practice: city of dialogues

The project in Nuuk was a continuation of and a negotiated reinvention of a line of thought developed through public architectural inquiries in the Norwegian Arctic city of Tromsø. Practice-based design research in the field of architecture has been conducted both within and outside academia. Assignments for various clients, teaching, idea-competitions, events, exhibitions, and participation in urban and planning discourse are all examples of venues for knowledge building, mediation and critique. Our learning from, commenting on and working with diverse urban and architectural projects, often in extended professional and transdisciplinary networks, has over time evolved into experience-based methods for staging a large public conversation on the future of the city. In these projects we employed a collection of communicative, narrative and visual approaches, which awaited a continuous process of experimentation, and poses a challenge to established practices and political and administrative institutions.

In Tromsø we developed experience-based methods for leading the large public conversation on the future of the city, *The Game of Tromsø* in 1995–7 and the City Development Year from 2005 to 2006, which were both made in larger collaborative networks with other architect practices and transdisciplinary teams. In the article 'Planning beyond the horizon: The Tromsø experiment', Torill Nyseth, John Pløger and Trine Holm investigated the City Development Year in Tromsø as a case that 'is a democratic experiment with planning as a more open, transparent and inclusive process, and it represented a break with institutionalized practices' (Nyseth et al., 2010: 223). *The Game of Tromsø* gave access to and visualized excavations in the city of the future by means of exhibitions and texts produced during two highly intensive years. The main rules of *The Game of Tromsø* entailed selecting places and endowing them with new meaning. The explorations served to challenge existing views on landscapes, forms of development, complexity, the programme of the city and the emerging urban geography. The project came out of a close cooperation and idea exchange between Knut Eirik Dahl and the Head of the Urban Planning Department, Erik Øwre, and aimed to explore the possibility of growth inwards as a response to the UN's Agenda 21 (Programme of Action for Sustainable Development). The City Development Year ten years later was, on the other hand, a result of external critique of a new municipal plan for the city centre that led to its rejection. 'It was an experiment which moved contingency and fluid planning into a political situation that could question the city's hegemonic planning discourse, not least because in charge of this experiment was a network of professionals and interest groups independent of local government and planning authorities' (Nyseth et al., 2010: 226).

The City Development Year stated that the city we see and experience now does not constitute the real town – this exists in the future space, which was being challenged by national and international strategies in politics, research and culture. From the viewpoint of the Norwegian government, the spotlight was directed at the future of the Barents Region 2020. The future city of Tromsø could only be traced and discovered within perspectives larger than the city itself. The small city centre is a major arena for interpreting the pressures on the city from the outside as architecture, while also affording a programme for studying this type of internationally oriented public space. The city core is a veritable battlefield for future interpretation. A number of the knowledge communities in Tromsø, which is home to Norway's youngest population and with a high level of education, now challenge conventional planning concepts by making entirely new statements about the future in full public view. They look with expectation towards what the city's response will be to the challenges it faces and how it will reshape itself by means of a new built reality – the impatience from the young population represents a pressure from within.

Both *The Game of Tromsø* and the City Development Year were projects that conceptualized civic dialogues. Oral knowledge exchange has a strong tradition in north Norway. The projects engaged this (sometimes mythologized) preference for storytelling, curiosity and excitement to learn about other people's livelihood and fields of expertise. The contemporary urban discourse culture was traced to unexpected venues where informal contact between people from different realms of knowledge took place. Informal

Envisioning dialogues of new urban landscapes in Nuuk 177

conversations enhance the general orientation and information level in the city and allow knowledges to migrate between disciplines and professions.

In criticizing the notion of innovation, Ingold and Hallam stated that 'even architects, however, are human beings. They move in the same circles as those who walk the streets of the cities they have helped to design. And it is surely in these movements, not in splendid isolation, that their ideas take shape' (Ingold and Hallam, 2007: 9). Architects has a special responsibility to immerse themselves in the civic discourse in order to be able to make designs relevant to the city. Yaneva argues that architecture must be seen as a part of society and that 'to depart from the divide between architecture and society, we also need to depart from an understanding of the society as a separate domain or context in which architecture can be formed' (2012: 4). In a similar fashion to how other academic disciplines employ literature critics to inform their research on a given topic, architects survey contemporary and historical architectural and urban projects that have dealt with similar design problems to the project at hand. For the architect, responsiveness evolves through being able to conceptualize the collective discourse, and to extract ideas that are possible to conjure into being as relevant architectural concepts or events to frame the civic discourse on legislation, plans, new technologies, and environmental, economic and social sustainability measures.

A question for the architect is: what informs your project? This involves an attention to multiple resources in the community. In the transformation of neighbourhoods, it must include an awareness and openness towards voices that often go under the radar of public meetings. All parties should be given a fair chance to shape the architects' imagination. Thus, it is a good idea for planners to put architects and citizens in the same room *before* the project is designed. It is about being aware of the multitude of influences and about seeking to be exposed, impressed and inspired.

Our method of conceptualizing dialogues is amplifying what we hear and see to new outputs in the form of new sketches, strategies and evocative statements, and to engage in graphical discourse. Smart diagrams, often employing statistics, used as arguments, as known from the Dutch urban architecture 'school' in the 1990s inspired by the milieu around Rem Koolhas and the Office for Metropolitan Architecture, can be compared to the depicted artefacts in classical 'conversation pieces' appearing in paintings from the Enlightenment, where group portraits would be arranged around a map or another artefact. It is a means of looking at what to create discussions around.

Conversation pieces can work as a preparation for contingency for future debates. What is does methodologically for architects is that it helps to sort out a design problem in one's own head, to communicate an idea within the design team and to communicate it to commissioners, stakeholders and interested parties. It opens op possibilities for creating relational spaces around items, pieces, works, creative texts and notions, representations that can inform public debate. In this way, citizens are engaged as co-creators and not merely as informants for the plan. In the next section we show how these methods were calibrated to the specific conditions in Nuuk and how new methods were created. The scale and scope of the *In Nuuk* project was to stage and materialize a civic discourse on the social, environmental, economic and architectural impacts of the transformation of the city centre. Involvement in such conversations means that the citizens as dialogue partners are able to recognize themselves in the project.

In the Middle of the World, in the Middle of Nuuk

Nuuk was subjected to a *political moment*. The government and the municipality asked new questions and searched for new answers. This openness was welcomed by citizens and capacities, including artists, social workers and cultural opinion makers, who eagerly participated in focus groups that became a continuous source of information. At one of our first focus group dialogues, one citizen stated: 'This is a window of opportunity for Greenland, at it may be open for some few years and then it will close – let's use it.' He also told this beautiful childhood story:

> When I was a boy, this area was marshlands called Little Plain and Big Plain. I often recall one warm summer day when I had learned to fold a new kind of paper plane. I went out on Little Plain to test one of which I was particularly proud. The grassy plain lay baked in the sun. I sent off my plane and it rose. It continued to rise in spirals on the upwards-drifting air current. I never saw it heading down. It left in me a concept of a perfect moment, of beauty, of eternity. I like to think that maybe it never landed.[3]

His story about the paper plane conceived both an analysis and an architectural concept. It became a metaphor that we used to visualize the research, documents, plans and ambitions that were then encircling Nuuk and Greenland. The interest from global companies setting the spotlight on Greenlandic resources is one. The annual report from the Department of Resources is another one, being relatively uncritically open to all kinds of investment, while a third is the report on infrastructure in Greenland, pinpointing Nuuk as the growing settlement. The hottest topic in Greenlandic politics at the time was the survival of the life forms of all the smaller settlements that have been broken up throughout history. A fourth paper plane is the stunning report that came out in our project period from the Tax and Welfare Commission. This report went to the core of the state of Greenland in relation to its vulnerable economy and the lack of education of the Greenlandic people in their own language, which no one had approached

Envisioning dialogues of new urban landscapes in Nuuk 179

Figure 10.1 Paper planes of whitepapers, reports and research as they circumscribe Nuuk

seriously or with empathy. Taken together; the challenges that had to be met in a short timeframe raised the question of how to avoid repeating wrongs from the past. One citizen asked: 'Why have we got the surroundings we have when there have been plans for everything?' We argued that it was time to leave idea of the zoning plan with separate programmes, and interpolate a spatial structure of low threshold learning (capacity building) and civic programmes in the new urban fabric.[4]

The dense urban fabric had been effectively mass-produced by the Danes and erected on Arctic wetlands close to the old city centre, the Colony Harbour. The greater part of the Nuuk population live in these residential slabs, described by the novelist Kim Leine as vertical villages (Leine, 2007). These neighbourhoods possess a strong sense of community and an intense mix of socially deprived and resourceful residents, children at risk and the ambitious next generation eager to create content for the Greenland of tomorrow. Once inhabited by residents from coastal villages that were closed down during the 1960s and 1970s, the white slabs were left without maintenance while the city was growing outwards. In 2010, when the political strategy of the Government of Greenland entailed a combination of demolition and revitalization, the whole city of Nuuk became a new type of

Figure 10.2 Blok P was Greenland's largest housing project, once inhabiting one per cent of the entire national population. A new horizon appears after the disappearance of this housing slab

game board imposing a possible nomadic situation for the poorest part of the population. The city had to respond to the challenges this posed on the central neighbourhoods and the city at large. In the Air Greenland magazine *Suluk*, we read a feature interview with the Prime Minister Kleist: 'His biological father was a Danish craftsman who, in the words of the Premier, was one of the workmen who built Greenland, while the Greenlanders watched' (*Suluk*, 2010, no. 1: 29). The interior of this expression is both dramatic and traumatic. Naalakkersuisut was determined to use the new and important opportunities emerging to build competence through coupling Greenlandic and international companies. The aim was to bring home and maintain this competence.

They shall see what we hear

The programme for the strategy plan and thinking was administratively formulated at the outset, but was twisted and challenged through the process. Our main concern was: where shall the inhabitants live, what new opportunities are they given and what is the city centre when social circles are broken up? In short, who has the right to the city? Everything seemed to be in a kind of flux, including the built environment. During the first five weeks of the city dialogues, the whole working group explored and expanded the brief for the project: a plan searching for other openings and stepping stones than those which were immediately apparent.

The architect team were not assigned with the task of designing "creative" solutions to already defined problems, but creatively took part in the trans-level public negotiations to articulate concerns as *design problems*. This implied not only finding solutions to challenges, but also finding challenges that were not apparent in the outset. There is a significant difference between advocating a finite project on behalf of the project owners and advocating the shared ideas and concerns of citizens towards the project design organization.

The project developed through conversations in the overlapping fields of different expanding collectives. The political board of the project, the Mayor of Sermersooq Municipality, the Minister of Infrastructure and Housing, and the Chairman of the Construction and Environment Committee, engaged and contributed actively throughout the process. The team of co-designers, guest architects and researchers expanded as the magnitude of challenges became evident. By the time of the final exhibition, the extended team was working all over the world, from Nuuk to Tromsø, Oslo, London and Tasmania, working online and in intense workshops in Nuuk and Tromsø. We were also attempting to initiate north-to-north cooperation between the municipalities of Tromsø and Sermersooq; we brought our landscape-architect students from the Oslo School of Architecture and Design to Nuuk. Additional resources, time and funding were provided both by the Greenlandic commissioners and the Norwegian Ministry of Foreign Affairs.

The first design move in Nuuk was to co-produce an activity plan to consolidate the participation process within the municipal administration of Nuuk and the Government of Greenland. The Danish-speaking project leader from the municipality, Jakob Exner, called this a *Dreiebog* ('storyboard'). In Norwegian, this word is associated with filmmaking. We were excited about making a *storyboard* because of its visual connotations. It developed into a textual and visual declaration with *seven reminders for the future*. The ambition was to get the people living in the neighbourhood and the people of Nuuk to enter into continuous dialogues on the city in becoming. This kind of participatory programming implied that during the course of the process, the citizens should 'see what we heard' as the strategy plan was being designed through the architect team's spatial interpretation of concerns raised in the city dialogues.

Who are you and what is your desire?

Did the methods employed in the project make the challenges regarding the renewal of the city centre apparent? One answer can be found in the team's shared eagerness to place emphasis on oral knowledge exchange. Helena Lennert, one of the Greenlandic architects in the team who spoke Greenlandic, wanted to find ways to creatively engage with the culture-specific forms of oral knowledge exchange in Nuuk. She told us about the *kamik post*, which refers to how news and gossip informally travels from person to person and illustrated this by using a local proverb: 'when we had kamiks [the traditional footwear], we could walk everywhere. Now that we wear shoes, we can only walk on the road'. She set out words on the town about upcoming events and said that more people would want to come if they heard about it through the *kamik post* than if they only read about it in the newspaper: 'Since timing is of the essence, and since, in any event, there is no clear-cut division of labor between planning and practice, much of this gathering and evaluating of intelligence takes place informally, by word of mouth, and involves the members of the group in an ongoing dialogue' (Friedmann, 2011: 72). Through city walks (Nuuk Safaris), and continued discussions with all kinds of groups of people, including all the architects, writers, artists, summer labs with young people studying abroad, etc., a broad tapestry of viewpoints was unfolded. She also came up with a solution to how we could meet residents in the area face to face and arranged *Kaffemiks* (social gatherings around a cup of coffee), where she, the Mayor and a journalist gave interviews in people's homes. Some of these interviews were published in the weekly newspaper for the whole of Greenland to read.

The media followed these activities closely and the two first *kaffemik* dialogues were published in the national newspaper *Sermitsiaq AG* in week five of the project. In an editorial entitled 'Democracy Commits', the editor commented on the project and the invitation to contribute and participate in the city dialogues. The article emphasised the importance of the direct, face-to-face dialogue between the politicians, architects, planners and all kinds of residents: 'We hope that the citizens accept the invitation, because, overall, the project is not only about how the city centre in the future should look like – it's also about how to involve citizens in the process before the decisions are taken. Hopefully the urban project in Nuuk [will] inspire processes and standards when it is a question of listening to citizens prior to political choices also in other crucial matters – be it, for example, the construction of an aluminum smelter, the extraction of uranium, or future mining permissions'.[5] The attention given to oral exchange was also reflected in the following public debate, as one citizen wrote in *Nuuk Ugeavis* (a Nuuk weekly publication): 'be patient when "developing" our capacities to organize. Plan and chair debates where we can employ our spontaneity and ability to be present here and now'. The writer continued by warning against rushing the

Envisioning dialogues of new urban landscapes in Nuuk 183

Figure 10.3 'Learning as catalyst' is the notion that opened up for inclusive and creative programming

process: 'Spend enough time to consult the master plan with the city. Make sure that as many uncertainties as possible are settled.'[6]

Learning as catalyst

Since an urban plan cannot be a record of everything that has been said or a collection of all good intentions, we searched for the statements and information that could be translated into programmes, spatial organization and architectural form. In this way, citizens' concerns were embedded directly into the programming of the city centre and the ideas for the spatial configuration of the programme. The notion of *learning as catalyst* entered the realm of the project and was accepted at the political level. It pointed directly at the tragic fact that until recently, Greenlandic schoolchildren had never been taught and educated in their own language, and that the way to a good life in modern society in Greenland could only be achieved by using the Danish language. The neighbourhood as a new type of knowledge centre was formulated. In an early phase, we made the following discovery: when Blok P disappears, the children's school stands alone as the heart of the changes to come. The schoolchildren will see the future appear and shall themselves take part in it. The notion of learning as catalyst makes it

Figure 10.4 Active city floor in the Blok P area is a question of the right to the city. Low threshold learning is the programmatic key

possible to imagine a green urban space that is a knowledge landscape in the footprint of Blok P:

> Everybody mentions 'learning' as an excellent notion to use when the project starts to organize the field. One mirrors oneself in one's surroundings; in what one is seeing. It is therefore important, especially in the middle of Nuuk, to set a physical framework that motivates the residents and other groups and individuals to live participating and unfolding lives. Learning on all levels may be such a mirror. (Minutes from the political reference group meeting. February 2010)

The question of the city centre as a new type of knowledge centre was formulated. This included speculating on a concept for innovative

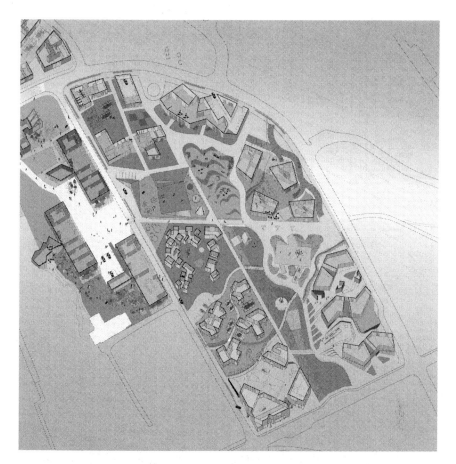

Figure 10.5 Civic landscapes indoors and outdoors at the ground floor of Tuujuk

relationships with other countries on the subjects of education and research. Insights and directions that came to the surface in the city dialogues were visualized continuously. In the design team, we experimented with how drawings could communicate that the ground floors in the future buildings and the outdoor urban landscape were intended to be one open plain or floor activated by various public or self-organized programmes. The Mayor later summed up the discussions as follows: 'we must make a city centre where people can meet, care and be concerned about each other and learn to be ambitious'. New representations triggered new discussions in a dialectic manner, both internally in the project organization and at the city level.

In the footprint of Blok P, a field of innovation and invitations was being conceptualized to give directions to the next step of development. All the ground floors of the area are designed in order to make being visible possible, of seeing each other, activating, learning and creating.

Figure 10.6 Ilaqutariit illuat – *The House of Families* – was planned to help young parents support their children and to be like a small society within the larger society

To explore the civic programming of the city floor through architectural form, we introduced the idea of *guest architect projects*. These were projects that tested the openness, limits and possibilities in the plan. As 'in between experiments', they were planned as stepping-stones from theory to reality. One of the guest projects, created by the group Fantastic Norway, was dedicated to a social programme entitled *The House of Families*, a home for young women in troubled situations and their children. It was previously decided that it would be built on the outskirts of the city, but when introduced into our concept at an early stage of the planning phase, everyone involved took notice of it.[7]

The discovery of original maps from 1948 and the story of the paper plane that descended over the plain of Arctic wetland brought about the idea of an Arctic waterpark with wetlands. The landscape concepts provided infrastructural armatures that organize the built structures of the future. Nuuk has open surface water systems, a very interesting feature that contemporary cities are re-introducing to mitigate against increased rainfall due to climate change. These water bodies are a part of the city's ecology. They are also part of the global ecology as Arctic wetlands are crucial as resting and grazing spaces for migratory birds. Tuujuk is named after a seabird of the gull family that migrates to Greenland; the park extends the landscapes of learning to relate to biodiversity and climate change in a 'greening Arctic'. In the footprint of Blok P, the Arctic wetland re-appeared and organized the urban pattern.

The advisory team, the political board and the municipal administration agreed to hold on to the ambitions in the strategy plan throughout the process of formalizing and, over time, realizing the new neighbourhoods.

However, the planning department in the municipality was given new leadership from Denmark and in the formal plan for Tuujuk and the Blok P area, they re-introduced zoning with separate programmes as well as allowing for a denser built-up structure. When urban plans are recast, it is often the case that the landscape infrastructure proves to be the most resilient element. Many of the citizens during the participation process had emphasised Tuujuk's qualities as a green, car-free area and wished for an open urban park open to everyone living in Nuuk. A Danish landscape architect office has now been commissioned to create the Arctic wetland park in Tuujuk that was part of the landscape armature of the strategy plan.

To exhibit is to open up

The creation of a strategy plan based on dialogue process is a way of collecting knowledge about the concerns, needs, and expectations of citizens towards the future urban environment. Synthetized and given material form as drawings, renderings, diagrams, texts and physical models, this conjures up shared mental images of the desired city.

The city planning department at the municipality hosted the final public exhibition of the strategy plan with a big physical model. An extensive project catalogue was published in Greenlandic, Danish and English. In addition to the citizens of Nuuk who made contributions, more than 100 people had been active as co-workers and helpers and dialogue partners in the making of the plan. The grand opening in Nuuk on 5 April 2011 was the starting point of the next phase and the endpoint for our engagement. The landing of the ambitions in the structure plan was going to be piloted by the politicians and planning authorities through the procedures of making juridical plans. The exhibited strategy plan was in itself part of the process leading up to juridical binding municipal plans. A plan is not an end point; the 'outcomes are volatile' (Hillier, 2007: 189). In 2011, the project was the winner in the 'Best Nordic Urban Plan' category in Northern Europe's first (and up until now only) fair for architecture and urban planning, *Arkitekturmässan*. The jury commended the 'clear and strong narrative that resulted from an intense research and exchange with the local community'.[8] In June 2015, a new juridical plan for Tuujuk doubled the building density, and in October of the same year, work started on building the first block. 'The story of process, of design in the making is, by the same token, a story of the making of the social' (Yaneva, 2012: 3). The making of city's architectonic project, its urban project and its landscape project goes beyond the plan. It is a collective work that can suffer and thrive under various planning regimes. As an inseparable part of society, the human-made environment is continually negotiated with internal and external forces that forge decay or revitalization.

Conclusion

This chapter has explored dialogical capacity building in negotiation and discourse at the city level. City dialogues, combined with visualization of futures, have a twofold capacity: to engage broadly and to inform the architectural project of the city. For the architect, the visualization of dialogues is about being aware of the multitude of influences and about seeking to be exposed, impressed and inspired.

The *In the Middle of the World, in the Middle of Nuuk* project gravitated towards continuous mediation between the team members, decision-makers, the administration, the media and citizens of Nuuk. Through designing spatial inventions based on the present, historical and geopolitical contexts as they came to the surface through the city dialogues, the advisory team attempted both to plan relevant venues and activities in the citizen participation process, and to embed the public concerns and findings that came out of the dialogues in the strategy plan. City dialogues are arenas where it is possible to train and cultivate one's intuition and sensitivity for city development that can open up possible contingencies and opportunities. The three dialogue projects mentioned in this chapter were activated by moments when the planning conditions changed and they lasted for around two years. They can be seen as intensifications of the long-term becoming of cities, where findings, themes, approaches and ideas time and time again take new forms in the conversation.

City dialogues prepare citizens and planners for decisions that need to be made in moments of rupture, crisis or opportunity. Citizen participation processes are important venues to keep the urban imagination alive. Memories from landscapes and cityscapes not yet constructed are created when planners, politicians, architects and citizens together imagine urban futures through sharing, discussing and visualizing concerns and ideas. When citizens learn to remember and articulate the future, they prepare the landscape and the city for what is to come and add to the contingency of the urban environment in the encounters with developers and forces of change. By combining broad city dialogues with methods of visualizing spatial interpretations of the expectations and concerns that participants share about the life they want to lead in the city, a mirror is created in which the future plans can be reflected and ambitions can be evaluated.

Notes

1 The credentials for all the figures in this chapter are as follows: Kommuneqarfik Sermersooq has in collaboration with the Government of Greenland prepared a comprehensive master plan for the Tuujuk and Blok P areas in Nuuk with advice from Dahl & Uhre Architects and *tegnestuen tnt nuuk*. Asplan Viak landscape and MDH Architects assisted with the structure plan. Energy advisors were Steinsvik

Arkitekter AS and INUPLAN A/S. The Norwegian Department for Foreign Affairs financed the guest architect projects made by Fantastic Norway, MDH Architects sa, 42 architects + Regional associates and *tnt nuuk* a/s + M:ARC ApS + Arkitekti ApS.

2 The quotation is taken from Kleist's public speech at the COP 15 side-event 'Greenland Sea Ice Sheet – Melting Snow and Ice: A Call to Action'. Available at: http://naalakkersuisut.gl/en/Emner/News/News_from_Government/2009/12/MeltingSnowandIceAcallForAction.aspx.

3 These stories are from two different events: the first is from the think tank with cultural workers and artists; the second is from a workshop when the landscape architects from the Oslo School of Architecture and Design visited Nuuk.

4 Statement from the citizen participation project, printed in the English translation of the exhibition catalogue, Nuuk, 2011.

5 Editorial in *Sermitsiaq*, week 5, February 2010

6 Ane Geraae, chronicle, *Nuuk Ugeavis* (Nuuk weekly paper), August 2010.

7 The guest project *The House of Families* was published on important websites on architecture and was an instant 'hit', so to speak, while the plan was still in the making. The magazine *Monocle* called us and asked: 'What is happening in Greenland?' A larger world was suddenly following the work in progress.

8 Jury report from Arkitekturmässan, 2011.

References

Friedmann, J. (2011) *Insurgencies: Essays in Planning Theory*. New York: Routledge.

Hillier, J. (2007) *Stretching Beyond the Horizon: A Multiplanar Theory of Spatial Planning and Governance*. Farnham: Ashgate.

Ingold, T and Hallam, E. (2007) Creativity and cultural improvisation: An introduction. In *Creativity and Cultural Improvisation*. New York: Berg, pp. 1–24.

Leine, K. (2007) *Kalak*. Copenhagen: Gyldendalske.

Nyseth, T., Pløger, J. and Holm, T. (2010) Planning beyond the horizon: The Tromsø experiment. *Planning Theory*: 224–47.

Sermersooq Municipality (2011) *In the Centre of the World in the Centre of Nuuk*. Nuuk: Scandinavian Books. Available in Danish at: http://issuu.com/sermersooq/docs/nunarsuup_qeqqani_nuup_qeqqani.

Yaneva, A. (2012) *Mapping Controversies in Architecture*. Farnham: Ashgate.

11 Social innovation as the common ground between social cohesion and economic development of small and medium-sized towns in France and Quebec

Abdelillah Hamdouch and Leïla Ghaffari

Introduction

Today, cities and towns are facing a multi-layered challenge. First of all, the interdependence of citizens and towns has become dramatically increased by the global economy and they have become either global winners or losers. While the individual's interests were mostly running in the same direction as those of the community and the city, today they no longer necessarily follow the same directions and rules (Reich, 1991; Kearns and Forrest, 2000), hence the emergence of a growing distance between self-interest and public interest. As a result, in most countries and places, the cohesiveness of society is threatened to some degree, which in turn requires the design and implementation of proper policies and plans dedicated to the (re-)creation of elements of sociability and cohesiveness (Stingendal, 2010).

Moreover, the global economy is putting pressure on cities and towns to be competitive. Cities and towns strive to find a role in the new global urban hierarchy (Kearns and Forrest, 2000). Still, this process of finding a new role is not always in the interests of the everyday life of the citizens and this phenomenon puts most cities and towns in an unbalanced situation between competitiveness and social cohesion. In fact, 'in many places public money is more invested in competitiveness than in welfare for inhabitants' (Cassiers and Kesteloot, 2012: 1912). The two-sided question that arises here is the relationship between economic development and social cohesion in cities. 'Does economic success lead to social success?' (Parkinson, 2007: 367). Symmetrically, can social cohesion contribute to economic success?

Although answering these questions is not simple, it should be taken into account that a knowledge-based urban economy can lead to the achievement of a more cohesive society (Parkinson, 2007). And of course a cohesive society offers a promising ground for economic development, but neither of these two processes occurs automatically, and the task of combining these two aspects requires that the issue be put on the agenda of the local policies of cities.

However, most urban studies focus on large cities and metropolises. Small and medium-sized towns (SMSTs) have always lived in the shadow of larger cities, which makes it much harder for them to find a role in the new urban hierarchy. Moreover, they have usually been considered less important in relation to national policy-making. This, combined with economic problems and global competitive pressures, results in a severe socio-economic situation (de-industrialization, unemployment, etc.) typical of many SMSTs (Demazière et al., 2014; Hamdouch and Banovac, 2014).

Considering the questions mentioned above concerning the relationship between social success and economic success, SMSTs are facing a different situation from those of large cities and metropolitan areas. The latter concentrate wealth and attract investments, which make them practically hegemonic in the urban hierarchy. In this study we claim that social cohesion in SMSTs plays a cardinal role in their socio-economic development. We suggest that the common ground between social cohesion and economic development is *social innovation*:

> Today ... when we talk about SI we refer to finding acceptable progressive solutions for a whole range of problems of exclusion, deprivation, alienation, lack of wellbeing, and also to those actions that contribute positively to significant human progress and development. SI means fostering inclusion and wellbeing through improving social relations and empowerment processes ... Socially innovative change means the improvement of social relations – micro relations between individuals and people, but also macro relations between classes and other social groups. It also means a focus on the different skills by which collective actors and groups play their roles in society. (Moulaert et al., 2013: 16)

We believe that social innovation is essential for the survival of SMSTs as a means of promoting both social cohesion and local economic development. In order to improve the economic development and social cohesion of SMSTs through social innovation, we believe that the institutional structure has a fundamental role to play. In particular, local policies are need to support and give space to social innovations so that they do not remain a micro-scale activity, the result of which fades away.

The remainder of the chapter is organized into four sections. First, we discuss planning in SMSTs from different perspectives. In this section, our objective is to place social cohesion and economic development in a relationship, to emphasize the differences between large cities and SMSTs, and to analyse the role of planning and policy-making in the process of social cohesion and local development. Second, we examine the actual status of SMSTs in the contemporary global economy and outline some development patterns. In doing so, our goal is to identify the processes of social innovation that can help SMSTs to survive. The role of social innovation

192 *Abdelillah Hamdouch and Leïla Ghaffari*

and proximity is highlighted in this section. Third, we derive insights from French and Canadian SMSTs to see how our analytical framework might be applied to these cases. Finally, we conclude by tracing some pathways for further research.

Planning in SMSTs: toward a cohesive society

In this section, we briefly examine planning issues in SMSTs, the role of local policies of social cohesion in the development of SMSTs and the importance of social innovation in these towns.

SMSTs

SMSTs are defined differently in different contexts. In France, the threshold for SMSTs was defined by the Federation of mayors of medium-sized towns (FMVM): small towns have a population of between 3,000 and 20,000 inhabitants, and medium-sized towns of between 20,000 and 100,000 inhabitants. The Inter-ministerial Delegation for Territorial Development and Regional Attractiveness (DATAR) uses, in turn, a larger threshold of 30,000 to 200,000 inhabitants for medium-sized towns. In the Canadian context, we use different terms, which are Small Population Centres, Medium Population Centres and Large Population Centres. According to Statistics Canada, medium-sized towns are those having a population between 30,000 and 99,999; small towns have a population between 1,000 and 29,999; finally, large cities are those with a population of 100,000 or more.[1]

The distribution of the population is again different in Canada and in Europe. About 72 per cent of Europeans live in SMSTs (OIR, 2006). This number drops to 21 per cent for Canadians according to the 2006 census.

What is common in almost all SMSTs is that they are different from big cities and metropolises. This difference creates specific potentials as well as specific weaknesses for the development of SMSTs (Demazière et al., 2014). The problems of metropolises and large cities, such as pollution, high living costs, crime, and traffic congestion may be less present in SMSTs, but at the same time, in the globalization process, they do not have the same status as big cities and it is more difficult for them to redefine their role in a new urban hierarchy. As a consequence, planning in towns deals with different challenges and it becomes important for them to find a way to differentiate themselves from other cities. As the report on the TOWN project concludes (Servillo et al., 2014: vi), SMSTs (specifically in Europe) share the following characteristics:

> Industrial employment has a greater proportion of employment, while the service sector has a smaller proportion of employment; a significantly smaller proportion of jobs [on average] in private marketed services and

in public services in comparison to [large cities and high-density urban areas]; a higher economic activity rate; a higher proportion of pensionable adults and more children; a lower proportion of working age adults with a degree; employment in the retail sector is significantly lower than in [large cities and high-density urban areas]; SMSTs have a lower proportion of people who live and work in them than the [large cities and high-density urban areas] that are located in the same regions and countries; unemployment rates in SMSTs tend to be lower than for [large cities and high-density urban areas in some] countries; higher proportion of school age children; higher shares of secondary or holiday homes.

Therefore, SMSTs occupy a more precarious situation, having fewer resources in comparison with large cities. This is the reason why the economic growth of SMSTs is related to social innovations based on local resources and comparative advantages (Knox and Mayer, 2009; Hamdouch and Banovac, 2014). In this process of mobilizing local potentials, as Demazière et al. (2014) stress, the institutional settings of SMSTs are important, and public policies and regulations influence the socio-economic development of SMSTs, as well as their attractiveness for investment and population. The role of institutional structure in the performance of SMSTs' economic systems is fundamental.

Governance and institutional structure

As David Harvey (1989: 4, quoted in Eizaguirre et al., 2012: 2001) states: 'The power to organize space derives from a whole complex of forces mobilized by diverse social agents.' Policies are one of the tools in the governance process, and governance not only refers to any form of coordination of interdependent social relations, but is also about the reflexive self-organization of interdependent actors. It should include alternative mechanisms of negotiation between various groups and networks, and equally embrace citizens who disagree with mainstream policy formulation and who present alternative creative strategies. In fact, instead of bottom-up and top-down practices, cities and towns have to start developing '"bottom-linked" practices which combine social and institutional innovation' (Eizaguirre et al., 2012: 2001). Policies relate bottom-linked processes to one another in various ways.

'Regional and local government, businesses, community, non-profit organizations (especially associations and social & solidarity economy enterprises, SSE), and even individuals are all involved in the objective of social cohesion' (Eizaguirre et al., 2012: 2005), and it is important that consistent policy-making creates the necessary links between relevant actors and develops a movement towards a cohesive society. In fact, if policies do not make these connections and do not create the space for innovative actions, lack of coordination minimizes the positive impact of these actions.

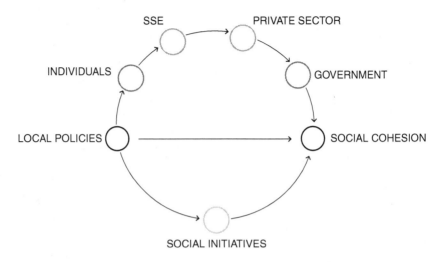

Figure 11.1 The role of local policies in feeding social cohesive dynamics

In other words, in order to create a cohesive society, all actions and efforts need to move coherently towards the object, and policies can make it possible (see Figure 11.1).

Moreover, 'urban governance and policy interventions can bring social cohesion when they go beyond the idea of creating spaces without conflict and take into account social and cultural differences' (Young, 1990, quoted in Eizaguirre et al., 2012: 2012). Here is where local policies have an important role to play: they are open to conflicting view and debate, and they can link the bottom-up and top-down processes. To achieve social cohesion, what happens at the local level and among individuals and associations plays an essential role, and it is crucial that local policies are attuned to what is going on in local civil society.

According to Andreotti et al. (2012: 1935), 'the empirical evidence stresses that innovative experiences are more likely to be planned and implemented at the local level. At a local scale, the territory with its resources and limits can indeed respond better to the local population's needs'. According to Cassiers and Kesteloot (2012: 1916), 'if the local level is not the most effective one for social cohesion policies, it is nevertheless the level where new practices emerge'. Still, 'local action ... must join and be joined by collective action in other spatial scales, thus interconnecting different levels of political struggle' (Cassiers and Kesteloot, 2012: 1916). So, policies are important in general for linking horizontal and vertical levels of social actions and local policies; in particular, they are important in giving space to and supporting innovative experiences. Policies can support social innovations, and institutions can be a kind of social innovation themselves by creating novel paths for participation and inclusion.

In sum, local policies can have three kinds of approaches to fostering social cohesion, all of which can be socially innovative: a direct approach, an interconnecting approach and an indirect approach. The direct approach is about local policies which address the effects of insufficient social cohesion, e.g. policies which try to solve the housing problems of marginalized groups. The indirect approach concerns policies which try to give space to innovative initiatives and actions, and support them to thrive. Subvention policies are one example of this kind of approach. Finally, the interconnecting approach concerns policies aiming at inter-relating social actions at different scales. For example, policies that encourage private firms to cooperate with educational institutions to enhance the employment of newly graduated students form part of this category. However, none of these approaches is sufficient on its own; they need to complement/combine with one another in order to achieve a coherent responsive policy system for fostering social cohesion. Moreover, it should be taken into account that all these local policies are affected and oriented by national and European policies.

Social cohesion and socio-economic development

Parkinson explains the strong relationship between social cohesion and socio-economic development: 'Cities with more jobs tend to have less poverty and social exclusion. The search for economic competitiveness does not exclude a concern with social cohesion. A high value added, knowledge based high skill economy can lead to the achievement of wider social goals. It is easier to redistribute wealth than poverty. But it does not automatically happen. It requires policy intervention' (Parkinson, 2007: 5). Social cohesion and socio-economic development have a two-sided relation. They both affect and are affected by one another.

According to Jenson, 'a careful monitoring of international statistics shows increasing rates of income inequality and homelessness, street crime and other forms of lawlessness, intractably high rates of youth unemployment, intergenerational dependency on social assistance, climbing rates of child poverty and a disturbing slide of some basic indicators of population health' (Jenson, 1998: 6). And the author continues: 'There is now a broad discussion of the dependence of economic growth on investments in healthy social relations, rather than treating social spending as simply a hostage to economic growth' (1998: 6).

Nowadays, considering the economic crisis, many countries, cities and towns 'may come under pressure to cut social protection. While social protection needs to be economically sustainable, it should be taken into account that it creates the basis for stable and sustainable societies and it is a wise investment for future economic sustainability and not just a burdensome cost' (European Committee for Social Cohesion (CDCS), 2004: 10).

So, on the one hand. 'social cohesion ... contributes to socio-economic development. A stable society is a favourable environment for business enterprise. The market economy depends on having people with money to spend; poverty is not a sound basis for economic development. In other words, what is good for social cohesion is also good for business' (European Committee for Social Cohesion (CDCS), 2004: 11). In other words, 'social quality is necessary to good economic policy as much as good employment policy is necessary to social quality' (Beauvais and Jenson, 2002: 44).

Social cohesion has two types of effects on socio-economic development; direct and indirect. Direct effects happen through creating jobs, improving education and answering the needs of the labour market. Indirect effects occur through improving society, a society in which people have place attachment, participate and care, a society which is tolerant and where people are entitled to be different, and a society in which the environment is respected and a standard level of ecological quality is provided for all. Such a society, when encouraging the above-mentioned values and aims, has a better socio-economic development basis and creates a promising base for new investments.

On the other hand, economic growth makes it easier to achieve social goals. Sustainable economic development depends on sustainable social development and also on a sustainable environment. Disparities and inequalities in wealth are 'tolerated as long as people feel that they have an equal chance to improve their situation. If, however, the differences become too flagrant, and if, above all, the less privileged feel that they have little real hope of bettering themselves, that they are trapped in a situation of poverty and social exclusion, that they have no stake in society because society has nothing to offer them, then socio-economic disparities will start to put social cohesion seriously at risk' (European Committee for Social Cohesion (CDCS), 2004: 10). Moreover, as the report of the *Confédération des Syndicats Nationaux* (CSN) of Canada mentions, 'one of the best ways to ensure social cohesion is to create jobs. Economic exclusion – for more than a temporary period of unemployment – leaves people fragile, isolated, and apathetic' (quoted in Jenson, 1998: 24).

Furthermore, 'the economy may be regarded differently, as a set of particular social practices constituted in social institutions and activities ranging from the everyday of family and community life to norms of consumption and social regulation of work habits and professional practice' (MacCallum et al., 2009: 1). From this point of view, social cohesion and socio-economic development are intimately interconnected.

As mentioned above, one of the ways in which policies can help to foster social cohesion is by giving space to social innovation. 'By encouraging these initiatives, policy makers strive to have a triple triumph; a triumph for the individuals and the society by providing high quality, affordable and beneficial services which will add value to the daily life of people; a triumph for government by making the provision of those services more sustainable in the long term; and a triumph for industry by creating new business opportunities and new entrepreneurship' (BEPA, 2010: 7).

The role of policies has become of increasing importance because social needs are more pressing now: 'At a time of budgetary constraints, social innovation is an effective way of responding to social challenges, by mobilizing people's creativity to develop solutions and make better use of scarce resources. Social innovation can also promote an innovative and learning society. It is a starting point for creating the social dynamics behind technological innovations' (BEPA, 2010: 6).

Moreover, innovative processes are essential for the survival of SMSTs and institutional settings are important for mobilizing the potentials of social innovations. It is this connection of social innovations and social cohesion policies that can help SMSTs distinguish themselves in a globalizing world.

The role of social innovation in the socio-economic development of SMSTs – a suggested analytical framework

As mentioned above, economic development and social cohesion are connected and influence one another. And local policies which support social innovations have an essential role to play in fostering social cohesion. Looking at the economic profile of SMSTs, we can see that in these towns, innovation has a special role, as the towns have to distinguish themselves in the new urban hierarchy and, being in different situations, they need to highlight their potentials. Social innovation is where economic development and social development are united, and SMSTs need innovation as a tool of survival. This need comes with an easier base for growing innovation since in SMSTs the strong proximity of local actors is observable (Hamdouch and Banovac, 2014).

The situation of SMSTs is different from those in large cities and metropolises, and this difference can be observed at all layers. But they themselves are different from each other and it is important to treat them according to their specific context and background. Many SMSTs have a manufacturing tradition and have gone through a process of de-industrialization due to globalization, delocalization and advancements in technology. In general, when SMSTs are mainly based on a productive economy, which is mostly connected to international markets and less connected to the local markets, they become fragile and dependent on all changes that occur in the global market (Cooke, 1989). Attracting investment and businesses by generating specific resources can be a driver of the local economy for SMSTs (Knox and Mayer, 2009; Pecqueur, 1989), but this boost in the economy is vulnerable (Demazière and Hamdouch, 2012). Specialization is not always encouraged by economists. Some (e.g. Krugman, 1991) argue that diversity in economic activities attracts more investors and consumers and makes the town less fragile (Demazière et al., 2013).

The literature on local economic development shows success in building networks and economic cooperation between local actors instead of specialization in selected industries or diversifying without networking (Carrier and Demazière, 2012; Demazière et al., 2013). The existing proximity between actors in SMSTs, which is inherently stronger than it is in large cities, can be a base for cooperative economic activities. As Léo and Philippe (2011) explain, SMSTs have a better chance of success by providing economic activities that can support each other. And they have the advantage of their small size, which facilitates administrative processes and also creates a stronger community life (Demazière et al., 2013).

Moving away from production and focusing on consumption, we can observe that today the mobility of people is increasing and this mobility is less and less job-oriented. People who are mobile search for a better quality of life. This is what gives SMSTs which are well connected and have environmental assets an advantage. The geographical circulation of income and the geographical circulation of production are different, which means that generating income and the actual spending of this income may take place in two different places (Davezies, 2008, cited in Demazière et al., 2013). This fact forms the basis for the residential economy and it plays an important part in the development of SMSTs. Attracting people to consume (i.e. to spend their income) in a place is a way of improving the local economy. Tourists, pensioners and young professionals are subject to this economy. And with their higher natural quality of life, SMSTs have the potential to attract the income being generated elsewhere. As Demazière et al. (2013) mention, in many SMSTs, tourism represents an important source of income. Incidentally, innovative processes are essential in order to have an outstanding and distinctive tourism industry. The importance of this economy depends on the attractiveness of the town to residents and tourists (Demazière and Hamdouch, 2012) and this attractiveness comes with innovative approaches that highlight the town's potential. A town that is well connected to larger cities may work on attracting young professional commuters by giving them enough reasons to live there. A town with a large elderly population and a potentially suitable environment for such people can focus on attracting wealthy pensioners in order to boost its economy. And there are SMSTs that are tourist-oriented because of assets such as natural and architectural heritage (Demazière and Hamdouch, 2012). Activating each of these potentials requires innovation. According to Davezies (2010), in times of economic crisis, SMSTs may profit from the residential economy because it captures the income spent locally in services that are not directly influenced by global competition (Demazière et al., 2013).

As mentioned above, in both the productive and the residential economy in SMSTs, innovation is essential. But innovation may act as the base of an economy itself in a knowledge-based society. As Demazière et al. (2013: 16) explain: 'Knowledge and innovation constitute a long-term opportunity for SMSTs with the potential to become a new foundation of their economy.' Benefiting from a knowledge-based economy requires a strong coordination among actors who are heterogeneous and geographically diverse (Hamdouch and Depret, 2001 cited in Demazière et al., 2013: 16). In this context, we can see that the existing close proximity between actors in SMSTs works in their favour and prepares the ground for a knowledge-based economy. In these towns, not only does spatial proximity exist, but also it is combined with an 'organized proximity' (i.e. a proximity based on intentional coordination devices such as negotiation and cooperation among the actors), giving, as Hamdouch and Ghaffari (2015) call it, a *co-constructed proximity*.

Building on the above considerations and arguments, we propose in this chapter an analytical framework suggesting a relationship between the development of SMSTs, social innovation and the proximity of actors (Figure 11.2). We suggest that for SMSTs, social innovation is not just a matter of choice but a necessity and a matter of survival to a greater extent than for large cities. Incidentally, considering the existing proximity of actors in SMSTs, it may be easier to initiate, implement and sustain social innovations in these towns than in large cities.

This chapter also suggests that social innovation creates a common ground between economic development and social cohesion (Figure 11.3). In other words, an economic development plan based on local potentials is likely to foster social cohesion as well. On the one hand, boosting the local economy by socially innovative approaches can improve the social cohesion of the town in general. On the other hand, policies which aim at fostering social cohesion through social innovation improve the economic situation of the town, since these actions help the local population to integrate in society and in the marketplace, and also establish a sense of attachment to the place which encourages them to come up with new ideas.

The argument sustaining this analytical framework is that proximity facilitates social innovation. Social innovation is used as a means of survival for the development of SMSTs; in turn, the improvements in the development of SMSTs reinforce the proximity of actors. Although this circular relationship may appear solid, as mentioned above, the support provided by policies to social innovations is essential for their success.

Brief insights from two case studies in France and Canada

In this section we will focus mainly on two cases: a French medium-sized town (Châteauroux) and a Canadian medium-sized town (Drummondville).

Châteauroux is situated in the south of the Centre region of France, in the Indre department. It has 46,386 inhabitants and the whole agglomeration of Châteauroux has a population of 76,600 (Demazière et al., 2014). In this town, social innovations connect social cohesion and economic

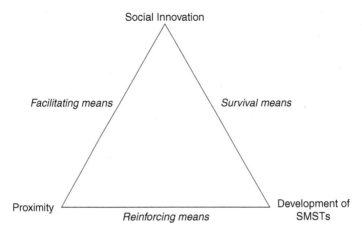

Figure 11.2 Analytical framework: the role of proximity and social innovation in the development of SMSTs

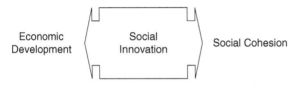

Figure 11.3 The place of social innovation in social cohesion and economic development

development and they have been supported by the policies of social cohesion. The Urban Contract of Social Cohesion ('Contrat Urbain de Cohésion Sociale' or CUCS), for example, follows nine thematic topics that form the basis of policies and also for calls for projects and actions (CUCS, 2013).

One of these thematic topics is access to employment and economic development. This topic follows a four-level policy. Indeed, over the last 30 years, Châteauroux has been following an approach of connecting the social and economic worlds. According to this approach, social cohesion policies which are clearly connected to the economic sector are defined. The first level is about connecting the economy and the social sector. In Châteauroux, this means that social actors mobilize the people excluded from the labour market (15–20 per cent of the active population) in order to enhance and then facilitate their economic integration. The 'maisons de quartier', social centres, charity associations and the associative movement in general try to find the inhabitants who have the capacity to valorize their competences so that they become aware of what they have and become engaged in the inclusion process.

This is important because what often happens at this level is that some people say that they do not have the capacity, when in fact they have skills that only need to be improved. Cooking workshops, dressmaking workshops and volunteer workshops are some examples of action at this level (Ghaffari, 2013).

The second level is to create fluidity in the processes. Châteauroux is in a highly partitioned system, meaning for example that people undertake successive training sessions in different fields for having a skill; very often, the training finishes and then nothing follows. The idea is then to try to avoid interruptions in the processes using the education sector, the skill improvement sector, company internships, etc. so that the person can enter the regular labour market step by step (Ghaffari, 2013).

The third level of action is to create dynamism in these processes by anticipating the needs of companies. Even if the unemployment rate is high, companies may have difficulties in finding the people who are employable. This means that, as Coatrieux explains, 'we have to foresee the needs of companies so that we can adapt our training programmes and prepare people to be available for the future needs of these companies' (Ghaffari, 2013).

Finally, the fourth level is helping job creators, be they large companies that want to locate in the territory or develop their existing activities, or small entrepreneurs who want to create their own economic activity. This means reducing the risks taken by job creators through favouring advantageous real estate offers and suitable premises. Mobilizing and coordinating all possible institutional subsidies and financial support for job creation is another important key (Ghaffari, 2013).

The Châteauroux case shows how policies try to improve the productive as well as the residential local economy, while at the same time addressing social issues. In fact, policies try to engage local actors in this process in order to bring about more sustainable growth. This is how the innovative component of local policies should be highlighted in order to contribute to the successful development of SMSTs.

The Châteauroux case also shows that, along with policy supports, the existing proximity of actors in this town facilitates the process of innovation and development. As mentioned above, one of the differences between metropolises and big cities on the one hand and SMSTs in the other is the scale of the city, which brings about a difference in relations. Due to their limited size, SMSTs offer their inhabitants a more human living environment and allow for stronger social relationships than in big cities.

Châteauroux constitutes a rather human living environment where most people know each other and meet easily in public space. So, naturally they work together. As Coatrieux explains:

> We exclude no one from our work and every time that we have a workshop we invite a lot of actors and they come. Actors such as 'les chambres consulaires', 'les organisations professionnelles', 'les

syndicats coopératifs', 'les acteurs sociaux', 'les centres sociaux', 'les acteurs socio-culturels', 'les chefs d'entreprise', 'les services de l'Etat, et du département'. There is no privileged actor. All actors who have the expertise on the subject that we are working on are invited. We are in a human scale and normally we work in a network. (Ghaffari, 2013)

Apart from working in networks, financial support is one of the means that connect authorities to local actors. In Châteauroux, the town allocates subsidies to social actors. 'La communauté d'agglomération' has an intervention domain called 'the town policy' ('La politique de la ville'). The town council calls for projects and supports the projects and actions with time limits. In fact, it allocates its aides to actions with precise objectives and outcomes suggested by local actors. Calls for projects and actions are adapted to the capacity of local actors (Ghaffari, 2013).

In Châteauroux, the subsidies are not allocated specifically to a domain; they update their specifications every year. However, the most important indicator for choosing projects is the involvement of inhabitants. In fact, 'la Communauté d'Agglomération' prioritizes projects that consider the needs of inhabitants (Ghaffari, 2013).

In terms of policy approaches, we can see a dominance of direct policies in the political body of Châteauroux, but we can also identify interconnecting policies even though it is possible to detect a lack of policies for connecting private sectors to the social and solidarity economy (SSE) or to the community.

Moreover, we observe that in Châteauroux, there is quite a strong horizontal relationship among different associations. We can see that implementing one action sometimes requires more than three associations or actors in general working in partnership. Thus, Châteauroux is an example where this dynamic of proximity, social innovation and development of an SMST works.

In Canada, Drummondville is a quite similar case, which we will briefly outline now. Drummondville is a medium-sized town situated in the Centre-du-Québec region. It is located between two important cities: Montreal and Quebec City. The location of the town is favourable for its development and its population has been increasing in recent years. According to the Institut de la Statistique du Québec, Drummondville had a population of 99,674 persons in 2011.[2] It is one of the manufacturing towns that have survived the economic crisis and have overcome de-industrialization and globalization shocks by spurring/benefiting from innovations embedded in strong social networks.

A total of 49 per cent of the workforce in Drummondville still works in manufacturing fields. Until 1960, more than 90 per cent of the workforce were employed in the textile industry and this lack of diversity brought about a great decline in the town's fortunes, which led to an unemployment rate of 25 per cent in 1970 (Champoux, 2003). But in recent years, the town has become an economic pole again due to national and regional economic changes, and also because of the presence of a strong innovation network embedded in the social context of the town. In other words, the town's geographical situation and the relational proximity among actors helped the local innovation networks survive and remain sustainable (Carrier et al., 2012). The research undertaken by Carrier et al. (2012) also shows that there is local cohesion in the network of economic actors that contributes greatly to their collective success. According to the Annual Report of the Society of Economic Development of Drummondville (SDED), since 2010 the number of jobs created in the manufacturing sector has been increasing, reaching 1,069 new jobs in 2014, and the dominant sector has switched from textile to machinery industries (SDED, 2014).

Moreover, at the local policy level, we can observe diverse programmes and funds which encourage innovation for a better economic development; those such as the Local Investment Funds, the Young Business Developer's Funds, the Social Economy Funds and Self-employed Workers Support have been particularly important (www.sded-drummond.qc.ca/index2.asp).

The focus of the SDED is on the economic development of Drummondville, while the Community Development Corporation (CDC) focuses on social development. But there is a relationship between these two organizations, which makes it easier to empower the local population. The CDC is the administrator of the 'social economy' section of the SDED and it receives a significant budget in order to support entrepreneurship and economic integration among the inhabitants (CDC, 2014).

Among other organizations that foster social cohesion at various scales in the town, the CDC implements numerous activities in order to foster social cohesion within the community. This is organized using different committees that work on different social issues, such as women, poverty, social development, solidarity and social inclusion (CDC, 2014).

The presence of higher scales of intervention in Drummondville is stronger than in the case of Châteauroux. This presence is not limited to financial support and different regional organizations take part in the activities coordinated by the CDC or the SDED.

In terms of policy approach, Drummondville shows a dominance of indirect policies, which are mostly focused on financing social initiatives. However, direct policies and interconnecting policies are also present. What is interesting in the case of Drummondville is the inter-relationship between different organizations. As an example, the CDC and the SDED work with a significant number of community partners in order to achieve their objectives. To name just a few, we can see the collaboration of community centres and youth clubs ('Maisons des Jeunes') of different neighbourhoods (CDC, 2014). This proximity at the local level is one of the keys to the success of local development of this town.

The cases of Drummondville and Châteauroux are therefore instructive illustrations of the facilitating influence of co-constructed proximity in the innovation process and, as a result, in the development of SMSTs. The support coming from local policies is also a reason why these towns have been successful in maintaining/revitalizing a productive economy during a period of crisis and a more general context of new competitive pressure.

Conclusions and further research perspectives

In this chapter, we have tried to emphasize the importance of social innovations in the dynamic of social cohesion and economic development in SMSTs. We have argued that social innovation is the common ground that can foster both social cohesion and economic development/revitalization. On the one hand, it is a survival means for SMSTs, since they are usually subject to a more delicate socio-economic situation than large cities in a globalization and crisis context, and also because they need to (re)define themselves in the new urban hierarchy.

On the other hand, social innovation is easier to establish and sustain in SMSTs in comparison with large cities because in SMSTs, there is a strong proximity of actors. Based on the arguments we proposed on the relationships between social innovation, proximity and the socio-development of SMSTs, we developed an analytical framework that aimed to clarify the process underlying these relationships. In this analytical framework, proximity is conceptualized as a facilitating means for social innovation; in turn, it has been argued that social innovation is a means of survival for the development of SMSTs. Finally, closing the loop, we argued that this development could actually reinforce proximity while contributing to a more cohesive society.

Institutional factors play an important role in the efficiency of the explained process. Policies are needed to support social innovations so that they will have a chance to be implemented and to last. Policies are also needed to support and facilitate the proximity of actors by creating networks of actors who can share their knowledge and work together.

We tried to derive lessons from two examples of SMSTs according to our analytical framework. In the French case of Châteauroux, we could see how social innovations supported by strong social cohesion policies can foster the development of the town and how existing proximity of actors, resulting from the human scale of the town, facilitates the design and implementation of necessary actions.

In the Canadian case of Drummondville, one could observe a strong social network which supports the economic development of the town. Yet again in this case, we can see how proximity may be the platform for an innovative process that can greatly help a traditional manufacturing town to survive de-industrialization and devitalization.

Beyond the arguments and the case studies examined in this chapter, we believe that the analytical approach proposed still requires theoretical elaboration and empirical evidence to support it. Indeed, several important questions deserve further investigation. Particularly important is to better document the effect of growing size in terms of area on the ability of a town to preserve a high potential of local networking among actors that could support sustained social innovation dynamics. Likewise, the variability of national policies (especially in times of crisis and sharp global competition) in relation to the funding of SMST policies and actions favouring a virtuous loop between economic development and social cohesion may represent a threat to the efforts in place locally. Finally, the question may be asked as to whether SMSTs are able to develop and/or sustain planning approaches and local policies balancing economic development and social cohesion objectives when some key actors weaken their local engagement or simply 'fly away' to places (including large cities) offering better financial or institutional advantages. The functional role that SMSTs can play in evolving urban hierarchies is clearly an issue, as well as their ability to plan for sustained cooperative commitments with other cities and towns which they can complement/work with in the mid- to long term.

Notes

1 https://www12.statcan.gc.ca/census-recensement/2011/ref/dict/geo049a-eng.cfm.
2 www.bdso.gouv.qc.ca/pls/ken/Ken211_Page_Accu.page_accu.

References

Andreotti, A., Mingione, E., and Polizzi, E. (2012) Local welfare systems: A challenge for social cohesion. *Urban Studies*, 49(9): 1925–40.

Beauvais, C., and Jenson, J. (2002) Social cohesion: Updating the state of the research. *CPRN Discussion Paper*, F(22).

BEPA (2010) *Empowering People, Driving Change: Social Innovation in the European Union*. Brussels: European Commision.

Carrier, M. and Demazière, C. (eds) (2012) Les mutations économiques des villes petites et moyennes. *Revue d'Economie Régionale et Urbaine*, 2.

Carrier, M., Theriault, M. and Veronneau, E. (2012) Structure socio-spatiale des réseaux d'innovation en secteur manufacturier traditionnel d'une ville moyenne. *Revue d'Économie Régionale & Urbaine*, 2: 215–44.

Cassiers, T., and Kesteloot, C. (2012) Socio-spatial inequalities and social cohesion in European cities. *Urban Studies*, 49(9): 1909–24.

CDC (2014) *Annual Report 2012–2013, Community Development Corporation, Drummondville*.

Champoux, M. (2003) Histoire et culture régionale du Québec, Université du Québec à Trois-Rivières, available at: www.uqtr.uquebec.ca/~bougaief/Culture/textes/drum24ju.htm.

Confédération des syndicaux nationaux (1995) *Développer l'économie solidaire*. Montreal: CSN.

Cooke, P. (ed.) (1989) *Localities: The Changing Face of Urban Britain*. London: Unwin Hyman.

CUCS (2013). Appel à projets 2013 Programmation Contrat Urbain de Cohésion Sociale. Available at: http://sig.ville.gouv.fr/page/45.
Davezies, L. (2008) *La République et ses territoires*. Paris: Le Seuil.
—— (2010) *La crise et nos territoires: premiers impacts*. Paris: Caisse des Dépôts and Institut CDC pour la Recherche.
Demazière, C., Banovac, K. and Hamdouch, A. (2013) The socio-economic development of small and medium-sized towns (SMSTs): Factors, dominant profiles and evolution patterns. TOWN interim report: Appendix 4.
Demazière, C. and Hamdouch, A. (2012) *Observation des dynamiques économiques et stratégies des villes petites et moyennes de la Région Centre*. ODES Project, Interim Research for Région Centre, Université François Rabelais, UMR CITERES, Tours.
Demazière, C., Hamdouch, A., Banovac, K. and L. Daviot, L. (2014) *Analyse des Dynamiques de Développement de 16 villes petites et moyennes de la Région Centre*. Final Report, ODES Project, Vol. 1, Région Centre and UMR CITERES – Université François-Rabelais de Tours, Tours.
Eizaguirre, S., Pradel, M., Terrones, A., Martinez-Celorrio, X. and Garcia, M. (2012) Multilevel governance and social cohesion: Bringing back conflict in citizenship practices. *Urban Studies*, 49(9): 1999–2016.
European Committee for Social Cohesion (CDCS) (2004) *A New Strategy for Social Cohesion*. Brussels: European Committee for Social Cohesion.
Ghaffari, L. (2013) Interview with Gilles Coatrieux, the Director of Inclusive Development and Attractiveness of the Castelroussine conurbation, Châteauroux.
Hamdouch, A. and Banovac, K. (2014) Socio-economic and performance dynamics of European SMSTs: Methodological approach and lessons from 31 case studies. In L. Servillo (ed.), *TOWN, Small and Medium-Sized Towns in their Functional Territorial Context*. Luxembourg: ESPON, pp. 162–87.
Hamdouch, A. and Depret, M.-H. (2001) *La nouvelle économie industrielle de la pharmacie: Structures industrielles, dynamique d'innovation et stratégies commerciales*. Paris: Elsevier.
Hamdouch, A. and Ghaffari, L. (2015) La gentrification comme produit de la proximité entre acteurs dans les opérations de requalification-redynamisation des quartiers défavorisés? Le cas de Montréal. Paper presented at the 8th International Conference on Proximity: 'Building Proximities in a Global World', Tours, 20–22 May.
Harvey, D. (1989) From managerialism to entrepreneurialism: The transformation of urban governance in late capitalism. *Geografiska Annaler*, 71(B): 3–17.
Jenson, J. (1998) Mapping social cohesion: The state of Canadian research. *Canadian Policy Research Networks Inc.*, F(03).
Kearns, A., and Forrest, R. (2000) Social cohesion and multilevel urban governance. *Urban Studies*, 37(5–6): 995–1017.
Knox, P. and Mayer, H. (2009) *Small Town Sustainability: Economic, Social and Environmental Innovation*. Basel: Birkhauser.
Krugman, P. (1991) *Geography and Trade*. Cambridge, MA: MIT Press.
Léo, P.-Y. and Philippe, J. (eds) (2011) *Villes moyennes et services aux entreprises: enjeux et strategies*. Paris: L'Harmattan.
MacCallum, D., Moulaert, F., Hillier, J. and Vicari-Haddock, S. (eds) (2009) *Social Innovation and Territorial Development*. Farnham: Ashgate.

Moulaert, F., MacCallum, D. and Hillier, J. (2013) Social innovation: intuition, precept, concept, theory and practice. In F. Moulaert, D. MacCallum, A. Mehmood and A. Hamdouch (eds), *The International Handbook on Social Innovation: Collective Action, Social Learning and Transdisciplinary Research*. Cheltenham: Edward Elgar, pp. 13–24.

Moulaert, F., MacCallum, D., Mehmood, A. and Hamdouch, A. (eds) (2013) *The International Handbook on Social Innovation: Collective Action, Social Learning and Transdisciplinary Research*. Cheltenham: Edward Elgar.

OIR (2006) *The Role of Small and Medium-Sized Towns (SMESTO): Final Report*. Vienna.

Parkinson, M. (2007) Social cohesion in English cities: Policy, progress and prospects. Available at: www.bbsr.bund.de/BBSR/EN/Publications/IzR/2007/6Parkinson.pdf?__blob=publicationFile&v=2.

Pecqueur, B. (1989) *Le développement local*. Paris: Syros.

Reich, R. (1991) *The Work of Nations*. New York: Simon & Schuster.

SDED (Society of Economic Development of Drummondville) (2014) *Annual Report*.

Servillo, L., Atkinson, R., Smith, I., Russo, A., Sýkora, L., Demazière, C. and Hamdouch, A. (2014) *TOWN – Small and Medium-Sized Towns in their Functional Territorial Context, Final Report*. Luxembourg: ESPON.

Stingendal, M. (2010) Cities and social cohesion: Popularizing the results of Social Polis, Malmö University, Department of Urban Studies, available at: www.socialpolis.eu/uploads/tx_sp/Cities_and_Social_Cohesion_-_final__web_.pdf.

Young, I.M. (1990) *Justice and the Politics of Difference*. Princeton, NJ: Princeton University Press.

12 Renewed sustainable planning in the Arctic

A reflective, critical and committed approach

Gisle Løkken and Magdalena Haggärde

Introduction

Arctic landscapes, cities and societies are heavily affected by global incidents beyond local influence or control. Well-known and severe environmental challenges due to overpopulation, escalating urbanisation, economic crisis and over-exploitation of nature have evoked awareness of changing ecosystems and increased vulnerability.

In our practice as architects in Arctic landscapes, we have seen a need to develop experimental, subversive and open planning approaches that adopt a *hands-on* attitude to the reality of the landscape. Decades of inadequate understanding of correlating complex systems justify a critical evaluation of a dominant Western, modernist-capitalist planning model. The modern episteme and a notion of human superiority over nature has hence triggered what Bruno Latour (2004) describes as a necessary shift *from matters of fact to matters of concern*, with the aim of developing new positions in line with Gregory Bateson's statement: 'We are not outside the ecology for which we plan – we are always and inevitably a part of it' (Bateson 1972/2000: 512).

Our theoretical foundation for a renewed approach is based on the notion of the landscape as a derivation of time and space, following the ideas of Doreen Massey (2005) and simultaneously the use of concepts such as complexity and a non-hierarchical understanding of society, inspired in particular by the writings of Michel Foucault, Henry Lefebvre, Gilles Deleuze and Félix Guattari. It is a prerequisite for gaining new recognition in planning to accept a non-hegemonic approach where the subjective perspective is also valid, which means that we challenge what might be considered strictly scientific methods. However, landscapes, nature, people and society in general behave unpredictably, which opens up the possibility for alternative approaches, including experimental mapping and drawings. These are investigation methods tested in several projects, competitions and master studios from our office, which we have further elaborated upon in several publications (70°N arkitektur, 2012, 2014; Haggärde and Løkken, 2008, 2009, 2010, 2011, 2012, 2014).

To exemplify the different methodical approaches applied in different contexts and landscapes, we will use examples from a master studio at Bergen School of Architecture conducted in Finnmark and at the Kola peninsula (Haggärde and Løkken, 2011), and a competition entry from the invited international planning competition about the relocation of the mining city of Kiruna (70°N arkitektur et al., 2012). These are two very different examples: the first has a didactic purpose, while the second aims to make a plan that will greatly affect the future of the citizens involved. These examples show that every case needs to be investigated and treated individually, and that investigation tools and research language have to be developed and applied to each situation.

The purpose of the investigation will always be to gain deep, profound and critical contextual knowledge for planners and architects to create new, adaptable and dynamic solutions.

First, we will discuss a general theoretical background for the approach and thereafter present the two cases as examples of implementation in different contexts.

Knowledge from the landscape: time / space / change

The speed of change and the fact that some changes in the landscape have reached beyond the point of no return have gained increasingly greater focus. It is essential to detect the complexity of the transforming forces evoking and determining this development, and to continuously strive to find and develop appropriate tools to understand and work with these matters. A comprehension of complex issues presupposes a thorough investigation of the landscape, where a multitude of elements are put into play and connect along different trajectories of speed and time. The landscape itself holds vital information for planning – information about resilience and vulnerability that can form patterns of resistance in planning processes. An informed and complex spatial planning approach contains ideas of space and time as interwoven, but at the same time ongoing, incomplete and inconsistent dimensions throughout history. In the same way as Doreen Massey describes time, landscape and history as 'full of holes, of disconnections, of tentative half-formed first encounters. Loose ends and on-going stories' (2005: 107), our planning should be seen as an ongoing and susceptible process that never reaches completion.

Our approach as architects and planners in Arctic landscapes requires knowledge, curiosity and an open mindset. Doreen Massey states that: '"Everything is connected to everything else" which should be a salutary political reminder that whatever we do has wider implications than perhaps we commonly recognise' (2005: 107). While in the nineteenth century there was a concern in science to eliminate chance and create equilibrium and stasis, by the end of the twentieth century, acceptance of the idea of seeing science as made up of open systems, irreversible time and of indeterminacy has grown (Massey, 2005: 114). This has created a foundation on which the landscape must be investigated and understood as an assemblage of spatial narrations, events and practices – an experience that acknowledges both the objective and the subjective, including natural processes and history. The experiment is holistic and almost encyclopaedic: 'Whatever the starting point, the matter in hand spreads out and out, encompassing ever vaster horizons, and if it were permitted to go on further and further in every direction, it would end by embracing the entire universe' (Calvino, 1988: 107).

The belief in a modernist superiority

The latest 100 to 150 years of implemented urban concepts in the North are seemingly a transfer of technology, architecture and urban patterns known from other provenances imposed in an endless endeavour to conquer and civilise through urbanisation. An underlying colonial belief in superiority over local knowledge and behaviour has resulted in town planning that shows little creativity, sensitivity, ability or desire to develop urban structures on the premises given in the landscape or in terms of local and social conditions. Henry Lefebvre (1996) discusses the legitimacy of planning in the light of what he calls the practice *to inhabit* and emphasises the establishment of 'highly localized, highly particularized and centralized units' to re-establish an urban unity. He warns against a pretentious expert regime that is not in contact with real life and experience as a critique of a modernist notion of superiority and (quasi-)scientific beliefs: 'Architects seem to have established and dogmatized an ensemble of significations, as such poorly developed and variously labelled as "function", "form", "structure", or rather, functionalism, formalism, and structuralism.' Lefebvre believes that it is a tendency not to elaborate knowledge from the 'significations perceived and lived by those who inhabit, but from their [the experts] interpretations of inhabiting'. The result of such a top-down orientation is, according to Lefebvre, that 'their system tends to close itself off, impose itself and elude all criticism'. He warns about the limitations of analyses and systems 'put forward without any other procedure or precaution, as planning by extrapolation' (Lefebvre, 1996: 158).

The Arctic utopia

The few examples in architecture history of experimental approaches towards Arctic urban planning show a tendency to turn the northern or Arctic city into an urban utopia through idealisation of *pure life* under harsh conditions. Some of the best-known examples are Ralph Erskine's prospect for Resolute Bay (1958) and Frei Otto's generic proposal for an *Arctic City* (1971). Erskine's example shows enclosed assemblies of buildings gathering intimately to gain protection against the allegedly harsh outside. Likewise, Frei Otto takes the notion of the unfriendly Arctic conditions to the extreme and proposes a huge dome covering the whole city in order to provide total climate control for its inhabitants. Even though both these architects are excellent designers with a humanistic approach, the ideas represented in these utopias show an absence of basic contextual understanding in order to *live with* and to develop life in *accordance with* the natural given conditions. Instead, they carry an underlying notion of a Western, modernist culture battling against nature (culture vs. nature) – a battle to gain control over natural forces. Latour describes it as a Western character trait that 'we are the only ones who differentiate absolutely between Nature and Culture, between Science and Society, whereas in our eyes all the others ... cannot really separate what is knowledge from what is Society, what is sign from what is thing, what comes from Nature as it is from what their cultures require' (Latour, 1993: 99).

The right to the city – the right to the territory you inhabit

A renewed Arctic urbanity has to focus on the quality and the reality of everyday life. Increased attention towards the inhabitants' right to their own city (or territory) and individual emancipation regardless of social status challenge private property rights and the traditional economic systems. The becoming of urban life does not follow a coherent line or a consistent ideology, but demands participation and adaptation related to the reality of the citizens, and where the notion of becoming is an open opportunity: 'Becoming is a rhizome, not a classificatory or genealogical tree. Becoming is certainly not imitating, or identifying with something; neither is it regressing-progressing; neither is it corresponding, establishing corresponding relations; neither is it producing a filiation or producing through filiation. Becoming is a verb with a consistency all its own' (Deleuze and Guattari, 2004: 263).

The criticism of Western modernism can be applied to twentieth-century urbanisation (colonisation through urbanisation) in the north, with its distancing from inherited knowledge about living in the landscape according to its given natural conditions – a displaced knowledge in Western civilisation since the Enlightenment. There is a lack of improvisation skills and an absence of an open-minded ability to adaptation, to the unforeseen spatial changes applied to the landscape from annual cycles, and from the complexity of what is inevitable to become (with or without the will of man). According to Manuel De Landa, Deleuze gives new conceptual tools that free us from the constraints of a constructivist view on nature:

> unlike social constructivism, which achieves openness by making the world depend on human interpretation, Deleuze's approach achieves it by making the world into a creative, complexifying, problematizing cauldron of becoming. Because of their anthropocentrism, constructivist philosophers remain prisoners of what Foucault called the 'episteme

of man', while Deleuze plunges ahead into a posthumanist future, in which the world has been enriched by a multiplicity of nonhuman agencies. (De Landa, 1999: 41)

Extended Arctic urbanity

Most northern cities and settlements are very small and are located in scarcely inhabited, large landscapes, often constructed on the basis of one predominant industry such as a mine, a factory (metallurgic industry), fisheries or military activity (strategic or political presence). Even today, after decades of strong post-industrial changes in the global economy, industrial structures and demography, these cities are to a large extent highly dependent on a few essential sources of income. As a consequence, these cities are extremely vulnerable to fluctuations in global economies, public policies and climatic or environmental changes. In addition to a skewed gender distribution due to the prevailing single industries, many of these cities have experienced difficulties in maintaining their population and a healthy demographic diversity.

The habitation of Arctic landscapes seems to blur the notion of city life into something we might call an *extended Arctic urbanity*. The inhabitants seem largely to define their urban lives in a more extensive territory than the physical limitations of the actual city. This means that they define their lives in relation to the shifting seasons in the surrounding landscape (the time spent with different outdoors activities), the changing light conditions and the cyclic shifts in nature's production (fishing, berry picking, hunting, etc.) to a much higher extent than is often considered.

Learning from the landscape – benefiting from the Arctic commons

Natural resources in the north have historically largely been treated as *common pool resources* (CPR) and have been managed as a shared benefit either regarding offshore or coastal fisheries or the inland resources of hunting, gathering and grazing. However, according to Nobel laureate Elinor Ostrom (1990), these systems of reasonable ecological durability require a certain level of agreement and common interest among the actors. A well-governed CPR system works within certain principles, such as clearly defined boundaries, rules regarding the appropriation and provision of common resources, collective-choice arrangements, effective monitoring, and mechanisms of conflict resolutions and sanctioning of appropriators who violate community rules. The dilemma of the commons, also described by Garrett Hardin (1968) as *the tragedy of the commons*, implies that free access and unrestricted demand for a finite resource ultimately reduces the resource through over-exploitation, whether temporarily or permanently. The metaphor illustrates that the commons are implicitly highly vulnerable from actors or interests that have not endorsed the *rules* that have been unconsciously agreed upon. In the case of contemporary reindeer husbandry, the internal threat from overpopulation and overgrazing represents a possible ecological tipping point. However, in our contemporary globalised society, the most present and severe threat is, as previously pointed out, the implementation of new and heavy infrastructure and mining as irreversible changes in the CPR systems – a total *deterritorialisation* (Deleuze and Guattari, 2004), and for the landscape a possible point of no return. Deterritoralisation is defined by Deleuze and Guattari as the movement by which one leaves a territory in the sense of a physical shift in habitat (migration from one condition of habitation to a radically different one), or the fundamental shift or evolution in any other significant cultural or technical condition. To map landscapes in different stages or levels of transformation, in the span from relative deterritorialisation to absolute deterritorialisation, gives a good understanding of the radical changes in the landscape when it is exposed to strong transforming forces. This dichotomy is made crystal clear by a reindeer herder in Biedjovággi (Kautokeino), Isak Mathis Triumf: 'Mining industry and reindeer husbandry can never go hand in hand. Reindeers cannot eat rock. Everything living in nature needs earth to live. There will only be rocks left if they start mining' (Bjercke and Larsson, 2013).

New hierarchies – complex reality/rhizome understanding

There is an inconsistency between the subjective experience of life through individual everyday practice and the normative way in which the formal society is organised and governed. Politics, economic systems, laws and planning processes appear to be essentially hierarchical and feature linear authority, in many cases resulting in limitation, stagnation and regression. This can be seen in strong colonial systems such as former Soviet Union or Greenland, but regression can also be the long-term consequence in smaller communities facing the power of national and multinational capital and industrial interests. Through the concept of the rhizome lies the ultimate metamorphosis of a hierarchical system, which Deleuze and Guattari denoted as a tree structure:

> unlike the trees or their roots, the rhizome connects any point to any other point, and its traits are not necessarily linked to traits of the same nature; it brings into play very different regimes of signs, and even non-sign states ... Unlike the graphic arts, drawing, or photography, unlike tracings, the rhizome pertains to a map that must be produced, constructed, a map that is always detachable, connectable, reversible, modifiable, and has multiple entryways and exits and its own lines of flight.
> (Deleuze and Guattari, 2004: 23)

Through a rhizome thinking, hierarchical systems will no longer be valid, and new ideas of validation, new encounters and new priorities will become evident and relevant: 'In this open interactional space there are always connections yet to be made, juxtapositions yet to flower into interaction' (Massey, 2005: 11).

Beside the formal governing systems of order and bureaucracy, based on linear methods of investigation, there are infinite parallel systems of informal networks, knowledge and *weak voices* that are not so easily observed and recognised. In our search for a profound understanding of the landscape, we need to work with these voices of otherness to find new approaches to comprehensive knowledge and to the changes explicitly going on. We need to investigate and experiment, to map and to research along lines and trajectories that have not necessarily been investigated before. We desire to make connections and juxtapositions that are not obvious, and to find spatial connections and openness that are not prejudiced or limiting. According to Deleuze and Guattari (2004), we can even undertake mapping of *realms that are yet to come*.

'Make a map, not a tracing', state Deleuze and Guattari in their text about the rhizome: 'What distinguishes the map from the tracing is that it is entirely oriented towards an experimentation in contact with the real ... A map has multiple entryways, as opposed to the tracing, which always comes "back to the same". The map has to do with performance, whereas the tracing always involves an alleged "competence"' (2004: 13–14). This means that our mapping will not be complete or conclusive, but will follow tracks or *lines of flight*. According to Doina Petrescu:

> Guattari and Deleuze's 'lines' challenge the usual designer thinking about 'lines'. They are an abstract and complex enough metaphor to map the entire social field, to trace its shapes, its borders, its becomings. They can map the way 'life always proceeds at several rhythms and at several speeds'. They map individual cracks and collective breaks within the segmentation and heterogeneity of power. The 'line of flight', *ligne de fuite*, is defined not only as a simple line, but as the very force of a tangle of lines flung out, transgressing thresholds of established norms and conventions, towards unexpected manifestations, both in terms of socio-political phenomena and in individual destinies.
> (Petrescu, 2004: 44)

The conception of the northern landscape

The concept of the *North* has always been afflicted by colonial imagery and perceptions, and hence formed by romantic notions of exoticism, myths about beauty and the idea of the *sublime*. These notions are still present today, amplified by a growing tourist industry, and not least by the rhetoric from multinational mining and oil companies. Today researchers describe the extensive changes taking place in the Arctic as a series of *tipping points*, which in the form of extreme consequences are *points of no return*. This entails the permanent extinction of species and a permanent loss of known ecological systems, such as alterations in marine micro-ecology resulting in changed migration patterns of fish stocks, or a permanent loss of natural landscapes because of mineral extraction or the construction of heavy infrastructure.

Historically speaking, little attention has been paid to these *pre-industrial* landscapes by architects or landscape architects. The northern landscapes caught the attention of painters and writers in the romantic period of the late nineteenth century because of their sublime beauty, but have never traditionally been represented as landscapes until they were appropriated by the energy-producing, mining or metallurgical industries and mediated as commodity landscapes (Ponte, 2014). Today the notion of the commodity value of the landscapes seems stronger than ever, expressed by politicians and stakeholders in the mining industry and the financial services industry. 'What local people?' responded the Chairman of Beowulf Mining, Clive Sinclair-Poulton, when he was asked about the *local people's* opinion about his company's plan for an iron mine in the mountains of Gállok in northern Sweden - a comment that has since become a slogan for strong local resistance (see www.whatlocalpeople.se). The tendency to diminish the value of people living in these landscapes and the lives they have pursued for centuries has largely been implemented in the rhetoric from official authorities associated with the new energy and mineral industries. In a chronicle in the Tromsø newspaper *Nordlys*, political scientist Bente Aasjord points out that unlike the fisheries in the North, which have been treated as a common resource for centuries, now 'The competition for the Arctic resources has never been greater' (Aasjord, 2012). In a search for apparently new and virgin landscapes to exploit, a new map of the North has been drawn, resulting in a shift in the landscape rhetoric from *common* to *province* (oil and gas province).

A new language

As the landscape in the North does not fit into traditional landscape terms and descriptions from more domesticated landscapes, it is necessary to uphold continuous research and experimentation. It is crucial to develop a new etymology and a language that is better suited to describe the reality of those living in the landscape. From a mining developer's point of view, the landscape is understood in terms related to the mineral content and the landscape's commodity value, whereas the same landscape in a Sámi reindeer herder's cognitive perception contains a comprehensive understanding of movement and changing seasonal conditions for the herd, as well as layers of culture, history and narratives.

A key example of adaptive language inextricably linked to the landscape is shown in the doctoral dissertation by Inger Marie Gaup Eira (2012); 'The silent language of snow'. The work describes the multitude and complexity of a practitioner's knowledge of a landscape connected to the reindeer industry, through no less than 318 words for snow. These are short words and concepts describing seasonal changes, different snow qualities and layering, weather conditions, movement and conditions for transportation and food supply that are absolutely vital for survival: 'The use of Sámi snow concepts mirrors reindeer herders' traditional knowledge of the management of the herd on snow covered ground and how herders deal with these complex systems. This kind of knowledge has contributed to the survival of reindeer herding since time immemorial' (Gaup Eira, 2012).

Examples from the landscape

Based on the theoretical outline above, we will delve into two different cases briefly explained in the introduction. The two examples are based on the same conceptual understanding, but they are contextually different and demand a partly subjective approach. The investigation and mapping methods are developed on an interdisciplinary basis to achieve relevant planning tools that connect to reality, but also easily adapt to future changes.

To achieve a comprehensive understanding, we have tried to create a broad spectrum of concepts for investigation, including contextual narratives. These are stories that in many cases can generate strong counter-forces in contrast to the dominant narratives often presented from an outside perspective. The investigations follow the trajectories or *lines of flight* that are expected to reveal new knowledge, which in turn connect to other conceptual trajectories. It is in the nature of a non-hierarchical method that the potential number of concepts are endless, which means that the analyses and the outcome will never be concluded, but it still aims to be an operational planning tool and a work in progress.

The first case from Finnmark and the Kola peninsula is basically a testing of research methods for an Arctic landscape, while the second case in Kiruna aims to show how the methods of investigation can be transformed and implemented as operational planning tools.

Emerging Arctic Landscapes at Bergen School of Architecture (Haggärde and Løkken, 2011)

The aim of the master studio *Emerging Arctic Landscapes* was to broaden our understanding of complexity – to learn how to use complexity as a planning tool and to extend our cognitive and critical means as planners, architects and not least as human beings. The investigation concepts were developed and adapted in accordance with the didactic intentions of the studio, the landscape context where the studio was conducted, and also the contemporary political issues at stake in the North.

Mapping of the unforeseen: in the studio we mapped not only the extraordinary and peculiar, but also *the everyday normal* – layers of everyday experience and everyday practices – as well as *the hyper-normal* – which eventually have formed the landscape's spatial appearance. A hyper-mapping might be more subjective and focus on values related to the plan's context rather than being strictly neutral and objective. Furthermore, hyper-mapping continuously investigates layers of information that often reach beyond our immediate perception of the landscape.

In the studio we defined architecture and planning as ongoing and never-concluded processes as an acknowledgement of the fact that we ourselves – and everything around us – are in continuous and inevitable transformation. We enforced our awareness of the transforming energies forming complex spatial patterns, which in turn are intricately connected to changes in the landscape – a landscape that possesses inherent enigmas concerning time and history. The studio was an open and inviting testing ground for experimental approaches and critical discussions of both the landscape and the practices taking place within it. We introduced and discussed the need for openness and experimental investigations of the landscape in a way that also considered and accepted the subjective experience, the trivial and not least the unexpected as relevant for a spatial understanding.

The studio started with having the students formulate individual expectations towards the territory – tested and developed along a road trip from Hammerfest to Murmansk. This was meant to be a narration and a movement through a cross-section of seemingly remote arctic landscapes and intrusive developments: from the oil-driven growth of Hammerfest, via the core areas of Sámi culture in Kautokeino and Karasjok, which are heavily dependent on unspoiled landscape pastures, to the decaying (slowly transforming and arising) and mythical city of Vardø, through the highly multicultural Kirkenes, struggling between the old mining industry and a pending new oil economy, to the Kola peninsula and the heavily polluted landscapes in Nikel, and finally Murmansk, a city in decline and transformation from its status as an industrial harbour and military stronghold to an open and uncertain future.

The other world (DAV): in-between completing assignments of a more conceptual nature, we searched for a deeper encounter with Sámi philosophy. Gathered around the bonfire inside the circular space of the *lávvu* (the Sami tent) and through his rhetorical practice, the modern shaman and Sámi jurist Doctor of Laws Ánde Somby led the students towards an alternative understanding of space and landscapes through his *joik thinking*.

Research concepts developed to infuse the investigation with a sense of anticipation

Throughout the studio, new concepts were introduced and superimposed as new layers of an increasingly deeper landscape understanding.

Vulnerability: the notion of vulnerability is invariably related to the concept of life – whether it is human life or life in nature as such. The consciousness of mortality is disturbing and exposes life as fragile. Life does not exist in closed systems, but always relates to other life forms or systems of varying extents and sizes – in these relationships, dependency occurs, not least a continuous struggle for a position of survival. It is a slow drama that has been going on since the creation of the earth, encompassing all natural systems of all scales from the smallest biotope to global circuits (see Figure 12.1).

New hierarchies: the ascendance of the information industries and the growth of a global economy are inextricably linked, and have contributed to what Saskia Sassen calls 'a new geography of centres and margins' (2001: 13). This means that former structures of the economic or political hegemony have radically changed (and are still changing rapidly), resulting in a displacement (in an economic sense) in both the geographical significance of cities and places, and the value of different kinds of labour. These are phenomena that have been clearly observed in the geography of the North and have caused historical alterations in demography and migration patterns – tendencies that are increasing in every way (see Figure 12.2).

Flexibility: when adverse global forces and global economic fluctuations influence even the most remote places, it seems more necessary than ever to create flexibility outside the global consumer economy – to be resilient to economic alterations, to be prepared for devastating environmental impacts and to foresee the future effects of expected climate changes. Gregory Bateson expressed the need for flexibility in his book *Steps to an Ecology of Mind*: 'There shall be diversity in the civilization, not only to accommodate the genetic and experimental diversity of persons, but also to provide the flexibility and "preadaptation" necessary for unpredictable change' (Bateson, 1972/2000: 503). Bateson makes an accurate prediction of the coming climate changes and foresees the challenges that planners and architects will have to deal with concerning profound ecological matters. For him, the survival of our civilisation is closely linked to our understanding of natural processes, as we are inevitably a part of it (see Figure 12.3).

This notion of flexibility leads to the studio's final assignment formulated as *reorientations* – providing ideas about new openings through new cartographies and layers of disruptive knowledge. This means that our findings and learning appear to be exercises in new dynamic approaches and entryways to the landscapes and to the complexity of spatial practices – a dynamism that Stan Allen expresses so well: 'Bateson talks about survival not in resisting change, but in terms of accommodating change. It means that your thinking has to be every bit as fluent and adaptive as the kind of systems you are talking about … It is a way of thinking that mirrors the dynamism of ecological systems themselves' (Allen and Sauters, 2007: 138).

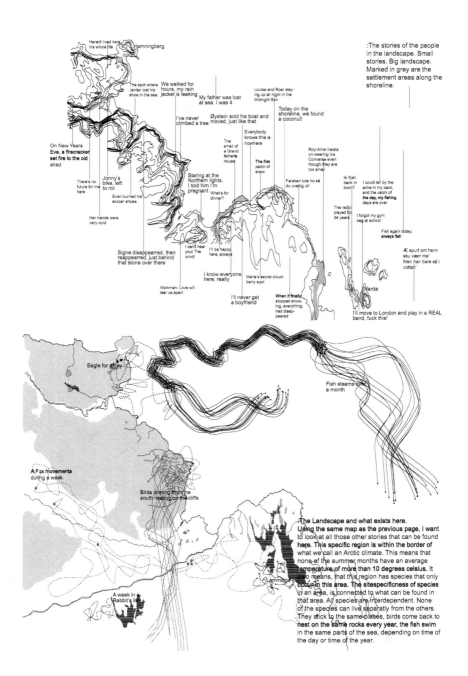

Figure 12.1 The stories of the people in the landscape. The landscape and what exists here – the other stories. From the student project *No-one belongs here more than you* by Marianne Lucie Skuncke

Source: Haggärde and Løkken (2011)

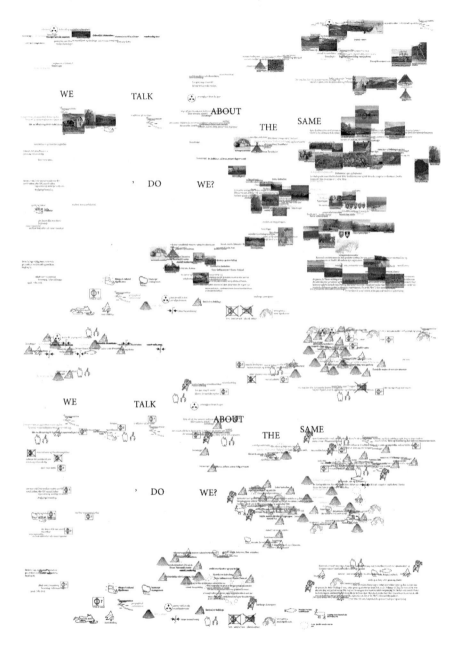

Figure 12.2 From the student project *Extracts of culture – we talk about the same, do we?* by Silje Ødegård

Source: Haggärde and Løkken (2011)

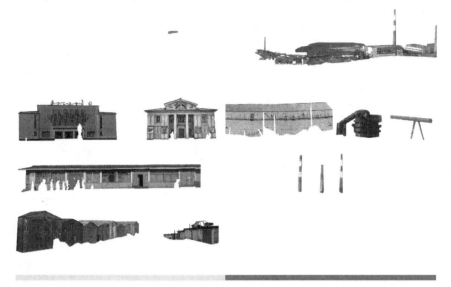
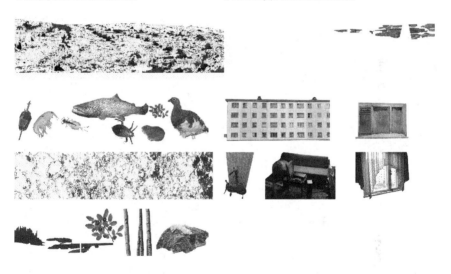

Figure 12.3 The delight space in the cultural landscape. The crude space in the industrial landscape. The dying space in the drained landscape. The dwelling space in the cultural landscape. From the student work *Flexibility in contradictory landscape* by Guðrún Jóna Arinbjarnardóttir

Source: Haggärde and Løkken (2011)

Kiruna – a constructed modernist city (70°N arkitektur et al., 2012)

The mining town of Kiruna was founded in the beginning of the twentieth century, and has existed and developed on the conditions of the mine ever since. The Kiruna mine is one of the world's most profitable underground ore mines, and when the owner of the mine, LKAB (owned by the Swedish state), needed to expand its activity under the existing city centre, there was no alternative other than to abandon the old city and construct a new one away from the undermined and expanding collapse zone.

Today's population of nearly 20,000 inhabitants has a relatively short history and is dominated by immigrants (first, second or third generation) to the area originating from all of Scandinavia, but primarily from northern Sweden.

Our initial fieldwork conducted in August 2012, named Kiruna Stories (70°N arkitektur, 2012), consists of time spent with people in the city and its surrounding landscape. Conversations with the population about daily life showed significant opinions about the city, the city life, the relationship with the mine (closely connected to opinions about the mining company) and not least the integrated relationship between the use of the city and the surrounding landscape. These are all parts of a self-determined vernacular Kiruna identity where 'All roads lead to the mountain/mine. In all public buildings, at the end of all streets, there is an opening, a view, a window, towards the mountain or the mine. When we talk to people, this is one of the things they point out: it's a mountain city' (70°N arkitektur, 2012). The city itself rests in a big landscape, with the nearest city 120 km away, which means that the inhabitants are continuously using and interacting with the landscape – through their cabins (most people have access to one), through leisure activities and through harvesting of the land's resources: 'Being close to the nature is one of the most important things [about] living here' (70°N arkitektur, 2012).

The fieldwork formed the foundation for our entry in the competition and provided crucial insight into the mindset of the inhabitants of Kiruna, which in turn was of vital importance for our response to the competition brief. Our most fundamental methodical approach was to make brief but thorough investigations related to concepts and findings in the landscape, and always offer a contextualisation of the concepts on the basis of people's everyday life, their experiences and their wishes for a new city (see Figure 12.4). We found Lefebvre's vision of the right to the city *as a transformed and renewed right to urban life* (1996: 158) a universal approach to urban life, which was highly applicable to Kiruna. According to Mark Purcell, this vision is a 'radical transformation of urban social and spatial relations. It would transform both current liberal-democratic citizenship relations and capitalist social relations ... the dominant model of citizenship is entirely upended by the right to participation' (2002: 99).

Figure 12.4 Kiruna is dying – fight!!!! Bye. I'll be here forever. Historic and contemporary messages on the walls of Kiruna

Source: 70°N arkitektur et al. (2012)

If the inhabitants are to *have a right to participation*, facilitating institutions must be created and institutional rights to participation must be introduced, which in turn will change the whole idea of planning, and the commonly accepted governing system of today. This counts for an acceptance of the complexity in landscape and society, and a methodical approach to handle and to make use of complex knowledge in the planning of new urbanities.

Concepts for investigation and transformation

Embracing the complexity of the landscape and the reality of the inhabitants evokes a new vocabulary to communicate the process and the plan. In the following, several concepts of investigation relating to the method will be presented and elaborated.

/ time / landscape / practice /

There is a crack in everything That's how the light gets in is our entry in the Kiruna competition (70°N arkitektur et al., 2012). The city of Kiruna has existed for 100 years in the paradigm of the mine and now the relocation of the city uncloses a new space of action where the city could be transformed. The relocation of the city implies a possible metamorphosis of unknown implications. At the same time the change creates an inherent possibility to make a new city that can confirm an identity that the citizens have supported for a long time – as residents in a vast, eternal and coherent landscape (see Figure 12.5). The people of Kiruna define their territory independently of the city's boundaries and relate their lives to multiple places in the landscape, depending on time, activity and season – as the inhabitants of these mountainous areas have always done. 'The everyday practice forms the landscape, and the lives of each particular is mutually influenced by the landscape and its coexistence with the city' (70°N arkitektur, 2012).

/ move / abandon / border /

The border between the new and the abandoned city is proposed as a dynamic and shifting territory, more than just a demarcation between now and then, here and there. The abandoned Kiruna contains a unique story of processes and an economy that will forever be intertwined with its future. The retraction is going to happen over a long period of time with a necessary flexibility and humbleness towards the existing and what is left behind. The reconstruction is an experiment to be created and developed through several coincidental processes, where programmes and buildings are constantly reinvented, repositioned and reshaped. The proposed concept of *spaces of action* represents openness, activity, participation and democracy (see Figure 12.6).

Figure 12.5 The eight seasons of the Sámi landscape – time, space and practice connected

Source: 70°N arkitektur et al. (2012)

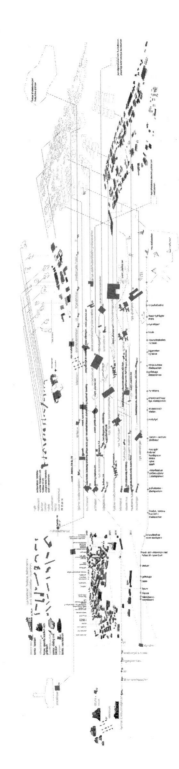

Figure 12.6 The move – a city inventory: programmes, buildings, functions to relocate, reinvent, reinforce, replace
Source: 70°N arkitektur et al. (2012)

One of the first and most significant buildings to be moved is the town hall, which signifies an early-stage possibility to redefine Kiruna's democratic project through hands-on interaction and collaboration between the politicians, the planners and the citizens. The new town hall can be defined as several temporary *embassies* in different parts of the city during the transformation process and, as such, 'the abandoning of the town hall offers a unique opportunity for the municipality to, in close collaboration with the citizens, plan and prepare the emerging Kiruna and to be present in its own future' (70°N arkitektur et al., 2012).

/ gap / entrained / new /

Under the label *nostalgia*, we propose the creation of an archive of artifacts in categories such as *everyday*, *icon*, *contour*, *tactile* and *message*. The existing is being noted, discussed and proposed a possible future: inscribed in a new context, as a memory documented, archived or preserved. It will always link both back and forth in time, coexisting with what is to come, enshrining the new in the known, and letting its history be touchable, visible and accessible (see Figure 12.7).

The existing highway through Kiruna, E10, is going to be moved to another position, and the diversion of the road will liberate space for a new city centre. Freed from heavy traffic, the area transforms in our proposal into a new heart of Kiruna: one with nature, which can emphasise the city's closeness to the surrounding landscape. The new *green heart* of Kiruna enables a compact city: it redefines the city structure, restructures the former industrial area, and allows patterns of walkways, efficiently connecting the centre to the whole city and its surrounding landscape (see Figure 12.8).

To launch the transformation, we propose an act of *premature gratification* (Shonfield 2001: 19) – a sauna as the very first gift from the new Kiruna to its population, being a *point of departure* (Haggärde and Løkken, 2010) both for imagining the new city and a catalyst for developing its new centre and recreational infrastructure. The sauna is, not least, a symbol for the collective use of the new *green heart*, but also a democratic redevelopment of Kiruna:

> The gap represents an opportunity to act in spaces of otherness and chance, both in time and space. Being hands-on a democratic process demands a relocation and regeneration of *vast* city space into a new vibrant city centre. By densification and remodelling of the existing tissue of an industrial area, a new compact and interconnected city will emerge. (70°N arkitektur et al., 2012)

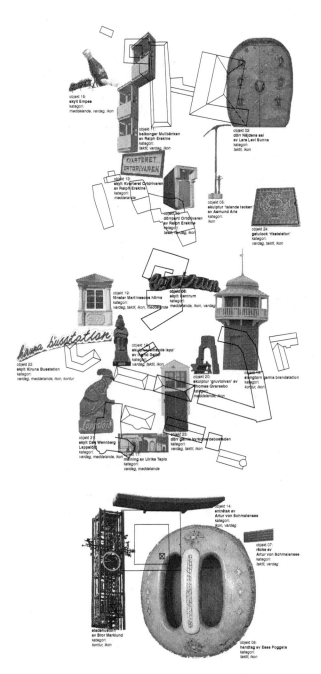

Figure 12.7 The entrained – iconic items of nostalgia: mapping the existing/archives for the future/present history

Source: 70°N arkitektur et al. (2012)

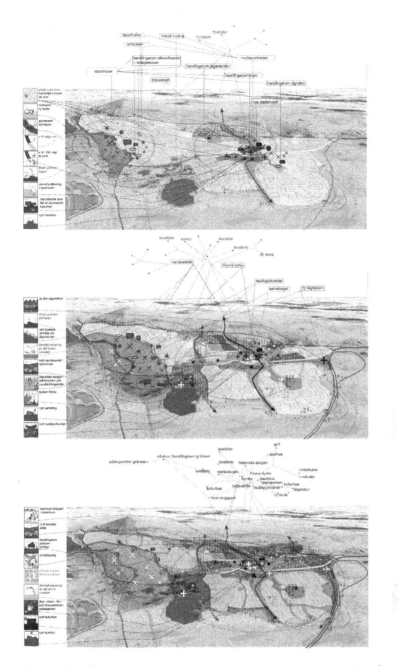

Figure 12.8 The new – new programmes in existing context/existing objects in new context/new programmes in the new city centre/happenings and acts of attention, adieus and establishings

Source: 70°N arkitektur et al. (2012)

/ city / everyday life / movement /

Everyday life will transform and be transformed by the use of the city. It can lead to more dynamic, sustainable and enjoyable patterns of movement and transportation. By reinforcing the existing qualities and adding new programmes, excitement and variation is provided in the city-close nature network – providing and connecting activities and venues, making them accessible all year around – and creating a compact city with multiple, parallel possibilities of movement such as skiing, driving snow mobiles, biking and using dogsleds (see Figure 12.9).

Attractive spots create new habits, movements and nodes, integrating the new centre as an active part of the inhabitants' everyday life from the start – 'emphasizing the city's connection to the landscape, and the landscape's presence in the city – in an everlasting coexistence' (70°N arkitektur, 2012).

Summary

The intention in this chapter has been to address what we often experience as a dysfunctional contemporary planning regime in obvious need of renewal, to draw a possible new theoretical framework for a better understanding of the landscape and to show examples of new methods of investigation. A renewed form of sustainable planning in the Arctic has to be open to the inherent knowledge in the landscape, to be susceptible, performative and operational, and to initiate and facilitate rather than restrict. In the spirit of Deleuze and Guattari's notion of 'What distinguishes the map from the tracing', we are trying to be 'oriented toward an experimentation in contact with the real'. And the plans we make are intended to be like a map that 'does not reproduce an unconscious closed in upon itself; it constructs the unconscious' (Deleuze and Guattari, 2004: 13). Planning must always be driven by strong engagement based on consciousness and visions rather than political dogmas, which by nature will always be restrictive. The Deleuze-Guattarian concept of *lines of flight* and the simultaneous acceptance of society as a non-hierarchical complex rhizomatic structure (or rather non-structure) opens up new views on planning in accordance with Doina Petrescu and *atelier d'architecture autogerée*'s guiding statement: *losing control, keeping desire* (Petrescu, 2004).

An open, inviting and experimental planning approach must aim to be highly relevant for the local inhabitants, based on real issues and extensive participation, and simultaneously recognising the extent of strong global transforming forces. Because the nature and the reality of life are by no means static, the purpose of future planning primarily has to be formulated as a tool in a process that is always looking for new knowledge, making use of this knowledge and at the same time facilitating experimentation with new solutions. The plan and the architecture must strive towards a continuous reformulation and renewal and thus must always emerge as a work in progress.

Figure 12.9 The everyday life – integrated movement, landscape, items of nostalgia
Source: 70°N et al. (2012)

References

70°N arkitektur (2012) *Kiruna stories*. Preparatory fieldwork for competition entry, with Marianne Lucie Skuncke.

—— (2014) *Focal Point Biedjovággi*, master studio at the Tromsø Academy for Landscape and Territorial Studies. http://focalpointb.blogspot.n./.

—— et al. (2012) *There is a crack in everything. That's how the light gets in*. Entry in the prequalified competition on the future of Kiruna by 70°N arkitektur, Ecosistema Urbano, Ljusarkitektur, Kristine Jensens tegnestue and Rambøll.

Aasjord, Bente (2012) Prinsen i provinsen. *Nordlys*, 10 February.

Allen, Stan and Sauter, Florian (2008) Theory, practice and landscape. In Josep Lluis Mateo (ed.), *Natural Metaphor – Architectural Papers III*. Zürich: Actar/ETH, pp. 132–41.

Bateson, Gregory (1972/2000) Ecology and flexibility in urban civilization. In *Steps to an Ecology of Mind*. Chicago: University of Chicago Press, pp. 503–12.

Bjercke, Bente and Larsson, Karl-Gøran (2013) Giske vil bestemme hvor gruvene skal ligge. NRK Sápmi. Available at: www.nrk.no/sapmi/_-staten-kan-overstyre-kommunene-1.10946221.

Calvino, Italo (1988) Multiplicity. In *Six Memos for the Next Millennium*. Cambridge, MA: Harvard University Press, pp. 101–24.

De Landa, Manuel (1999) Deleuze, diagram, and the open-ended becoming of the world. In Elizabeth A. Grosz (ed.), *Becomings: Explorations in Time, Memory, and Futures*. New York: Cornell University Press, pp. 29–41.

Deleuze, Gilles and Guattari, Félix (2004) *A Thousand Plateaus*. London: Continuum.

Erskine, Ralph (1958) *An Ecological Arctic Town*. Prospect for Resolute Bay, commissioned in early 1970s by the Canadian government.

Foucault, Michel (1984) Of other spaces, Heterotopias. *Architecture, Mouvement, Continuité*, 5: 45–9. Available at: http://foucault.info/doc/documents/heterotopia/foucault-heterotopia-en-html.

Gaup Eira, Inger Marie (2012) The silent language of snow. Sámi traditional knowledge of snow in times of climate change. Available at: www.uarctic.org/news/2012/5/inger-maria-gaup-eira-doctoral-defence-in-kautokeino.

Haggärde, Magdalena and Løkken, Gisle (2008) Öppenhet och. Experiment paper given at the Architectural Inquiries conference, Gothenburg.

—— (2009) Om framtidens landskap – Mosaïc::Region. Article in Kungliga skogs- och lantbruksakademins Tidskrift #5, Stockholm.

—— (2010) Findings – using complexity as investigation tool: The plan as dynamic process. Paper given at the World in Denmark 2010 – As Found conference, Copenhagen.

—— (2010): Points of departure – en kontinuerlig reformulering av planens mål og virkemidler, Det store rum. In Skou Kvorning and Christensen Møller (eds), *Debatbog om regional planlægning*. Copenhagen: RealDania, pp. 196–221.

—— (2011) *Emerging Arctic Landscapes*, master studio at Bergen School of Architecture (assisted by Tone Berge), http://emergingarcticlandscapes.blogspot.no.

—— (2012) För en ny arktisk mytologi. *Glänta*, 1(12).

—— (2014) Openness and participation as key factors in sustainable planning in the north. Paper given at the Artek Event: Urbanisation and Infrastructure in the Arctic conference, Sisimiut.

Hardin, Garrett (1968) The tragedy of the commons. *Science*, 162(3859): 1243–8.

Latour, Bruno (1993) *We Have Never Been Modern*. Cambridge, MA: Harvard University Press.
—— (2004) Why has critique run out of steam? From matters of fact to matters of concern. *Critical Inquiry*, 30(2): 225–48.
Lefebvre, Henri (1991) *The Production of Space*. Oxford: Blackwell.
—— (1996) *Writings on Cities*. Oxford: Blackwell.
Massey, Doreen (2005) *For Space*. London: Sage.
Ostrom, Elinor (1990) *Governing the Commons*. Cambridge: Cambridge University Press.
Otto, Frei (1971) *Arctic City*. Feasibility study commissioned by Hoechst AG.
Petrescu, Doina (2004) Losing control, keeping desire. In Peter Blundell Jones, Doina Petrescu and Jeremy Till (eds), *Architecture and Participation*. London: Routledge, pp. 43–64.
Purcell, Mark (2002) Excavating Lefebvre: The right to the city and its urban politics of the inhabitant. *GeoJournal*, 58; 99–108.
Ponte, Alessandra (2014) *The House of Light and Entropy*. London: Architectural Association.
Sassen, Saskia (2001) The global city: Strategic site/new frontier. *Quaderns/Borders*, 229. Available at: www.rrojasdatabank.info/saskiasassenglobalcity.pdf.
Shonfield, Katherine (2001) Premature gratification and other pleasures. In *This is What We Do: A Muf Manual*. London: Elipsis, pp. 14–24.

13 Quality of life and attractiveness issues in small and medium-sized towns

Innovative or commonplace policies?

Hélène Mainet and Jean-Charles Edouard

Introduction

This chapter aims to develop critical perspectives on the role of quality of life in attractiveness discourses and policies of small and medium-sized towns (SMSTs). In changing contexts linked to the economic restructuring process, accurate effects of metropolization, but also a growing residential mobility of population linked to social demand for better amenities and quality of life, the local actors in SMSTs face challenges in relation to the implementation of development policies. They are now confronted with different and sometimes ambivalent options: to develop productive and/or residential economies; to retain and attract businesses and/or people; to compete or cooperate with policy-makers in neighbouring towns; or to reproduce successful models and/or try to promote innovative actions.

In a context of de-industrialization and global economic challenges, the attractiveness of places is indeed more topical than ever. In the current competitive context between places and cities, SMSTs are sometimes said 'to be doomed to decline because of a lack of critical mass and density in terms of economic and institutional resources' (Selada et al., 2012). However, the development of residential economy and creative class models illustrates the fact that other models of development are possible, based on an understanding of factors that enhance people attraction. As quoted by Bailly and Bourdeau-Lepage (2011), 'the *homo oeconomicus* is now substituted by the *homo qualitus*, trying to maximize his personal and family well-being'.[1] The issue of quality of life deals with different aspects, such as the urban environment, social amenities, and commercial and service equipment and infrastructure from an objective point of view, but also the demands of inhabitants, especially newcomers, for standard and 'urban' equipment, and official discourses and marketing. At the same time, several measures and approaches are emerging in order to help the construction and promotion of local sustainable development programmes, such as Local Agenda 21, 'Healthy Cities' and *Cittaslow*, amongst others. Then, the issue of mobility becomes important, associated with extended commuting distances, which can become a constraint or an opportunity for small towns depending on how far removed they are from bigger urban centres.

In this general context of political and social demand for a better quality of life linked to the increasing impacts of sustainable development criteria, stakeholders in SMSTs seem to have the opportunity to take part in the competition for people by promoting amenities such as a good image, a 'natural' environment, affordable property prices, social solidarities, acquaintance forming, etc. The 'reason for this stems partly from progressive disillusionment with materialistic goals' (McCall, 1980) and from the search for a quality of life that is better than what the countryside or the metropolis can offer, which is made up of tangible but also intangible assets.

The stakes for SMST policy-makers are also closely correlated with new forms of governance and collaboration. It is therefore interesting to understand the capacity to implement local actions, to take into account the impacts of policies and trends like decentralization, privatization and liberalization, but also the reform of public services (and then the role dedicated to the first levels of the urban hierarchy in their polarizing influence). At the same time, regional cooperation tools are developed, such as inter-municipal integration in France.

It then becomes interesting to question the scope of innovative approaches in the implementation of quality-based actions, even those not directly addressing creative people. Are policies based on the promotion of quality of life in an attempt to attract new inhabitants and businesses really innovative or are they merely fashion-complying practices?

There are four main sections to this chapter. After the introduction, the second section reviews literature dealing with the place of quality of life in attractiveness policies. We then present and discuss research data derived from a large set of case studies analysed in recent works (the French PHC Campus France Polonium project and the AttracVil project). Some conclusions are finally presented so as to contribute to further reflections.

The place of quality of life in attractiveness policies: theoretical framework

Productive activities have for a long time been the focus of urban attractiveness (the attraction of economic actors to create employment). The concept is now widely open to residential aspects ('recruitment' of tourists and new inhabitants) and linked to issues of mobility and a higher social demand for quality of life.

The notion of 'place attractiveness', leading local development strategies, is now widely used by policy-makers and researchers, and even more so than the traditional notion of location in the urban hierarchy, to define and measure the influence of places. Both terms are different, but are closely linked when articulated as attraction and influence. Towns have always shown their capacity to attract all kinds of resources (very often at the expense of other towns or rural areas). The recent interest in 'attractiveness' can be explained by the fact that mobility and flows of resources, capital and people are accelerating. In the context of territorial competition, the capacity of attraction is highly strategic (Mainet and Edouard, 2014a).

The criteria for assessing attractiveness are therefore increasingly complex and combined. The attractiveness of a territory is, in traditional terms, its capacity to durably attract different forms of resources (human, economic and financial). This notion is nonetheless not that simple. Attractiveness must first be analysed through an objective focus determining the attraction of a place (in a similar way to gravitational attraction). This capacity allows for the arrival of resources on the territory (Hatem, 2004). Attractiveness is therefore the driver of movements and changes as well as a factor influencing settlement. It can be measured by the balance of in-and-out movements of people, capital, jobs, etc. But a more subjective aspect also exists: the appeal or desirability. Drivers of attraction are psycho-sociological and are based on individual and collective decisions depending on the representations, tastes and interests of various 'actors' (inhabitants, tourists and local stakeholders). Towns and places can be attractive because of obvious and real resources and opportunities, but also because of images, atmospheres and some seductive capacity. Two drivers are and have always been important. The first is centripetal. Historically, it explains the agglomeration of people and activities in towns. It is nowadays a powerful driver for metropolization processes to the benefit of large cities (with economies of scale and positive externalities). The second is centrifugal. It explains the sprawl of people and activities from urban centres to suburbs and peripheral areas (or even to rural communes). The process is based on short-distance but also long-distance mobility, explaining movements from large cities to other places (regional centres, SMSTs and villages).

The consequences are not only demographic. Mobility entails powerful mechanisms of redistribution of wealth between regions and towns. Places of settlement can benefit from consumption, but also from spending on facilities for populations or tourists. Territory competition is not only based on a productive economy (the production of goods), but also on a residential economy (the production of services for inhabitants), as analysed by economists (Davezies, 2008). This explains new demands for quality of life correlated with sustainable development preferences (Rogerson, 1999) and the attraction of highly qualified migrants and of the 'creative class' (Florida, 2005).

As pointed out by Niedomysl (2010), 'the attractiveness of places is currently gaining a high policy salience in policy makers' efforts to draw mobile capital'. In fact, many studies, whether empirical or theoretical, have been conducted in order to estimate or evaluate place attractiveness. There is frequent confusion between attractiveness and competitiveness as many studies are conducted based on economic perspectives. The focus is often on production factors and spatial planning in order to attract firms, investors or a qualified workforce, but analysing attractiveness is not a simple analysis of installation costs incurred by firms between places (Krugman, 1991). The development of studies on 'creative cities' has shown the importance of space amenities and infrastructures in attracting well-educated active people, the so-called 'creative class' (Florida, 2005). Urban performance depends not only on the city's endowment of hard infrastructure ('physical capital'), but also on the availability and quality of knowledge, communication and social infrastructure ('human and social capital').

In this changing context, with more commuting and quality-demanding households, criteria of quality of life, well-being and well-living are more frequently used by stakeholders as factors of attractiveness (Indlay and Rogerson, 1993). It is important to differentiate these notions. Well-being and well-living are linked to individual and personal aspects of life through elements of living conditions and standards (material and objective criteria) combined with value systems that match the needs, demands and priorities of individuals and families (McCall, 1975 and 1980; Tobelem-Zanin, 1995; Veenhoven, 2000). The notion of quality of life is directly linked to material and objective patterns of the space environment, even if it integrates a subjective dimension due to inhabitants' conceptions (Fleuret, 2006; Rogerson, 1999). 'Indeed, if the quality of life is geographically distributed, it is also socially differentiated'[2] (Borsdorf, 1999). Quality of life therefore refers to living conditions depending on space quality and opportunities for the well-being of inhabitants (such as public spaces, access to services, etc.). Public actors give increasing importance to the qualitative dimension of spaces. Space is not only considered from the angle of functional opportunities, but as a potential for well-being and well-living. Obviously, spaces differ with respect to their capacity to meet the needs and demands of inhabitants for high-quality surroundings (functionality, social links, emotional links, etc.) suitable for a personal and family (well-being) as well as collective blossoming (togetherness).

Many indicators have been developed in order to classify and rank cities according to such new and more combined criteria, but also to evaluate implemented policies (McCann, 2004; Niedomysl, 2007). The role of sustainable development agendas and the implementation of European Union policies are important in the construction of criteria and indicators (Musson, 2010). Notions or labels are created to qualify those new dimensions of attractiveness, such as 'Smart cities', 'Green cities', 'Quality cities', 'Healthy Cities' or 'Slow cities', depending on social, environmental or technical aspects. They can be applied to large cities, but also in some cases to small towns that tend to take part in the competition between spaces and towns.

From a strictly competitive viewpoint, most SMSTs seem to be disadvantaged or disqualified in comparison to bigger cities, which have more services and can offer more opportunities. But in fact, SMSTs can take part in the competition; they may have the potential to attract activities (often through specialization processes), inhabitants and tourists. The context of higher social demand for quality of life is even good for some of them as they can be promoted as less expensive, less polluted and less crowded spaces than metropolises, as places close to pleasant surroundings and offering a countryside feeling in urban spaces (Bell and Jayne, 2009; Knox and Mayer, 2009; Edouard, 2012).

As pointed by Jayne et al. (2010), the issue of liveability is regarded as important in studies of small cities in the USA, Canada and Australia, particularly 'in terms of competitive advantage based on "quality of life" indicators that are attractive not only to footloose businesses and tourists but also to "downsizing" urbanites (including the creative class) trading city incomes for a quieter life, better work/life balance, cheaper rents and inspiring hinterlands'. Many studies have addressed economic growth in small cities, the social implications of the in-migration of 'creative labour', and the importance of community and sense of place, as well as showing how urban regeneration is conceived and pursued in small cities (Bishop and Han, 2013; Selada et al., 2012; Waitt and Gibson, 2006). Indeed, quality of life opens up opportunities for small cities to follow the Floridian script and to pursue economic growth through cultural-economic activity (Jayne et al., 2010). If Florida sets the optimal size/scale for his 3Ts theory (technology, talent, tolerance) for larger metropolitan areas, his idea that people tend to select places first and then look for job opportunities is intellectually invigorating for small settings.

Even for SMSTs not implementing official policies dedicated to the attraction of the cultural economy or high-skilled workers, the liveability issue is now important in terms of their economic development (Van Heur, 2011). Attracting new inhabitants, especially if they are young, middle-class or upper-class households with children, is now a major objective for many local stakeholders. SMSTs are often described as 'places of well-being' and 'human-sized' towns (Kwiatek-Soltys and Mainet, 2014; Mainet 2011). But beyond a good image, the issue is to identify whether smallness is conducive to developing experiments for local sustainable and creative policies or if local actors only reproduce models successfully created and assessed in larger cities.

SMSTs: places where the living is easy? Research data and discussion

Methods

The research material is largely based on data collected within several research programmes[3] dedicated to attractiveness and quality of life in small towns. This chapter presents the results from the French case studies in the Auvergne region (the sample zone for the Polonium project). Specific fieldwork was conducted in SMSTs involved in dedicated policies such as Local Agenda 21 and *Cittaslow* membership (outside Auvergne). In the different programmes, the focus was on small towns defined according to the French classification as urban units with more than 2,000 inhabitants and fewer than 20,000. Sampling was made in order to get a variety of situations depending on demographic size, distance from bigger towns and socio-economic trends (declining and booming towns).

Table 13.1 Examples of images and words used to describe amenities in small towns

Words and notions used		Number	%
Total sample		83	100
Of which:	Location ('gate of', 'gateway', 'at the heart of')	38	45.8
Of which:	Living environment ('natural' and 'preserved')	20	24.1
	Quality of life	17	20.5
	History, heritage	15	18.1
	Dynamism of local economy	11	13.3

Sources: analysis of selected French websites of small towns (2010)

A first method consists of the analysis of official websites of small-town municipalities. Websites are undoubtedly among the most important media for place promotion nowadays. The description of towns, the pictures used, the kinds of information provided and target groups (investors, tourists and inhabitants) reveal the character and activity of the place and the policy-makers' orientations. Introductory Internet pages were systematically analysed for over 80 French small-sized towns.

To highlight inhabitants' perceptions of quality of life and place amenities, a survey was conducted in 12 small towns in the Auvergne region. A questionnaire was handed out to pupils and completed by parents (data was collected online and with the teachers' help). This method was chosen in order to address recent inhabitants, but with the bias of a relatively low proportion of senior inhabitants (only 1.5 per cent of respondents). A total of 328 questionnaires were returned, which was considered significant enough for an analysis of individuals' perceptions and representations.

Finally, meetings with local policy-makers were organized. Data was collected from semi-structured interviews in the same towns where the questionnaires were delivered, but also in towns previously identified based on the commitments of local actors to sustainable development and quality-based programmes.

Promotion of amenities in SMSTs

Environmental, social and heritage aspects are very often used in city branding (Table 13.1). The study of websites shows that the living environment (described as 'natural' and 'preserved') and quality of life references are more frequently quoted than economic aspects (Mainet, 2011). Local amenities are notably promoted.

The descriptions highlight a relaxed lifestyle, but also a bustling city centre. Short distances to surrounding natural and rural amenities allow people to enjoy the best of both urban and rural living. As noticed by Selada et al. (2012), the promotion is often twofold: endogenous amenities and

Table 13.2 Perceptions of quality of life by inhabitants of small towns

A Evaluation of quality of life	%
Excellent	49.0
Good	43.2
Rather good	4.2
Bad	1.2
B Components of quality of life	**Quotations rank**
Place amenities (quietness, living environment, etc.)	1
Personal aspects (family life, well-being, etc.)	2
Social aspects (neighbourhood, sense of security, etc.)	3
Job/work proximity	4

Source: authors' survey, 2012–13

territorial embeddedness. The territorial position and place accessibility are referred to in almost a half of the websites. In a context of globalization and metropolization, such amenities must be taken into account for territories to be attractive as good locations, but accessibility, proximity and connectivity to active nearby places are also important in attracting businesses and inhabitants. Local amenities are made up of three main dimensions: the natural and built environment, which encompasses the architecture of the place (with photos of monuments of interest or typical architecture), the climate, public spaces and other tangible and natural assets (pictures of surrounding places with rivers, forests or mountains); social and cultural capital linked to the community and its social interactions (*genius loci*, intangible heritage, identity, with pictures of festivals, fiestas and markets); and economic activities associated with the business climate. It is noteworthy that the dynamism of the local economy receives a low score (13.3 per cent) compared to sheer space identity qualities ('gateway', 'heart of'), with a score of 45.8 per cent. The image is definitely 'residential' rather than 'production-orientated'.

Inhabitants' views on liveability in SMSTs

Attractive images of the town and the importance of environmental aspects are also noticeable in inhabitants' representations and perceptions (Table 13.2). The survey conducted in small towns of the Auvergne region shows their evaluation of quality of life as 'good' and 'excellent', largely linked to the characteristics of the place and outdoor amenities, like the assets of the living environment. Social aspects are also important and are more significant than economic features such as the existence of job opportunities or work proximity.

The liveability factor should be mentioned in terms of quality of life components. For inhabitants of small towns, local amenities are an important part of the quality of life. The place itself, with its quietness, nice surroundings

Table 13.3 Residential mobility in French small towns

	Auvergne region
Length of residence in town (%)	
From birth/over 20 years	33.9
10–19 years	38.5
5–9 years	17.5
Less than 5 years	10.1
Previous place of dwelling (% of inhabitants with residential mobility)	
Rural area/village	30.5
SMST	29.2
Big city	40.3
Reasons for settling in the town (%)	
Work/job proximity	21.6
Nice surroundings	11.0
Proximity of bigger town	10.4
Nice living environment	9.8
Housing/rent prices	9.5
Family	7.3
Childhood place	7.3
Quietness	6.7
Housing	6.4
Marriage	3.4
Services, trades, urban infrastructures	0.3
Other (mainly linked to housing and family)	9.4

Source: authors' survey, 2012–13

and shops and services, is a key factor of residential choice (Table 13.2). It must indeed be linked to residential mobility and the fact that localization quite often results from a deliberate choice. Niedomysl (2010) shows how a life-course perspective needs to be integrated into quality of life analyses, since not only do migrants' needs, demands and preferences depend on their current life-course phase situation, but their resources and constraints are also likely to correlate with the life-course. The length of residence in a town can strongly influence the answers given. In this case, the structure of respondents is quite balanced between newcomers and locals (or people living in the town for several years). This data illustrates the fact that quality of life and quality of place can be key relocation factors in growing peri-urbanization and counter-urbanization processes (Table 13.3).

Quality-based strategies of public actors: a set of variation

Quality of life based on local amenities is promoted by policy-makers and appreciated by inhabitants, especially newcomers, as a key factor for residential choice. But beyond images and promotion, the analysis of policies implemented by local stakeholders shows that, at first glance, many actions are not original and are often mimetic when visibility and differentiation are at stake.

Amongst the most frequently observed policies are the measures dedicated to promoting city centres, with the upgrading of public spaces (namely the main square or the old town), revitalization and heritage promotion programmes, measures to prevent vacant houses, support given to local trades and services, etc. Official programmes exist, supported by national agencies (French schemes like OPAH (programmed operation for the improvement of the housing environment) or AVAP (protection of architectural, urban and landscape heritage)). Other endeavours focus on the control of urban sprawl on the outskirts of town centres. Master plans are important to open (or not) natural and agricultural spaces to urbanization and housing projects. In Issoire (a small attractive town of 15,000 inhabitants, located 35 km from the regional city of Clermont-Ferrand), sprawl control is a strategy used to protect landscapes, but also to avoid costs linked with the maintenance of excessive infrastructures and urban networks. Tools of action are quite limited: diversification of the housing market through the construction or rehabilitation of public flats and houses, upgrading of the old part of the town to increase its attractiveness for young families, etc. Policies dedicated to cultural life have been developing significantly in small towns since the 1990s (Edouard, 2008; Sibertin-Blanc, 2008). Summer festivities (the Friday 'After Boulevard' in Issoire from June to September and art exhibitions in Brioude), festivals (the 'La Pamparina' street music festival in Thiers every July or the Street Theatre Festival in Aurillac every August) and also cultural seasons (with specific programmes dedicated to young audiences or families). The business component of policies is also important. Besides classic plans like the creation of commercial or industrial zones, other schemes are developed, such as the 'Place aux Jeunes' in Brioude, which aims at attracting young entrepreneurs (the town supports their settlement) or funding for store-front upgrading (in Brioude, with the support of the association of communes and regional agencies).

Other small towns demonstrate more ambitious and holistic policies. Examples of this are small towns that implemented Local Agenda 21 or set a *Cittaslow* process. *Cittaslow*, the 'International network of cities where the living is easy',[4] is a quite interesting approach, dedicated to villages and towns of fewer than 50,000 inhabitants. The initiative was launched in Italy in 1999 and spread worldwide. In June 2015, the association consisted of 199 members, mostly in Europe. As stated by the official philosophy of the movement, 'good living means having the opportunity to enjoy solutions and services that allow citizens to live in their town in an easy and pleasant way' (www.cittaslow.org). Quality of life is central to the *Cittaslow* philosophy in its various dimensions of tangible and intangible components (natural and built environment, social and community aspects, cultural events, etc.). It has been studied in different national contexts (Mayer and Knox,

2006, 2009; Grzelak-Kostulska et al., 2011; Mainet and Edouard, 2014b). According to the survey conducted in the French *Cittaslows*, the objectives are to base local policies on local amenities and to use the *Cittaslow* charter as a guideline as well as an element of international visibility. The mayor of Segonzac (the first French *Cittaslow* in 2010) says it clearly: 'small towns are disadvantaged as they face the traps of anarchic development. What is interesting in *Cittaslow* is more the approach than the label. We have to take strategic decisions and Cittaslow helps us to have guiding principles and objectives'.[5]

Strategies of differentiation are also important (*Cittaslow* is slowly developing in France with only nine members and the curiosity for the name is still important). This is particularly the case for small towns that are integrated into the influence zone of larger cities. Local actors tend to promote quality of life assets and amenities with extreme vigour (this is the case for Segonzac in the vicinity of Cognac, Créon in the Bordeaux metropolitan area or Grigny in Greater Lyon).

The charter insists on endogenous assets to promote strong-willed policies. As stated in Labastide d'Armagnac, 'at a time when decisions are taken at national, European or international levels, it is important to root action at the local level'[6] (Labastide d'Armagnac leaflet giving the reasons for membership). Even if the measures themselves are not necessarily ambitious and remarkable, the objective is to emphasize the visibility and the differentiation of the place, its uniqueness and competitive assets, in the same way that 'Creative cities' develop quality-based actions. Even if creative people are not the main target, the tools used are quite similar. 'While the towns in *Cittaslow* are pursuing a variety of different goals, what unites them, what they have in common, is a desire to protect the unique and distinctive aspects of their communities' (Beatley, quoted in Mayer and Knox, 2006).

Discussion

The main findings show that plenty of SMSTs tend to formulate quite ambitious policies addressing images and promotions of places, but not many develop as really original or holistic actions. Amongst these, however, interesting examples have been analysed in different spatial contexts, showing the importance of the competence and commitment of local actors.

The reasons for implementing (or not) place promotion policies are very interesting to analyse from the viewpoints of actors in small towns. Small cities are at a distinct disadvantage when trying to enact sustainability policies due to capacity issues (staff time and skills, local revenue). They often have limited local government service delivery and planning capacity. Professional management (both in the form of a city/town manager and the specific dedication of staff time) increased the adoption of policies.

Furthermore, small towns depend more on citizen or political leadership. Local leadership is a decisive factor in promoting change and new strategic visions (Selada et al., 2012). If they are proactive, local leaders can be promoters or facilitators of creative ecosystems. The role of local leaders is very important in the decision to apply for programme participation or the labelling of such programmes. The role of citizens can also be important in small towns. For example, in the first French *Cittaslows*, the idea originated from citizens (a resident of Italian origin in Labastide d'Armagnac; people from local tourist information centres in Segonzac and Créon) before being promoted by municipal councils. Local governments that created an official citizen commission to oversee sustainability actions seem to adopt more ambitious policies. The example of Issoire is typical, with a 'Group 21' dealing with inhabitants and actors dialogues and organizing field workshops aiming at *in situ* observations of local issues. Such examples remain uncommon, as most local actors tend to inform and involve citizens once the decisions and processes have started and only to the extent that it is important to create conditions for the acceptance and legitimization of the transformation process.

According to policy-makers, having started such programmes, the main reasons are associated with the promotion and acknowledgement of measures already settled or implemented, often separately. The formalization of a programme (Local Agenda 21, *Cittaslow*, etc.) is a way to give coherence to a holistic policy. Another key reason is linked to the advantage of being part of an outreaching network and sharing experiences and good practices. Small towns need structures to provide technical and management assistance and support (at the regional or national levels). For example, in Auvergne, an eco-development network of SMSTs was created in 2013, with the support of the state in terms of funding and engineering. This network aims to bring together 19 towns of the Massif Central area on planning and development topics and issues (in November 2013, the first meeting was dedicated to the development of downtown areas). Another example is the collaborative organization 'Platform 21 for sustainable development', which was created as 'an animation, exchange and mutualisation tool on sustainable development ... accompanying public and private actors[7]' (www.plate-forme21.fr). Such networks help to further the sharing of good practices, but also take into account negative externalities of attracting people (especially for very attractive small towns), which can be very costly (charges, works) as budgets are often limited and incoming inhabitants can affect house prices, let alone the cohabitation between new and longer-established inhabitants. In that context, medium-sized towns might be expected to benefit more than small towns. As pointed out by Bishop and Han (2013), they contain a critical mass of population to attract businesses and services, yet are still small enough to enable strong partnerships and a personable and collaborative business network.

Finally, the studies show the need to take scales into account. SMSTs are constituted across multiple geographical scales. Possibilities always exist for residents, businesses and municipal authorities to engage in multi-scalar strategies through networks that rewrite how the 'local' is constituted and thus to 'rescale' smallness. For example, the availability of jobs rather than amenities appears to have attracted creative people in some circumstances. Bishop and Han (2013) and Niedomysl and Hansen (2010) highlight the debate within the literature on whether investments in amenities bring jobs or investments in jobs bring talent. All other factors being of equal importance (for example, jobs and affordable housing), they suggested that highly skilled people may have a preference for a place that is richer in amenities. The same process is noticeable in France and the issue of geographical scales is important. Our survey shows that job opportunities are important for residential mobility (Table 13.3), but also that households give priority to local amenities as the main elements of a good quality of life (Table 13.2). People tend to draw a quite large area of potential residence, closely linked with job accessibility and housing affordability, and then choose the specific place of residence by taking into account the available local amenities. This is particularly important for small towns in the vicinity of larger cities (with job opportunities), which can be attractive thanks to their natural, built and social characteristics and images.

The issue of scale is also important for policy-makers as they need to cooperate with other institutional actors. In the French context of the implementation of inter-municipal collaboration, local stakeholders can no longer think and work at the very local scale only, but must develop inter-territoriality actions, taking into account what is done and planned in the surrounding, often associated, municipalities.

Conclusion: quality of life and innovation for SMSTs

The main objective of this chapter was not to analyse policies dedicated to the attraction or retention of creative people or creative businesses, art and culture in SMSTs, but to study actions based on amenities to attract people, often young workers and households with young children, and ideally entrepreneurs, in a context of quality of life promotion, with local development objectives. The findings show that the attraction of people and businesses, whether creative or not, is a complex process.

Models of development should be based on the promotion of the uniqueness of the place and not on reproducibility. As analysed by Jayne et al. (2010), a great deal is at stake when small towns and cities seek to replicate creative city strategies of larger places. It is difficult for SMSTs to compete with large metropolises in terms of agglomeration economies, but it is possible, even crucial, to develop strategies based on specific assets. In recent years, many policy-makers have followed 'metropolitan imaginaries' (Selada et al., 2012) with often disappointing results, as the preconditions and resources of small towns differ considerably from those of larger ones.

Affordability (housing) and liveability stand out as the primary drivers of attraction for SMSTs, supported by specific qualities of community and place, including the non-economic dimensions of everyday life. Policies should be context-sensitive as investment in infrastructure and amenity needs to be contextual and well-adapted to local circumstances. There are suggestions that local and national governments need to pay closer attention to the local context rather than adopting a 'one-size-fits-all' approach (Bishop and Han, 2013). There is also an opportunity for more qualitative studies to examine the 'people climate' that is deemed attractive by (creative) people at different life stages.

Finally – and this is not the mere paradox – if quality of life is an important, if not the main, added value of SMSTs, considering that their strictly economic competitiveness can be comparatively limited, what is the limit point where growth (being spatial and functional) negatively affects quality of life? To follow Tesson (2010), the question for SMSTs is that being really innovative probably means building on quality of life, limited growth and controlled attractiveness. SMSTs could then become models of quality cities and towns and reference points for larger cities looking for solutions to improve their conditions for quality of life, and some already do so.

Notes

1 Original quotation: 'À *l'homo oeconomicus* semble se substituer *l'homo qualitus*, qui cherche à maximiser son bien-vivre et celui de sa famille.'
2 Original quotation: 'En effet, si la qualité de vie est géographiquement distribuée, elle est aussi socialement différenciée.'
3 The AttracVil programme was financed by Clermont-Ferrand MSH–USR 3550 in 2011–12 and was dedicated to the issue of attractiveness of SMSTs (definition, indicators); the Campus France PHC Polonium was conducted in collaboration with the Pedagogical University of Krakow (Poland) and dealt with issues of quality of life in SMSTs in France and Poland.
4 'Cittaslow–Rete Internazionale delle città del buon vivere.'
5 Original quotation: 'Les petites communes sont les moins armées face aux pièges d'un développement anarchique. Ce qui nous intéresse, c'est moins le label que la démarche. Nous avons des choix importants à faire. *Cittaslow* va donner un fil conducteur à notre politique d'aménagement' (Segonzac Mayor, *Le Monde*, 3 October 2010).
6 Original quotation: 'A l'heure où les décisions se prennent souvent au niveau national ou encore européen et international, il est important d'ancrer l'action au niveau local.'
7 Original quotation: 'Outil d'animation, d'échange et de mutualisation des informations et pratiques sur le développement durable … au service des acteurs professionnels et institutionnels du Massif central.'

References

Bailly, A. and Bourdeau-Lepage, L. (2011) Concilier désir de nature et préservation de l'environnement: vers une urbanisation durable en France. *Géographie, économie, société*, 13(1): 27–43.

Bell, D., and Jayne, M. (2009) Small cities? Towards a research agenda. *International Journal of Urban and Regional Research*, 33(3): 683–99.

Bishop, A. and Han, S.S. (2013) Growth of the creative economy in small regional cities: A case study of bendigo. Paper delivered at the State of Australian Cities Conference, www.soacconference.com.au/wp-content/uploads/2013/12/Bishop-Economy.pdf.

Borsdorf, A. (1999) La qualité de vie dans les villes alpines. Le cas d'Innsbruck. *Revue de géographie alpine*, 87(4): 81–91.

Davezies, L. (2008) *La République et ses territoires: la circulation invisible des richesses*. Paris: Le Seuil.

Eckert, D., Grossetti, M. and Martin-Brelot H. (2012) La classe créative au secours des villes? *La vie des idées*, www.laviedesidees.fr/La-classe-creative-au-secours-des.html.

Edouard, J-C. (2008) La petite ville: contexte scientifique et enjeux de développement/aménagement. *Bulletin de l'Association de Géographes Français*, 1: 3–12.

—— (2012) La place de la petite ville dans la recherche géographique en France: de la simple monographie au territoire témoin. *Annales de Géographie*, 1: 5–22.

Fleuret, S. (ed.) (2006) *Espace, qualité de vie et bien-être*. Angers: Angers University Press.

Florida, R. (2005) *Cities and the Creative Class*. New York: Routledge.

Grzelak-Kostulska, E., Hołowiecka, B. and Kwiatkowski, G. (2011) Cittaslow international network: An example of a globalization idea? In *The Scale of Globalization. Think Globally, Act Locally, Change Individually in the 21st Century* (Conference Proceedings, University of Ostrava), pp. 186–92.

Hatem, F. (2004) Attractivité: de quoi parlons-nous? *Pouvoirs locaux*, 61(2): 34–43.

Indlay, A. and Rogerson, R. (1993) Migration, places and quality of life: voting with their feet? In T. Champion (ed.), *Population Matters: The Local Dimension*. London: Paul Chapman, pp. 33–49.

Jayne, M., Gibson, C., Waitt, G. and Bell, D. (2010) The cultural economy of small cities. *Geography Compass*, 4(9): 1408–17.

Knox, P. and Mayer, H. (2009) *Small Town Sustainability: Economic, Social, and Environmental Innovation*. Basel: Birkhauser Verlag AG.

Krugman, P. (1991) Increasing returns and economic geography. *Journal of Political Economy*, 99(3): 483–499.

Kwiatek-Sołtys, A. and Mainet, H. (2014) Quality of life and attractiveness of small towns: A comparison of France and Poland. *Quaestiones Geographicae*, 33(2): 103–13.

Mainet, H. and Edouard, J-C. (2014a) Indicators of small towns' attractiveness: Issues of definition, criteria, based on French cases. In A. Kwiatek-Soltys, H. Mainet, K. Wiedermann and J-C Edouard (eds), *Small and Medium Towns' Attractiveness at the Beginning of the 21st Century*. Clermont-Ferrand: Clermont-Ferrand University Press, pp. 13–27.

—— (2014b) *Cittaslow*, une labellisation pour la qualité de vie des villes secondaires? In M. Fournier (ed.), *Labellisation et mise en marque des territoires*. Clermont-Ferrand: Clermont-Ferrand University Press, pp. 511–26.

Mainet, H. (2011) Les petites villes françaises en quête d'identité: ambigüité du positionnement ou image tactiquement combinée? *MOTS, Les langages du politique*, 97: 75–89.

Mayer, H. and Knox, P.L. (2006) Slow cities, sustainable places in a fast world. *Journal of Urban Affairs*, 28(4): 321–34.

—— (2009) Pace of life and quality of life: The Slow City Charter. *Community Quality-of-Life Indicators*, 1: 21–41.

McCall, S. (1975) Quality of life. *Social Indicators Research*, 229–48.

—— (1980) 'What is quality of life?', *Philosophica*, 25(1): 5–14.

McCann, E.J. (2004) 'Best places': Interurban competition, quality of life and popular media discourse. *Urban Studies*, 4(1): 1909–29.

—— (2008) Livable city/unequal city: The politics of policy-making in a 'creative' boomtown. *Revue Interventions économiques*, 37, available at: http://interventionseconomiques.revues.org/489.

Musson, A. (2010) Revue de littérature sur les indicateurs d'attractivité et de développement durable: vers un indicateur d'attractivité durable. *Géographie, économie, société*, 12(2): 181–223.

Niedomysl, T. (2007) Promoting rural municipalities to attract new residents: an evaluation of the effects. *Geoforum*, 38(5): 698–709.

—— (2010) Towards a conceptual framework of place attractiveness: a migration perspective. *Geografiska Annaler*, B 92(1): 97–109.

Niedomysl, T. and Hansen, H.K. (2010) What matters more for the decision to move: Jobs versus amenities. *Environment and Planning*, A 42: 1636–49.

Rogerson, R.J. (1999) Quality of life and city competitiveness. *Urban Studies*, 36(5–6): 969–85.

Selada, C., Cunha, I. and Tomaz, E. (2012) Creative-based strategies in small and medium-sized cities: key dimensions of analyses. *Quaestiones Geographicae*, 31(4): 43–51.

Sibertin-Blanc, M. (2008) La culture dans l'action publique des petites villes. Un révélateur des politiques urbaines et recompositions territoriales. *Géocarrefour* 83(1): 5–13.

Tesson, F. (2010) Etre une *Creative City* ou une ville de qualité de vie, http://ftesson1.perso.univ-pau.fr/tesson/images/Html_temp/Pdf/CreativeCity.pdf.

Tobelem-Zanin, C. (1995) *La qualité de vie dans les villes françaises*. Rouen: Rouen University Press.

Van Heur, B. (2011) Small cities and the socio-spatial specificity of economic development: A heuristic approach. in A. Lorentzen and B. Van Heur (eds), *Cultural Political Economy of Small Cities*. London: Routledge, pp. 17–30.

Veenhoven, R. (2000) The four qualities of life, ordering, concepts and measures of the good life. *Journal of Happiness Studies*, 1: 1–39.

Waitt, G.R. and Gibson, C.R. (2006) Creative small cities: Rethinking the creative economy in place. *Urban Studies*, 46(5): 1223–46.

14 Postscript
Pathways towards a critical and comparative approach to creative planning

Nils Aarsæther, José Serrano, Anniken Førde, Christophe Demazière, Torill Nyseth and Abdelillah Hamdouch

The chapters in this volume display a multitude of settings, developments and outcomes related to planning and development work in small and medium-sized towns (SMSTs). Geographically, the studies presented range from cities and towns in the Mediterranean to urbanized settlements in the ultimate Arctic. However, reading the chapters will convey an impression of if not commonalities, then recognizable dimensions and scales, as well as cultural, economic and political dynamics across the towns that are studied. What emanates from this volume then is potentially something different from merely observing deterministic trends related to globalization – or multitudes and complexities. As editors, we have observed something of importance, i.e. characteristics of processes taking place in the space between structural constraints and individual entrepreneurial motives. In the following pages, we will try to extract some generic aspects from the creativity and innovative moves in a number of towns and places. Finally, we will discuss how the findings may inform both theory and practice in planning. Hopefully, our contribution can be valuable to emerging and ongoing processes of urban development and transformation at the level of the SMST – within their respective national and regional contexts.

Innovative and creative actions, strategies and planning endeavours

Basically, the studies in this volume are all based on a common understanding of how important context and structure are if we want to describe, explain and compare creative processes. In this respect, the structural constraints related to environmental and climatic factors, to economic structure, to legislation and to a nation's administrative arrangements and scales play a part. As a crucial factor, we regard the political and regional culture that comes into play. Here, the chapters display a wide variety of contexts, in which the distinction between 'small' and 'middle-sized' towns should also be noticed. The middle-sized 'centre' with well-developed service functions offers other (but not necessarily better) opportunities for creative action than small urban settlements that are more or less enlarged villages or towns dominated by primary and secondary industries. Creativity has different expressions in 'industrial' towns compared to 'residential' towns. In this volume, the chapters vary with respect to the highlighting of structural traits and to the extent that structures – whether legal, economic or cultural – determine or restrict experimentation and creative moves.

However, the room for action – the room for *manoeuvre* – within a city or town depends on additional properties to those relating to size, occupational structure and position in an urban hierarchy. Across Europe, rigid hierarchies and central government control have increasingly given way to devolution, and a principle of decentralization has entered the legislative and administrative systems that are relevant to urban and local development. It is even a characteristic of decentralization that actors at the lower levels of national hierarchies may challenge and criticize what is seen as unnecessary and negative constraints imposed from above.

In some countries, taxation and financial transfers from the state may enhance the capacity for action. Another dimension is related to the stocks and dynamics of human and social capital – in short, the ability to cooperate and to form and participate in outreaching networks may augment the capacity for action significantly. The room for manoeuvre definitely should not be regarded as a constant. In today's 'networking society', formal rules and structures may be circumvented, challenged and to a certain degree modified. Finally, structures that are regarded as semi-permanent are increasingly exposed to processes of economic restructuring, with direct consequences for a city's viability. The overnight disappearance of the once-solid cornerstone factory is a very common experience in the age of globalization.

As we have learnt from previous research, theories of structural constraints and of potentials for action offered by the stock of human capital do not explain the occurrence of creative and innovative planning. Room for manoeuvre and action may or may not be invaded by creative and innovative moves. In this volume, the focus is on the potentials for creative, territorial action; how it is facilitated and linked to planning and development processes. In this respect, a first question pertains to how and by whom creative planning moves are initiated, and what is their main field or focus. Further, it is a matter of how initiatives are worked out and (at least tentatively) implemented. Then, some of the contributions are follow-up studies that analyse how creative planning fares when the forces and structures they challenge respond. And finally, what difference do creative development and planning make – both locally and in a wider context of learning and diffusion?

The main contribution of this volume relates to the exposition and analysis of innovative and creative actions, strategies and planning endeavours. But the emphases differ; some chapters focus on initiation, others on the implementation and some explicitly address the setbacks, effects and side-effects. By adhering to an understanding of the importance of stages in planning and development processes, a comparison across national systems, city sizes and thematic foci can be facilitated.

The discussion across cases in its turn, then, should contribute to a twofold learning process, first in terms of planning theory and the social sciences (what are the useful concepts and theoretical approaches?), and then in terms of planning practices (can certain ways of doing things work in other contexts?).

Initiatives, organization and implementation

The creative forces and actors: how does a creative development or planning endeavour start? Who are the ones who initiate and seek support to organize creative projects? To what extent do people in small- and medium-sized settings rely on or search for initiatives and policies originating outside of the town or municipality in question? What are the preconditions for local level creativity? How is creativity expressed in networks and informal relations between actors positioned at different levels and scales? From the chapters presented in this volume, it is possible to extract a relatively clear message: to the extent that creative moves are directly linked to municipal planning practices, the local politicians and planners are forging new relations and partnerships with actors in the community and at the regional level. In the city of Drammen (Norway), the municipal leaders worked together with private developers to reinvent the image as well as the physical expression of the city by employing a novel and creative riverside strategy, as reported in Chapter 4. A different approach was chosen by the municipal planners constructing the 'ideal' new neighborhood in the case of Fornebu. They developed a 'village centre' model largely by themselves, at arm's length from elected politicians, and by involving outside academic expertise (Chapter 9). In several chapters, creative moves are taken when the state or regional authorities makes funding available for innovative planning and development work, and in these cases innovative local actors exploit the potential of multilevel governance, mobilizing voluntary organizations at the community level, as well as actors in the region. We find creative initiatives of this type in several French cases, such as in Chapter 3, where the mayors in two small towns were also national political figures.

In all the chapters, territorial and comprehensive commitments are highlighted, but how to 'lift' your town or city most often means developing a strategic focus on projects in order to turn them into levers for a broader place-developmental process. In this respect, the organization of community centres and local medical centres in the Val de Loire region (Chapter 6), and the village centre strategy of the Fornebu project (Chapter 9) address the town/community with a 'comprehensive' aim. But, unlike the creation of a new urban neighbourhood in Fornebu, the new site for the Kiruna mining town in Arctic Sweden implies moving its present inhabitants, thereby highlighting how the continuity of Arctic-type identities can be maintained (Chapter 12). Moving up one level, the inter-municipal arrangements in France analysed in Chapter 7 also provide platforms for regional-level development strategies. However, most initiatives, including those of the comprehensive planning process, tend to become more strategic and 'leverage'-oriented than comprehensive. In Nuuk, the capital of Greenland, the focus is on the creative use of dialogues in an innovative and participatory housing development (Chapter 10). Sometimes one may wonder if the creative component is more proclaimed than real, for development ideas (for example, R. Florida's '3Ts': talent, technology and tolerance) often 'travel' from place to place, in a blueprint mode, as discussed in Chapter 13. Initiation then is not an either/or split between 'insiders' or 'outsiders'; local leaders may pick up ideas from other places and levels, and 'outside' scientists and professionals may offer their services to specific urban audiences (see the case of Kiruna in Chapter 12), but the point we want to emphasize is that innovative and creative processes almost invariably occur and proceed in a networking mode.

The implementation and organization: sometimes creative ideas and projects are attuned to the overall planning process, thus making a formal planning process into an arena of innovation and creativity. In other cases, projects that aim to enhance overall city development take place outside of, or at a critical distance from, the procedural rules of planning legislation. Creative planning orientations and actions may emanate within the local business community, within public sector departments or within the cultural/voluntary milieus. Formal planning work may in many towns be regarded as bureaucratic or irrelevant to local development. But, as demonstrated in studies of project-based and inter-municipal collaborations in Chapters 6 and 7, we also find examples of productive interaction between municipal planning processes and innovation.

The effects and responses: all too often, descriptions and analyses of novel interventions end in a phase still marked by enthusiasm and aspirations. What is often lacking is analysis of how structural barriers occur and how they may block implementation. From the initiative in Tromsø to create a new policy programme for cultural industries, however, we learn that an innovative and semi-autonomous organizational set-up was taken over by bureaucratic structures, and in fact the programme for innovation within the cultural industries was terminated (Chapter 5). Bringing a novel solution or process from the idea and start-up phase to implementation invariably means relating to power structures. These relations can take the form of legitimizing the creative effort, but more often it means negotiations with and the involvement of political and administrative actors and institutions. For creative planning projects to survive, its proponents must 'be able to "read" the structure of power in a particular community' (Brooks, 2002: 186). And in this respect, creativity will most often be a necessity in order to find ways to make potential hostile forces into co-operators.

Learning for planning theory

Behavioural planning theory has evolved from the criticism of a simplistic instrumental model based on the assumption that it was possible to apply scientific knowledge to action, in a linear mode, in order to control future developments. The critical approach highlighted instances with de-linking of ends and means (Banfield, 1973, Lindblom, 1973), the tendency for planning to comply with economic and bureaucratic power structures (Sager, 2013), and to seal itself off from alternative sources of knowledge and social groups (Brox, 2006). Further, the democratic anchoring of planning presupposes that a majority of elected representatives, and not the professional staff, are in fact the planning 'champions'.

However, the planning discourses drawing on these insights have left little room for understanding creativity and innovation. In particular, the incremental, 'muddling through' perspective, although it may offer valuable insights, links planning to the quest for consensus and alleged 'realism'. Innovation and creativity are exactly the opposite of incremental action. Accordingly, as planning and development work invariably and explicitly address the future, creativity should be discussed in relation to planning theories that move beyond the incremental modality.

As for rational 'planning system' models, the chapters in this book have shown that creative elements and moves may be compatible with the strategies which small towns and cities deploy within a rational planning perspective. In some cases, creativity is stimulated within the municipal planning organization itself, but more often, creativity occurs in networks that are formed in the intersection between planners, politicians, and outside partners. Innovative and creative action in imagining the future of a town may be directly as well as indirectly productive for municipal-level planning processes.

The communicative planning theory underlines the values of inclusion and deliberation. The communicative model and models emphasizing participation and collaboration all describe processes in which knowledges, perspectives and interests are thrown together, sometimes in a competitive and sometimes in a cooperative manner. The insights and perspectives of this volume argue for the transformative power of new collaborations and partnerships. This is in line with planning theory arguing for opening and challenging traditional planning structures by inviting 'outsiders' in (Forester, 1999, Nyseth, 2011). The case studies presented illustrate planning and development processes involving a multitude of actors. Broad networks including actors outside the formal policy-making structures seem more capable of producing new solutions and alternative ideas independent of institutional conventions, rules and regulations. But several of the chapters also demonstrate the challenges such creative and unconventional planning projects encounter in the implementation phase. Experimental planning and plans tend to be seen as irregular, administrative disorder. Thus, when the project period ends, experimental models are often being replaced with more traditional ones (see, for instance, Chapter 5 on policy programmes for the cultural industry, Chapter 9 on the Fornebu experiment, and Chapter 10 on the explorative planning projects in Nuuk and Tromsø). As the many case studies illustrate, creative planning approaches enter into a complex of encounters and contestations. Grasping this complexity also calls for more creativity in our research practices, theories and methods.

In recent years, many contributions to urban planning theory have argued for planning that acknowledges the complexity of contemporary cities and towns (Hillier, 2007, Nyseth, 2011, Pløger, 2004). This implies a form of planning that is open to new possibilities, and participation processes stressing openness, temporality and respect for difference (Pløger, 2004). Applying a territorial approach, the chapters in this volume emphasize and acknowledge the multitude of local contexts in SMSTs. This creates a means for a relational understanding of creativity as well as planning and development, where economic, social and ecological development processes are seen as interwoven. The perspectives on creativity and innovation drawn throughout the book challenge the dominant view that metropolitan cities are the sites for innovation by emphasizing the multiple agencies at work in SMST development processes. The case studies presented in this volume demonstrate the problems of 'one-size-fits-all' approaches, often based on metropolises, and the authors argue for more context- and complexity-sensitive approaches and models.

An important step towards achieving this aim is to continue exploring theories of planning as a process of becoming rather than fixing (Hillier, 2005) – a form of planning that takes into account the unknown. The case studies in this volume apply different approaches and perspectives, but share an understanding of plans and planning as continuous work in progress. Post-structural and post-representational planning theory offers perspectives to theorize about urban transformation and to explore the concept of becoming – as creative experimentation in the spatial (Hillier, 2007: 13). The focus on planning as becoming leans on an ontology acknowledging the dynamic, complex and relational aspects of time and space as a politics of the possible. It further emphasizes the acknowledgement of complexity and contestation. Such perspectives open up the way for seeing planning as experiments, focusing on the possibilities for creative change. The complexity of contemporary SMSTs and cities urge for dynamic approaches, for a planning that is flexible and able to compromise. This is challenging for spatial planners, who need to deal with the imaginations and desires of what the future city might look like. Post-structural perspectives recognize the partiality of our knowledge and models; we can never grasp the entire flow. Rather, we need to focus on understanding 'the whole' as being composed of many small stories. We can strive to avoid essentializing abstract units by focusing on concrete empirical examples (Law, 2004). This perspective on the partial has relevance to planning; even though a plan can never be perfect, we need to strive to make things better (Fainstein, 2005, Hillier, 2007). By offering insights into specific processes in specific contexts, our hope is that this book can contribute to a better understanding of both the partial and 'the impossible whole' by creative experimentation in the spatial.

The aim of this book has not been to compare different cities or local contexts. The comparative strength of this volume relates to collating creative approaches rather than outcomes. Creativity is understood as relational and situated, and, as such, difficult to compare. Nevertheless, by assembling studies of creative approaches to planning and development under different conditions and taking various forms, we hope that this book has contributed to an increased understanding of how creativity within this field can be enhanced. The aim is not to reveal the universal, but – as argued by Deleuze and Parnet (2002) – to find conditions under which something new is produced. The contribution to comparative approaches thus lies in the insistence on acknowledging the complex situatedness of every planning and development process, as well as the complexity of research practices, without giving up the systematic investigation of both planning processes and our approaches to them. Alvesson and Sköldberg (2000) call this *reflexive pragmatism* – bridging the gap between epistemological concerns and research methods, and balancing reflexivity in a multitude of situated cases with a sense of direction and a commitment to accomplishing results.

Learning for planners and practitioners

Can planning practitioners learn from the insights presented in this volume? To be realistic, the audience of academic publications is, first of all, to be found in academic circles. But planning research and the teaching of planning theory and methods are more closely linked to practice than are the activities within traditional academic disciplines. Municipal and town planners may of course keep track with what goes on in journals, books and conferences, but more likely they will be updated by reading professional periodicals and by attending dissemination events and courses offered by university extension services. By publishing a book like the current volume, the dissemination work is hardly more than half-done.

There are several lessons worth highlighting from the case studies presented. First, the view on the potentials of SMSTs should be reconsidered. Practitioners can have an optimistic perception of the strengths and autonomy of SMSTs, but must be reminded that SMSTs do not only occupy a subordinate position. National-level policies tend to give priority to metropolitan development and to the higher part of the urban hierarchy. Nevertheless, studies dedicated to SMSTs demonstrate that economic development also takes place outside the metropolitan areas (Tallec, 2014) and leading firms can be localized in SMSTs.

SMSTs have specific resources which can be activated by practitioners, in particular resources related to social cohesion. Social cohesion stimulates economic development because actors know each other; social and economic networks are stronger and operate more easily across sectoral divides. Network partners can invent new ways of social coordination, which in return encourage economic development (see Chapters 6 and 11). In the field of social cohesion, small size is a strength. Leaders and planners in SMSTs who are able to identify key sectors for their development are in a position to connect a wide range of private and public actors.

Further, we may be aware of the difficulties and the pitfalls for the development of SMSTs. From Chapter 8, we see the need to articulate and coordinate initiatives beyond the provision of infrastructure improvements. Synergies do not emerge automatically from infrastructure investments, and networking policies are necessary to connect local actors with actors from other territories and levels of government.

Heritage and identity are pointed out as specific assets of SMSTs and a means to anchor development projects in the local community. Here the risk is to reduce and essentialize identity and heritage by promoting it as a brand. In order to be efficient, public action depends on the ability to create coherence between the message/vision, the material characteristic of space and concrete changes (see Chapter 4). Without this coherence, public action can fail to stimulate and link various local actors. But policies of identity, heritage and social cohesion may function as vital elements within a comprehensive strategy for the area and its relationships with the wider environment.

The creative approach in planning is an open process. The final output is not defined in advance and planners have to accept adapting to new ideas, even the unknown. This implies risk, which may be disagreeable for professionals accustomed to deliver concrete results. Creativity can also be enhanced by replacing sectorial approaches with horizontal principles of organization (see Chapter 9).

Several cases presented here have focused on citizen participation (see Chapters 9, 10 and 12). Citizen participation is a good way to inform creative planning processes, and open dialogue is crucial. Citizens need knowledge, time and meeting space in order to be motivated and informed, and thus able to participate. During processes of participation and deliberation, ideas and objectives can be produced, criticized and modified. Involving citizens in the decision-making process contributes to rooting the process development in the local community. But practitioners still need technical and other types of expert knowledges in order to understand and act on space. However, acting together with citizens means that practitioners have to be good at listening as well as accepting a reduction in their level of control.

The final insight that we think are essential for practitioners to pick up from the studies presented here is as follows: learning from experiences and experiments across borders is also valuable for professionals working in specific urban and regional contexts. Town and municipal planners may, by networking, organize processes that include and bring in innovative and creative elements; you don't have to operate on the outside to be creative.

References

Alvesson, M. and Sköldberg, K. (2000) *Reflexive Methodology: New Vistas for Qualitative Research*. London: Sage Publications.
Banfield, E.C. (1973) Ends and means in planning. In A. Faludi (ed.), *A Reader in Planning Theory*. Oxford: Pergamon Press, pp. 139–49.
Brooks, M.P. (2002) *Planning Theory for Practitioners*. Chicago: Planners Press.
Brox, O. (2006) *The Political Economy of Rural Development*. Delft: Eburon.
Deleuze, G. and Parnet, C. (2002) *Dialogues II*. London: Continuum.
Fainstein, S. (2005) Planning theory and the city. *Planning Research and Education*, 25(2): 121–30.
Forester, J. (1999) *The Deliberative Practitioner*. Cambridge, MA: MIT Press.
Hillier, J. (2005) Straddling the post-structuralist abyss: Between transcendence and immanence? *Planning Theory*, 4(3): 271–99.
—— (2007) *Stretching Beyond the Horizon. A Multiplanar Theory of Spatial Planning and Governance*. Aldershot: Ashgate.
Law, J. (2004) *After Method: Mess in Social Science Research*. Abingdon: Routledge.
Lindblom, C. (1973) The science of muddling through. In A. Faludi (ed.), *A Reader in Planning Theory*. Oxford: Pergamon Press, pp. 151–69.
Nyseth, T. (2011) The Tromsø-experiment. Opening up for the unknown. *Town Planning Review*, 82(5): 573–93.
Pløger, J. (2004) Strife – urban planning agonism. *Planning Theory*, 3(1): 71–92.
Sager, T. (2013) *Reviving Critical Planning Theory*. London: Routledge.
Tallec, J. (2014) La construction socio-spatiale de l'innovation en ville moyenne face aux objectifs de compétitivité et d'attractivité des politiques d'aménagement. Unpublished PhD dissertation, Toulouse: Université Jean-Jaurès.

Index

Aarsæther, Nils xi, 6; *co-author of Introduction and Chapters 1, 9 and 14*
Aarschot 52–3
Aasjord, Bente 215
Adorno, T. 81–3, 93
Agenda 21 *see* Local Agenda 21
agglomeration 39–40
Aix-en-Provence 122, 126–7
Alba 50–1, 54, 56
Albrechts, Louis 14–15, 36
Allen, Stan 218–19
Alvesson, M. 88, 255
Andreotti, A. 194
archipelago concept 130–1
architecture 177, 210–11, 217
Arctic landscapes 8, 208–17, 251–2
Arinbjarnardóttir, Guðrún Jóna 221
d'Armagnac, Labastide 243–4
Athienou 50–1, 54, 56
attractiveness discourses 8, 234, 237–40, 244–5
AURORA – HUBERT CURIEN exchange framework xvi
Auvergne region 238–40, 244

Bærum 156–69
Bailly, A. 234
Banovac, Ksenija xi, 4–5, 40; *co-author of Chapters 3 and 6*
Barents region 176
Bateson, Gregory 208, 218
Beauvais, C. 196
Béhar, D. 25
behavioural planning theory 253
Belgium 39
Bell, D. 29
belonging, sense of 82, 100
biodiversity 6

Bishop, A. 244–5
Blois 26
'Blok P' 173, 180, 183–7
Bolay, J.-C. 38
Borsdorf, A. 237
Bourdeau-Lepage, L. 234
La Bourdonnais 129
Bourges 26
Brandýs nad Labem 53
Brioude 242
Brunet, Roger 24
business parks 6, 91, 120–30

Calvino, Italo 210
Camargue 124
Cambrils 52–4
Campbell, S. 13
Canada 7, 192
Capranzano, V. 94
Carlson, Yngve 67
Carrier, M. 203
Cassiers, T. 190, 194
Central Place Theory (Christaller) 38
Centre-Val de Loire 5, 26, 98, 104–6, 111
Châteauroux 26, 106–7, 110, 199–203
Châtellerault 28
Chicago 28
Christaller, W. 29, 38
citizen participation 174–5, 181–2, 187–8, 256
Cittaslow network 242–4
city centres 69–7, 72–4, 184–5, 242
city dialogues 7, 173–4, 185–8, 192
civil society 57, 72, 158–9
Clancey, G. 30
climate change 186, 218
Coatrieux 201–2

Index

collaboration between municipalities 103, 131; *see also* cooperation
Colwyn Bay 48–9, 54
common pool resources (CPR) 212–13
communicative planning theory 253
commuting 53, 119
comparative advantage 27, 56, 157, 238
Confédération des Syndicats Nationaux, Canada 196
confluence theory of creativity 135
Connolly, J. 28–9
consensus-building 4
contracts, use of 104–6, 111
Contrat Urbain de Cohésion Sociale (CUCS) 200
cooperation, inter-municipal 54–7, 65, 103–4, 115, 119–21, 131
Costa Daurada 53
'co-thinking' 16–17
Courlet, C. 115
creative cities 236–7
creative class, the 82, 100–2, 134, 234–8
creative industries 5
creative people 243, 245, 251
creative planning 14, 17–18, 134–5, 152, 254–6
creativity 2–6, 86–7, 91–4, 135, 253; definition of 15–16; three meanings of 14–16
Csikszentmihalyi, M. 135
cultural activities 98–102, 111
cultural anthropology 28
cultural industries 81–94, 252; definition of 83; as a tool for development 82–5

Dahl, Knut Eirik xi, 7, 176; *co-author of Chapter 10*
Dahl & Uhre Architects 173
Dali 47–8, 53, 56
Davezies, L. 198
decentralization 42–4, 47, 102, 105–6
de-industrialization 146–8, 197
De Landa, Manuel 211–12
Deleuze, Gilles 86, 174, 208, 211–14, 230, 255
Delladetsima, Pavlos Marinos xi, 6; *co-author of Chapter 8*
Demazière, Christophe i, xii, 3–5, 193, 198; *author of Chapter 2, co-author of Introduction and Chapters 1, 6 and 14*
Dendermonde 52–3
densification 69
Department for Cutlure, Media and Sport (DCMS) 83
deterritorialisation 213
development practices in SMSTs 45–55
devolution 16, 102
dialogue as a basis for planning 7
dormitory towns 54
Drammen 4, 61, 65–75, 251
Dreux 28
Drummondville 199, 202–4

East European countries 43
ecology 186, 214–15
economic development and social cohesion 199–200, 204–5
Edouard, Jean-Charles xii, 8, 27; *co-author of Chapter 13*
Eizaguirre, S. 193
embedded social relations 54
empowerment of citizens 159, 168
endogenous assets of towns 101
endogenous growth 56
entrepreneurialism 61–2
environmental challenges 8, 208
environmental protection 161
environmental sustainability 13
Erskine, Ralph 210
Étang de Berre 124
Eurocopter Company 128
Euromediterannée project 125
European Committee on Social Cohesion (CDCS) 195–6
European Observation Network for Territorial Development and Cohesion (ESPON) 39–45, 56
European Social Planning 41
European Spatial Development Perspective (ESDP) 37, 41–2, 55
European Union (EU) 4, 18, 37, 237
Exner, Jakob 181
expert knowledge 18
externalities *see* negative externalities; positive externalities

Fantastic Norway group 186
federalized states 43
Finnmark 209, 216
Les Florides 125–9
Florida, Richard 14, 238, 252

260 Index

Førde, Anniken xii, 5; co-author of Introduction and Chapters 1, 5 and 14
Fornebu area 155–6, 160–9, 251
Forrest, R. 99
Foucault, Michel 174, 208, 211–12
France 4–7, 22–7, 31–2, 97–8, 102–3, 110–11, 118, 192, 235, 238–45, 251–2
Friedmann, John 168, 174, 182

Gaudin, S. 27
Gaup Eira, Inger Marie 215–16
gemeinschaft and *gesellschaft* 29
geology 208
Germanic group of countries 43, 103
Ghaffari, Leïla xii, 7, 199, 201; co-author of Chapter 11
Global Analysis of World Cities (GaWC) group 30
global cities 29–32, 116
global financial crisis (2008) 97–8, 165
globalization 1, 22–3, 29–30, 101, 116–18, 192–3, 213
governance structures 4, 61–2, 65–7, 75
government, role of 61
Greece 136, 148
Greenland 173, 178–83, 186, 213
Guattari, Félix 86, 174, 208, 211–14, 230

Haggärde, Magdalena xii–xiii, 7; co-author of Chapter 12
Halbert, L. 116–17
Hallam, E. 15, 87
Hamdouch, Abdelillah i, xiii, 4–7, 40, 44, 199; co-author of Introduction and Chapters 1, 3, 6, 7, 11 and 14
Han, S.S. 244–5
Hansen, H.K. 245
Hardin, Garrett 212
Harvey, David 193
Hauge, A. 87
Healey, Patsy 62, 65
Hildreth, P.A. 27, 38, 40
Hillier, Jean 14, 85–6, 94, 174, 187
Holm, Trine 175–6
homo economicus 234
Horkheimer, M. 83
The House of Families programme 186
human capital 237
Hundsund 163–4

image of a place 71
industrial districts 28, 115
industrial heritage 57
Ingold, T. 15, 87, 177
innovation 3, 5, 8, 14–15, 86–8, 91–4, 135, 177, 198–9; in cities 40; as a driver of the economy 98–102; *see also* social innovation
Innovation Norway 85, 89
Institut national de la statistique et des études economiques (INSEE) 25, 40
institutional structures 42–4, 55–6, 102, 204; and governance 193
integrated development 4, 17–18, 75, 161–8
integrated policy-making 65
interdependence between territories 116
Interleuven 53
'interterritoriality' (Vanier) 120
INTRO programme 82–94
Issoire 242, 244
Issoudun 109–10

Jayne, M. 29, 238, 245
Jenson, J. 195–6
Jessop, Bob 62
job creation 201
joik thinking 217

kamik post 182
Kearns, A. 99
Kesteloot, C. 190, 194
Kirkenes 217
Kiruna 209, 216, 222–7, 251–2
Kleist, Kuupik 180
knowledge-based economies 198–9
Knox, P. 100
Kola peninsula 209, 216–17
Koolhas, Rem 177
Kramvig, Britt xiii, 5, 87–8; co-author of Chapter 5
Krugman, P. 29, 198

Lajugie, J. 26
land-use planning 1
landscape: commodity value of 215; protection of 242; study of 208–17, 230
Latour, Bruno 208, 211
Law, J. 88
leader firms 116
learning as catalyst 183–4
Lefebvre, Henri 208, 210, 222
Leine, Kim 179

Leipzig Charter (2007) 42
Lennert, Helena 181–2
Léo, P.-Y. 39, 198
'lines of flight' concept 216, 230
'liveability' concept 238, 240
Ljubljana 39
local actors 234, 243–4, 251
Local Agenda 21 176, 234, 238, 242–4
local amenities 239–40, 243–5
local authorities, role of 54, 61–2, 72, 98, 103, 127, 244
local contexts and policies 197, 205, 243, 254
Loire Valley 104; see also Centre-Val de Loire
Løkken, Gisle xiii, 7; co-author of Chapter 12
London 28
Los Angeles 28
Loukakis, John xiii, 6; co-author of Chapter 8
Lynd, R. and H. 28

McCall, S. 235
MacCallum, D. 196
Mainet, Hélène xiii, 8, 24; co-author of Chapter 13
mapping 214–17
Marignane 119, 127–30
Marseille 6, 114, 119–29
Massey, Doreen 208–9, 213–14
Mayer, H. 100
medium-sized towns 23–8, 104–5, 192
Meijers, E. 65
metropolises 17, 116–19
Meyer, S. 86, 91
la Mézière 119, 130
Michalko, M. 15
mixed profiles of SMSTs 49–53
mobility, residential 240–1, 245
modernism 210–11
Moulaert, F. 44
multiplanar theory (Hillier) 85
Muncie 28
municipalities, French and German 103
Murmansk 217

Nahrath, S. 13
'Napoleonic' group of countries 43
negative externalities 126
'negotiation' between cities or towns and their environments 18
neo-liberalism 1, 14, 16, 81, 157

networks and networking 39, 71, 75, 92, 198, 204–5, 252–3, 256–7
new public management 157
Newman, P. 4, 43, 55–6
Niedomysl, T. 236, 241, 245
Nordic group of countries 43
Norway 4–5, 61, 69, 74, 81, 83, 93, 157, 167–8, 176
Nuuk 7, 173–5, 178–82, 187–8, 252
Nyseth, Torill i, xiv, 4, 174–6; co-author of Introduction and Chapters 1, 4 and 14

Oakley, K. 86, 92–3
Ødegård, Silje 220
Olympic Games 151
optimal city size theory 29
Orléans 106
Österreichisches Institut für Raumplanung (OIR) 37
Östersund 48–9, 54
Ostrom, Elinor 212
Otto, Frei 210–11
Øwre, Erik 176

Paralimni 54
Paris 28, 106
Parkinson, M. 190, 195
Parnet, C. 255
participation see citizen participation
partnership working in public service provision 159–60, 163–8
Patras 6, 135–52
Pecqueur, B. 115
'people climate' 246
peri-urbanization 119–20, 241
Petrescu, Doina 214, 230
Philippe, J. 198
'place attractiveness' 235–6; see also attractiveness discourses
place development 251
place promotion and marketing 62–5, 71, 75, 239, 243
planning, opposition to 14
planning codes 43
planning process 150–1, 155, 252; see also spatial planning
planning theory 85–6, 94, 251–5
'Platform 21' organization 244
Pløger, John 175–6
'poles of centrality' 105
positive externalities 29
postmodernism 85
post-structuralism 254

Index

power structures 252
proximity's role in development of SMSTs 199–201
Purcell, Mark 222
Putnam, R.D. 159

quality of life 8, 198, 234–46
Queffélec, C.-N. 32

Rabinovitch, A. 38
RadArt network 87, 90–1
Radovljica 50–4
'reflexive pragmatism' 255
regional development policy 41–2, 53, 56–7, 104–5
regionalized states 43
reindeer husbandry 213–16
reinvention of places xvi, 63–5, 70, 74
Rennes 6, 114, 119–27, 130
residential profiles of SMSTs 48–9, 56–7
resilience strategies 5
rhizome concept 213–14, 230
Rio-Antonio Bridge 138, 142–5, 152
Robinson, J. 29–31
Rulleramp (company) 90
rural areas, towns in 54

Sassen, Saskia 218
Sauters, Florian 218
Schéma de Cohérence Territoriale (SCoT) 122–6
Scott, A.J. 36
secondary cities 30–2
Selada, C. 101, 234, 239–40
Sermitsiaq AG (newspaper) 182
Serrano, José xiv, 6; *co-author of Introduction and Chapters 1, 7 and 14*
service economy, growth of 149
Servillo, L. 25–6, 39–43, 54
shopping centres 69–72
Sinclair-Poulton, Clive 215
size of towns and cities 7, 29
Sköldberg, K. 255
Skuncke, Marianne Lucie 219
Slovenia 39
small and medium-sized towns (SMSTs) xvi, 1–5, 8, 17–18, 22–32, 37–42, 55–6, 100–5, 114–21, 127, 130–1, 191–3, 196–201, 204–5, 234–46, 254–6; advantages of 198–201, 204; characteristics of 38–42, 192–3; criteria for identification of 24–6; definition of 192; disadvantages of 117, 237; place in the new urban hierarchies 118–19; places where the living is easy 238–45; role in development 104; role in inter-municipal cooperation 119–21; role of proximity in the development of 199–201; social innovation in 196–7; socio-economic development of 197–9; as a subject for research 28–31
social and solidarity economy (SSE) 202
social capital 23, 237, 240; *bridging* type of 159
social cohesion 5–7, 98–100, 110–11, 190–5, 255–6; definitions of 99; and economic development 199–200, 204–5; and socio-economic develop-ment 195–6
social constructivism 211
social innovation 165, 191–2, 196–9, 204
social policies 194–5
social protection 195
socio-economic characteristics of towns 40–1, 45–7
socio-economic development 4, 36–7, 55–6, 111, 191, 195–9; and social cohesion 195–6
Somby, Ánde 217
space seen as a resource 115
'spaces of action' concept 224
spatial planning 36–7, 55
specialization, economic 40, 157, 197–8
Stead, D. 65
Storøya 163
strategic planning 13, 36, 44, 55
subsidies 103
suburbanization and suburban towns 38–9, 53
sustainability 6–7, 13; ecological and social 16
sustainable development 135, 196, 235, 237

Tallec, J. 31
Tarrega 49–50, 54
taxation 103
technocratic practices 14
Telemark Research Institute 93
Tennøy, A. 69
Territorial Agenda 2020 (EU) 42

territorial approach to public services 158–62, 165–8, 254
territorial development 103–5, 116–19
territorial economic theory 115
tertiary sector employment 149
Tesson, F. 246
Thornley, A. 43
3Ts theory 238
tipping points 214
Tønnesen, Anders; xiv, 4; *co-author of Chapter 4*
Tönnies, Ferdinand 29
tourism 198; cultural 98
Tours 106
TOWN project 192
traditional planning model 13
tragedy of the commons 212
transactive planning 174
transformation of places 63–4
Tromsø 5, 7, 81–5, 88, 93–4, 173–6, 181, 252
trust, levels of 99
Tuujuk 173, 185–7

Uhre, Kjerstin xiv, 7; *co-author of Chapter 10*
unitary states 43, 47
urban centres 39
urban hierarchy 30, 118–19, 190–1, 197, 235–6

urban sprawl 119, 130, 242
urban studies 4, 22–3, 28
urbanisation 30, 211

Val de Loire region 251;
see also Centre-Val de Loire
Vanier, M. 120
Veblen, T. 159
Vendôme 107–10
Vierzon 108–10
Vigar, G. 16
Vike, Halvard xv, 6; *co-author of Chapter 9*
Vilafranca del Penedes 53
village centers 161–7
vulnerability, concept of 218

Ward, Stephen 63
Weaver, C. 168
websites of towns 24, 239–40
well-being and well-living 237
West, G. 29
wildlife, protection of 123–4, 130
world cities 29–32

'x-factor' in culture 89, 94

Yaneva, A. 177, 187
Young, I.M. 194

zoning 43, 157, 179, 187

Taylor & Francis eBooks

Helping you to choose the right eBooks for your Library

Add Routledge titles to your library's digital collection today. Taylor and Francis ebooks contains over 50,000 titles in the Humanities, Social Sciences, Behavioural Sciences, Built Environment and Law.

Choose from a range of subject packages or create your own!

Benefits for you
- Free MARC records
- COUNTER-compliant usage statistics
- Flexible purchase and pricing options
- All titles DRM-free.

Benefits for your user
- Off-site, anytime access via Athens or referring URL
- Print or copy pages or chapters
- Full content search
- Bookmark, highlight and annotate text
- Access to thousands of pages of quality research at the click of a button.

REQUEST YOUR **FREE** INSTITUTIONAL TRIAL TODAY

Free Trials Available
We offer free trials to qualifying academic, corporate and government customers.

eCollections – Choose from over 30 subject eCollections, including:

Archaeology	Language Learning
Architecture	Law
Asian Studies	Literature
Business & Management	Media & Communication
Classical Studies	Middle East Studies
Construction	Music
Creative & Media Arts	Philosophy
Criminology & Criminal Justice	Planning
Economics	Politics
Education	Psychology & Mental Health
Energy	Religion
Engineering	Security
English Language & Linguistics	Social Work
Environment & Sustainability	Sociology
Geography	Sport
Health Studies	Theatre & Performance
History	Tourism, Hospitality & Events

For more information, pricing enquiries or to order a free trial, please contact your local sales team:
www.tandfebooks.com/page/sales

 Routledge Taylor & Francis Group | The home of Routledge books

www.tandfebooks.com